Beginning Flash® Game Programming For Dummies®

Cheat Sheet

Y0-CAP-554

Common Keyboard Shortcuts

File Menu Commands

Command	Windows	Mac
New	Ctrl+N	⌘+N
Open	Ctrl+O	⌘+O
Open as Library	Ctrl+Shift+O	⌘+Shift+O
Close	Ctrl+W	⌘+W
Save	Ctrl+S	⌘+S
Import	Ctrl+R	⌘+R
Publish	Shift+F12	Shift+F12
Quit	Ctrl+Q	⌘+Q

Edit Menu Commands

Command	Windows	Mac
Undo	Ctrl+Z	⌘+Z
Redo	Ctrl+Y	⌘+Y
Cut	Ctrl+X	⌘+X
Copy	Ctrl+C	⌘+C
Paste	Ctrl+V	⌘+V
Paste in Place	Ctrl+Shift+V	⌘+Shift+V
Clear	Delete/Backspace	Delete/Clear
Duplicate	Ctrl+D	⌘+D
Select All	Ctrl+A	⌘+A
Deselect All	Ctrl+Shift+A	⌘+Shift+A
Copy Frames	Ctrl+Alt+C	⌘+Option+C
Paste Frames	Ctrl+Alt+V	⌘+Option+V

View Menu Commands

Command	Windows	Mac
Timeline	Ctrl+Alt+T	⌘+Option+T
Snap to Objects	Ctrl+Shift+/	⌘+Shift+/
Work Area	Ctrl+Shift+W	⌘+Shift+W
Hide Panels	F4	F4

Drawing Toolbox

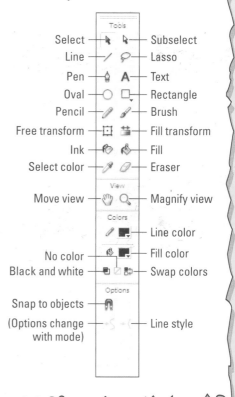

Select — Subselect
Line — Lasso
Pen — Text
Oval — Rectangle
Pencil — Brush
Free transform — Fill transform
Ink — Fill
Select color — Eraser

Move view — Magnify view

Line color
No color — Fill color
Black and white — Swap colors

Snap to objects
(Options change with mode) — Line style

Beginning Flash® Game Programming For Dummies®

Common Keyboard Shortcuts (continued)

Insert Menu Commands

Command	Windows	Mac
Convert to Symbol	F8	F8
New Symbol	Ctrl+F8	⌘+F8
Frame	F5	F5
Remove Frames	Shift+F5	Shift+F5
Keyframe	F6	F6
Blank Keyframe	F7	F7
Clear Keyframe	Shift+F6	Shift+F6

Modify Menu Commands

Command	Windows	Mac
Document Properties	Ctrl+J	⌘+J
Bring Forward	Ctrl+up	⌘+up
Bring Back	Ctrl+down	⌘+down
Bring to Top	Ctrl+Shift+up	⌘+Shift+up
Bring to Bottom	Ctrl+Shift+ down	⌘+Shift+ down

Control Menu Commands

Command	Windows	Mac
Play	Enter	Return
Test Movie	Ctrl+Enter	⌘+Return

Window Menu Commands

Command	Windows	Mac
Align	Ctrl+K	⌘+K
Color Mixer	Shift+F9	Shift+F9
Color Swatches	Ctrl+F9	⌘+F9
Info	Ctrl+ I	⌘+I
Transform	Ctrl+T	⌘+T
Actions / Code window	F9	F9
Library	Ctrl+L/F11	⌘+L/F11

For Dummies: Bestselling Book Series for Beginners

Beginning Flash®
Game Programming
FOR
DUMMIES®

by Andy Harris

WILEY

Wiley Publishing, Inc.

Beginning Flash® Game Programming For Dummies®

Published by
Wiley Publishing, Inc.
111 River Street
Hoboken, NJ 07030-5774

www.wiley.com

For general information on our other products and services, please contact our Customer Care Department within the U.S. at 800-762-2974, outside the U.S. at 317-572-3993, or fax 317-572-4002.

For technical support, please visit www.wiley.com/techsupport.

Wiley also publishes its books in a variety of electronic formats. Some content that appears in print may not be available in electronic books.

Library of Congress Control Number: 2005927728

ISBN-13: 978-0-7645-8962-1

ISBN-10: 0-7645-8962-8

Manufactured in the United States of America

10 9 8 7 6 5 4 3 2 1

1O/TR/RQ/QV/IN

WILEY

About the Author

Andy Harris earned a degree in Special Education from Indiana University/Purdue University–Indianapolis (IUPUI). He taught young adults with severe disabilities for several years. He also taught himself enough computer programming to support his teaching habit with freelance programming. Those were the exciting days when computers started to have hard drives, and some computers connected to each other with arcane protocols. He taught programming in those days because it was fun.

Eventually, Andy decided to teach computer science full time, and he still teaches at IUPUI. He lectures in the applied computing program and runs the streaming media lab. He also teaches classes in whatever programming language is in demand at the time. He has developed a large number of online video-based courses and international distance education projects.

Andy has written several books on various computing topics and languages including Java, C#, mobile computing, JavaScript, and PHP/MySQL.

Andy welcomes comments and suggestions about his books. He can be reached at `aharris@cs.iupui.edu`.

Dedication

This book is dedicated to Heather, Elizabeth, Matthew, Jacob, and now Benjamin.

Author's Acknowledgments

Although writing a book often seems like a lonely endeavor, it really takes a lot of talented and dedicated people to make a book on a topic as complex as this. Fortunately, I am blessed by my companions in this process.

First, I give thanks to Him from whom all flows.

Even nonfiction books have heroes. My hero is my wife, Heather. You are the unending delight of my life. Thank you for who you are and for all you do. Thanks also to all my kids. I know it's rough when Daddy spends so much time writing. I'm done for a little while. Let's go play! I love you guys.

Thanks to my dear friend Melody Layne who helped me once again take my writing career to a new place.

Thanks to acquisitions editor Katie Feltman. Even when I couldn't find the restaurant where we had our first meeting, you had faith in me and encouraged me all through the process. Thanks also to project editor Pat O'Brien, the Drill Sergeant For Dummies who can turn even me into an author worthy of the incredible *For Dummies* series. I'm still learning, Pat. One day, I'll really get it. Seriously, thanks for all the guidance. I really appreciate learning from you and working with you. Another big thank you goes to copy editor Teresa Artman: I'm amazed how she can take my mush and turn it into something that actually sounds good. And a big thanks to Scott Hofmann for technical editing.

The production process that goes behind a book is dizzying and impressive. I'd like to thank everyone at Wiley for their professionalism. The folks in layout, composition, graphics, proofing, cover work, marketing, and everyone else who worked on this book all deserve three cheers for their terrific work.

Thanks to Macromedia for developing Flash in a way that is adaptable for games and accessible to people who are not wealthy.

Thanks to John Gersting for looking over my code and giving me such good advice and guidance.

A very special thanks to my students, especially those in Web Game Development N451. You always teach me way more than I can ever teach you. Thank you for letting me be your teacher.

Publisher's Acknowledgments

We're proud of this book; please send us your comments through our online registration form located at www.dummies.com/register/.

Some of the people who helped bring this book to market include the following:

Acquisitions, Editorial, and Media Development

Senior Project Editor: Pat O'Brien

Acquisitions Editor: Katie Feltman

Senior Copy Editor: Teresa Artman

Technical Editor: Scott Hofmann

Editorial Manager: Kevin Kirschner

Media Development Specialist: Laura Moss

Media Development Manager:
Laura VanWinkle

Media Development Supervisor:
Richard Graves

Editorial Assistant: Amanda Foxworth

Cartoons: Rich Tennant
(www.the5thwave.com)

Composition Services

Project Coordinator: Adrienne Martinez

Layout and Graphics: Carl Byers, Andrea Dahl, Joyce Haughey, Stephanie D. Jumper, Barbara Moore, Barry Offringa, Lynsey Osborn

Proofreaders: Leeann Harney, Jessica Kramer, Joe Niesen, Carl William Pierce, Rob Springer, TECHBOOKS Production Services

Indexer: TECHBOOKS Production Services

Special Help: Rebecca Senninger

Publishing and Editorial for Technology Dummies

    Richard Swadley, Vice President and Executive Group Publisher

    Andy Cummings, Vice President and Publisher

    Mary Bednarek, Executive Acquisitions Director

    Mary C. Corder, Editorial Director

Publishing for Consumer Dummies

    Diane Graves Steele, Vice President and Publisher

    Joyce Pepple, Acquisitions Director

Composition Services

    Gerry Fahey, Vice President of Production Services

    Debbie Stailey, Director of Composition Services

Contents at a Glance

Table of Contents

Chapter 1

Why You Want to Write Games in Flash

Computer programming can be a whole lot of fun. That's why I got into it way back when, and it's why I still do it. Truth be told, the main reason I learned how to program was to write games. I couldn't buy much software for my first computer (a TRS-80 Model 1, still in the garage . . . sigh). I wanted to play games, so I had to create them myself. Admittedly, I was pretty bad at it, and I failed a lot, but I kept trying. As I grew up, my programming skills were marketable in the "serious" world, but I never lost my fascination with computer games.

Here are some very good reasons to write games:

✔ Computer games made more income in 2003 than the movie industry.

✔ Game programming is technically challenging.

✔ Making a game is *fun!*

Most other game development books can be divided into two camps:

✔ Some talk about the game design process, storyboarding, coming up with game ideas, and the visual side of gaming. That's pretty good stuff to know, but it doesn't help you actually make a game.

✔ Other books assume that you're already good at C++ and advanced math. That's pretty good stuff, too, but you don't need to start there.

I believe that newcomers to programming can master the essential ideas of programming at the same time they're learning to build games. I also feel that those with some programming experience will truly enjoy the uniquely creative aspects of game development. You don't have to know anything about programming or Flash to use this book. (However, if you know these things, you'll still probably see something new.)

In this chapter, I give you an overview of the basics of game designing and planning, writing, and programming in Flash (with ActionScript). Most of all, you're going to have a lot of fun.

Designing and Writing Games

If you've asked around about how to get started in game programming, people have probably told you to learn C++ and take lots of math classes. That's not bad advice, but I have an easier way. The truth is that making games isn't really about any particular computer language. After you learn how to write games, you can transfer those concepts to any environment you wish. There are surprisingly few main concepts behind game development. If you truly understand these ideas, you can translate them to any programming language you want.

In this book, I show you how to program games in Flash. I like Flash because it simplifies the visual side of programming, works on almost every computer made, and has a powerful and reasonably easy programming language. I talk about this more in the upcoming sections, "Game Programming in Flash" and "Game Programming 101."

Too, game programming is different than other kinds of software development. For one thing, games need to be fun. And games are all about communicating with the player as well as providing some sort of immersive world in which the player participates. As a game programmer, you get to be creative and think outside the box.

Making artificial worlds

Typical business programming relies heavily on certain conventions and metaphors. If you're writing a database application, it's *de rigueur* to make your program much like all the other programs users have seen. In game programming, though, you're often trying to "hide" the computer from the player. For example, if you're making a spaceship game, you want the controls to look and feel like spaceship controls. Imagination is a really important part of playing and writing games.

Introduction

I'm sure you bought your computer to do all kinds of serious work. Computers are good for homework, e-mail, work, and other perfectly respectable endeavors. But face it: Computers are also all about games. I love games, and I always have. As soon as I started to learn about computers, I wanted to use them to play games. I soon found it even more fun to make games than to play them. Even though I have a (somewhat) respectable career as a computer science teacher, the gaming aspect of computing has stayed with me.

If you're like me — with a love of games and curious how to write them — this book is for you. Most books on computer programming are pretty boring, but not this one. For example, I show you how to blow up stuff (as in *Kaboom!*, not as in enlarging a photograph). Most books on computer gaming are really technical, with endless descriptions of graphics primitives and indecipherable function calls. Not this one, though. I get things going as quickly as possible and let Flash do all the dirty work.

Yup, you read right, *Flash*. The Flash environment has emerged as a terrific tool for writing Web-based games. I dedicate this book to how games are made using this terrific tool. Along the way, you can glean some skills that might be useful in more ordinary programming contexts, too.

Okay, geek-speak disclaimer: Sometimes I have to use geeky words and even a little (gasp) math. Don't worry, though. Everything I show you has a purpose, and there won't be a quiz later. I speak English, too, so I promise to explain everything in regular English, with lots of fun analogies. (My favorite is the dog that does trigonometry.)

What's Really (Not) Required

If you're not sure you know everything you need to get started, don't worry! Here's what I *don't* assume you know upfront:

- ✔ **I don't expect you to be an ace computer user.** You should, though, be comfortable with all the ordinary computer operations, like saving/loading files and getting around in your operating system.

- ✔ **You don't need a super-high-speed computer.** Any system that can run Flash MX 2004 will do. These games work on even more humble machines.

✔ **You don't have to be a Flash master, either.** If you know how to make really great Flash animations, that's wonderful but not really necessary. Game programming is different from animation.

✔ **You don't need the most expensive version of Flash** (Flash MX 2004 Professional). This version of Flash does add some special features, but you really don't need any of those features to write wonderful games.

This book was written using Flash MX 2004 with the latest updates available. If you're running an earlier version of Flash, some of the programs will still run, but you won't be able to open the FLA files from the Web site.

✔ **You definitely don't need to be a pasty-faced, mega-caffeine-swilling computer programmer.** (However, if that describes you, you're still going to have a great time, you l33t haxor!) I start from the very beginning, using game programming to teach the basic tenets of programming in any language. *Teaser:* Stick around for more catapulting cows here than in any COBOL book you've ever seen.

So what is required? Only a copy of Flash MX 2004, some determination, and a lot of imagination.

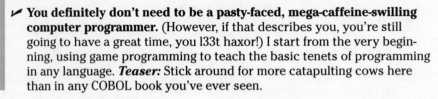

About This Book

Each chapter in the book describes a particular facet of game development. You can read the chapters in any order you wish, especially if you already have some knowledge of Flash or programming. If you're just starting, however, I recommend reading this book from front to back, simply because programming is a cumulative skill.

If you want, you can just download files from the Web site and start playing away. Most of the examples in the book are much more interesting in real life than I can show in a screen shot. Keep in mind that most of the example games on the Web site are left very simple to illustrate one particular idea. Still, they are pretty fun, and after you play them, I bet you'll want to read how they were made so you can change them and make your own variant.

Another fun alternative is to start at the very last chapter, which shows how to write ten different styles of games. Choose a game type that you want to master and go back to those chapters you'll need to pick up the necessary skills. This approach allows you to get to the game you want quickly without having to wade through anything that doesn't relate directly to that game.

How This Book Is Organized

I organized this book by writing a sophisticated Bayesian filter, artificial intelligence algorithm. Just kidding. Really, I sketched it on a napkin at the breakfast table. Still, I think it makes sense to break the book into a series of sections.

I lovingly named these parts as follows.

Part I: Basic Flash

This part gives you a programmer's introduction to the Flash environment. You see the various doohickeys and thingamabobs on the screen — and which ones you can ignore. You read how to make text appear and change onscreen, how to respond to button presses, and how to build a basic adventure game.

Part II: Getting with the Program

Time to experience some traditional programming skills (but nothing too boring). In this part, you master text-based input and output, see how to build random numbers, and make the computer perform the basic mathematical operations you'll use to build space muskrats in later games in the book. I show you how to make a sophisticated math game that generates random math problems. After that, I promise — no more educational games.

Part III: Sprites, or Movie Clips

Here you can use the most important element in Flash: the movie clip. Read here to find out what a sprite is and how you can use movie clips to make them easily in Flash. Then see how to build and control basic movie clips, making them move around onscreen, bashing into walls and each other. For a little ramble down Nostalgia Road, stick with me here to build the all-time classic *Pong* game.

Part IV: Getting Control of the Situation

Games aren't much fun if the user doesn't do anything. This section shows you how to respond to keyboard input and control sprites onscreen via player input. You also see how to add sound effects to your games (so anybody playing your game at work runs the risk of being fired). You discover more sophisticated ways of moving and animating your sprites to make them more realistic. Follow along as I walk you through building a complete game — Monster Traffic — complete with monsters, flames, car alarms, destruction, and mayhem.

Part V: Phun with Phuzzy Physics

Don't worry — this isn't anything like Physics 101 with Professor Baldnoggin. Oh, no. The stuff in this section is much more cool than that. Sure, I've got to use words like *mass* and *vector* at some point, but it's worth it because you use these ideas to build vehicles that turn realistically, boats that skid around on water, spacecraft that orbit planets realistically, and all kinds of other geeky fun. You also become the true master of your universe as you see how to create and destroy sprites at your slightest whim (Muhahahaha!).

Part VI: The Part of Tens

The famous Part of Tens is a staple of any book in the *For Dummies* series. The two chapters in this part are pretty handy. The first one outlines the ten most important math concepts for a game programmer. These are ideas that you see throughout the book. Master these, and you master game development in any language. The last chapter is my favorite in the whole book. I wrote starter code for ten different games. I didn't finish any of them — that's your job! I did get the basic framework down so you can add your own flourishes. You'll find several classics (such as *Space Invaders, Zelda,* and *Asteroids*) and a couple of original ideas. You can think of this section as a recipe book to get you started on your own games.

Icons Used in This Book

Certain concepts in any book ought to stand out on the page. With that in mind, this *For Dummies* book includes a number of margin icons for certain situations:

Tips are suggestions to make things easier.

Sometimes I have to talk about certain technical things in order to keep my *Self-Important Computer Science Instructor Certification*. These things are interesting but not crucial, so I mark them with this icon. You don't need to read them if you don't want, but memorize some of these paragraphs before you go to your next computer science party. The guests will love you.

Be sure to read text marked with this icon! If you do not follow a warning, bad things could happen: Puffs of black smoke might come out of your monitor, your workspace could be deluged by a plague of frogs, or your program simply won't work right.

These tidbits denote info you ought to think about, but it's not going to cause a disaster if you don't pay attention.

If you're gonna be a programmer, you gotta have code. Of course, I give you all the source code files for this book, located handily online at

```
www.dummies.com/go/flashgameprogrammingfd1e
```

Where to Go from Here

My recommendations on how to proceed? Mainly, have some fun and write some games.

- Begin by simply downloading the software and playing the games I've put there.
- If you're really new to all this stuff, jump in and start writing games. I put the easiest game programming tasks at the beginning, but you can start wherever you want. If you start in the middle and get confused, just back up until you're comfortable.
- For all other concerns, use the index or jump straight to the chapter you need. (You can always return later at your leisure.)

A Final Word

Thank you for buying this book, and I hope that you find *Beginning Flash Game Programming For Dummies* fun and valuable. I had a great time writing this book, and I think you'll have a lot of fun using it to write really terrific games. Have fun, learn a lot, and let me know what you've made!

Part I
Basic Flash

In this part . . .

You discover the basic toolset of the Flash environment as a programmer sees it. You give your programs various states and take a tour of all the beginning tools. You finish the section with a complete adventure game.

Chapter 1 shows you how to start thinking like a programmer. I explain how Flash and ActionScript are like other programming languages and some key ways they are different. If you've never programmed before, I prepare you with some wisdom about the programming process.

Chapter 2 is about creating Flash projects. You make a button and have it respond when the user clicks it. You find out how to embed your Flash games into Web pages.

The importance of interactivity

Games need to react to the player. The player should manipulate a virtual presence, and the game should react accordingly. Some games are turn based, and some are in real time, but all require more immediate feedback than traditional types of programs.

Games are about objects

Many games involve objects bonking into each other, shooting each other (with other objects), avoiding each other, and simply milling around. While you're writing a game, you usually think about objects, their characteristics, and how they interact with the player as well as with each other.

Players compete with the programmer

When you play a really great game, you're not really playing against the computer. Rather, you're really engaging in a stylized conversation with the programmers. As a game developer, you get the chance to set up worlds. The players interact with a stored version of your thoughts and imagination.

Game Programming in Flash

Macromedia Flash is a very good environment for learning basic game programming ideas. Here are a number of reasons for starting with Flash:

- ✔ **Flash offers robust multimedia support.** Flash, which was designed to support animation on the Web, supports various kinds of images easily. (Think JPEG images and custom drawings.) See how to use the drawing features of Flash in Chapter 9. Flash also has great support for various kinds of audio files, such as MP3 and WAV formats. You incorporate audio into your games in Chapter 8.

- ✔ **ActionScript is related to the influential C language.** The ActionScript programming language built into Flash is closely related to JavaScript and ECMAScript, which are two extremely common programming languages. All these languages are based on the C programming language, so the coding conventions you'll master are much like those in other languages.

✔ **Flash is designed for the Web.** By working in Flash, you have a ready distribution network. Because Flash was designed for the Web, all your games can be easily published on the Web, and anybody with a Web browser and a Flash plug-in can enjoy your games. And you won't have to worry about what operating system your users use. (All the programs in this book have been tested in Windows XP and Fedora Core Linux, but they should work in any OS with a Flash plug-in.)

Comparing ActionScript with Animation

Maybe you've used Flash to build Web animations without ever going into its programming features. Many books on Flash (as opposed to ActionScript) focus on the powerful animation features of Flash. These books often mention ActionScript but don't dwell on it heavily. Animation is primarily about creating moving images; user interaction in animations is minimal. When creating an animation, you generally create some sort of visual symbol onscreen and then use a tool called a *motion tween* to indicate where this object should be at a specified point in time. You can also use a tool called a *shape tween* to change the shape of an object over time. You can do this with many objects at the same time to make a complex animation. In order to track all these objects, Flash animators often arrange them into separate *layers.* Thus, a typical 30-second Flash animation might have hundreds of frames of animation in over a dozen layers.

Animation is cool because it allows you to build movies. However, to create games, you must discover how to program.

If you treat Flash as a programming environment (as I do in this book), you see things quite differently. You still use Flash to create objects, but instead of relying on the Flash environment to control what those objects do (via animation), you control the objects directly by writing programming code. The ActionScript programming language built into Flash lets you do anything that can be done with animation — and many things that cannot be done by using animation techniques alone.

In a nutshell, programming is what makes games interactive. You can

✔ Control what's onscreen, what size it is, where it is, and how it's rotated

✔ Detect whether two things touch each other

✔ Accept input from the user

How You Make a Game

The goal of game development can be summarized in one sentence:

Games are stories that use the player as a primary character.

Like any interesting story, a game needs these plot elements:

- ✔ A character (at least one)
- ✔ A conflict
- ✔ A goal

Game play must be compelling, but game elements don't need to be complex. Simple games like *Tetris* and *Pac-Man* have had phenomenal success.

Making a playable game

A good game has a good story, and it also has some form of user interaction. In Flash, the player uses the mouse and keyboard as primary input devices. Although these devices might seem limiting (compared with a more sophisticated joystick or driving console), you can do many things with these basic forms of input.

Although Flash doesn't directly support joystick input, users can easily use modern joysticks with the games you can write in Flash. Most joysticks now come with programs that allow the user to map keystrokes to keyboard commands. In effect, by allowing keyboard input, you also allow rudimentary joystick input.

A game should also look good and sound good, but these things don't matter if the game isn't fun.

Some of the best games ever have incredibly limited graphics and sound. If you've never played *NetHack* (as shown in Figure 1-1), download a copy (free for just about any computer ever made) and play it. At first, you might be thrown by the complete lack of graphics and sounds. *NetHack* uses plain text without any graphics or sound effects, but the game is amazingly absorbing. I bet that you get caught up in the incredible game play and find yourself actually scared of the capital D coming at you.

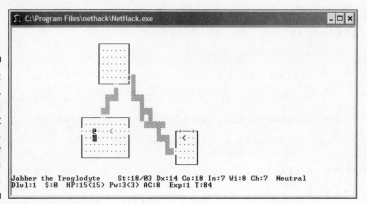

Figure 1-1:
A
captivating
game isn't
always
about flashy
graphics
and sound.

Most of all, games should be fun. I can't really tell you how to make a game fun. You need to test a lot for a game that's fun to play.

Starting with a plan

Before you worry at all about the details of your game, come up with a theme.

Think about what you want your game to be about. Outline and define the following components:

- **The main character:** Don't forget the kinds of obstacles this character will encounter. You can read how to build a main character throughout the book, but the topic is covered most deeply in Chapter 9.

- **The overall look of the game:** Consider the setting. What colors will you use? What overall look and feel are you looking for? (Retro? Cartoon? Gothic? Maybe a Gothic retro cartoon?) Chapter 7 describes how to set up the visual feel of a game.

- **The main screens:** Most games have

    • A main play screen (or two)

    • An instruction screen

    • Some sort of introduction

    • A Game Over screen, or maybe two: one for when the player wins and one for when the player loses

    Chapter 7 describes how to build multiple screens for your games.

Draw these visual elements on paper.

- **The objects on each screen:** You have to build everything in your game. The visual design part is important but relatively easy.

✔ **The role/behavior of each object:** Decide these details upfront for each object:

- • How the object moves

- • Whether it's controlled by the user or the computer

- • Whether it does something when it interacts with other objects

- • Whether it makes sounds

- • What happens when it leaves the screen

After you finish defining these objects, convert your sketches into reality. This sounds like a pretty easy step, but it's the one that might cause you a lot of grief. You probably know exactly what you want all the screen objects to do, but a computer is incredibly stupid.

You have to convert your clever ideas to statements so clear that even an idiot computer can understand them.

Learning to code

Mountain climbers train before they scale the big mountains:

✔ **Learn:** They learn the tools of the trade, practicing on small hills and isolated, safe areas before testing their skills on actual mountains.

✔ **Pace:** When they're ready to climb Mt. Everest, climbers don't go for the top in one day. They build a solid base camp at the foot of the mountain. Then they create another camp higher up, and another even higher.

✔ **Progress:** At each camp, the ultimate goal is still the summit, but the intermediate goal of the next camp is the task at hand.

A mountain climber concentrates on the next step.

The same advice is really good for all programmers, beginning or advanced:

✔ **Master the tools of the trade.** There's no getting past the fundamentals (which this book shows).

You need to know both

- • The basic ideas of programming

- • The principles of game development

✔ **Know the goal.** That's why you start with a written description of your program.

✔ **Use small steps.** Concentrate on mastering one task at a time.

In this book, chapters show you specific skills and apply those skills in simple games, so you can

- Learn the skills you need for complex games.

- Practice these skills in isolated programs.

✔ **Enjoy the view.** Game programming is supposed to be fun.

Celebrate your progress! When you succeed at a viable chunk of code, do a little Hampsterdance. (If you don't know what I'm talking about, visit www.hampsterdance.com.)

✔ **Pace yourself.** Your first program won't be the next version of *Quake,* but there's plenty of fun in writing games that are a little less ambitious. Eventually, you'll build your skills so you can write something way better than *Quake.*

Game Programming 101

Game programming is a process. All the programs in this book use the Flash environment, but the details of Flash programming aren't the most important factor. When you want to make a game, you need to choose an environment that will work as well as decide a strategy for creating the game.

Selecting a language

If you're reading this book, you've chosen Flash as your environment. Excellent choice!

✔ **Flash is an ideal environment for beginning game creation.**

Flash makes a lot of the implementation easier, so you can concentrate on the content of your games instead of all the details of memory management, image drawing, and reading the input devices. (Fancier environments make you put a lot of work into such details instead of mastering the craft of game development.)

✔ **Most commercial games are written in 2-D, using C++ and graphics engines like DirectX or OpenGL.**

Those are really great environments, but they aren't necessarily what you need while you're learning the process of game development.

If you want to be a racing champion, you don't just show up in Indianapolis with a helmet. Starting your driving career in a high-performance machine is foolhardy and dangerous. You begin your career racing karts and then advance through more challenging vehicles. That's why you should start programming with Flash and ActionScript:

- C++ is like a Formula 1 car — fast and difficult to handle.

- Flash and ActionScript are like a go-kart (albeit a souped-up, Internet-enabled go-kart that outperforms any computing environment NASA had during the moon program).

Planning tasks

Game programmers prepare by planning several parts of the game:

- **Encapsulating objects onscreen:** All the things that move around on the computer screen are called *sprites* by game programmers.

    Chapter 6 shows you what need to know:

    - What a sprite is

    - How to create a sprite with Flash tools

    Flash has a great object called a *movie clip* that can easily be used as a basis for sprites. Chapter 6 shows how to use it.

- **Accepting input from the user:** There are all kinds of user input devices, but Flash games concentrate on the mouse and the keyboard.

    Chapters 2 and 6 show how to get information from the mouse, and Chapter 8 describes reading the keyboard in Flash.

- **Moving things realistically:** Game programmers must

    - Understand the physics properties of position, velocity, and acceleration, and attach these characteristics to a sprite so that it moves in a realistic fashion.

    - Simulate such useful physical properties as gravity and friction.

    Chapter 6 shows how to manage basic motion in Flash. Read about more sophisticated motion in Chapter 9 and see how to create realistic vehicles in Chapter 12.

- **Dressing up the user's experience:** Graphics, sound, and animation matter. Chapter 9 shows you how to use graphics, and Chapter 8 shows you to use sound effects.

✔ **Keeping the action fun:** Every game must be able to adapt to the user's ability level.

Find places to adapt the computer's ability so the computer always gives users an interesting challenge. As I describe each game in the book, I give hints how you can make the game easier or more difficult.

Chapter 2

Cruising and Using the Flash Environment

*T*he Flash development environment has a lot of powerful features that can be intimidating to a beginner. For example, the default screen has 12 different panels with over a hundred buttons, icons, and menu choices. Fortunately, there's a lot of stuff you won't have to worry about, and the following sections present the essential interface features — such as the Stage and Timeline — so that they begin to make sense very quickly. The best way to find out about the Flash MX environment is to use it to write some programs. This chapter helps you build a basic adventure game, and along the way, you get chummy with the basics of the Flash interface.

Creating a New Program Project

The ideas in this chapter can be put together to build the classic first program, one that declares your programming prowess to the world. Figure 2-1 illustrates my take on this masterwork.

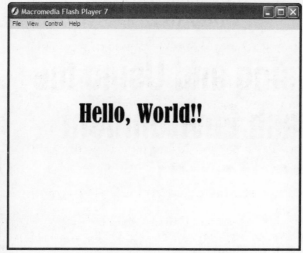

Figure 2-1:
This is a
very friendly
program.

When you first open Flash, you see a screen much like the one shown in Figure 2-2, which displays a list of project templates that you can create. The choice that you make here determines the starting characteristics of your project, but you can change most of the settings after you learn to manipulate objects and their properties.

To begin a new game project, just click Flash Document in the Create New column.

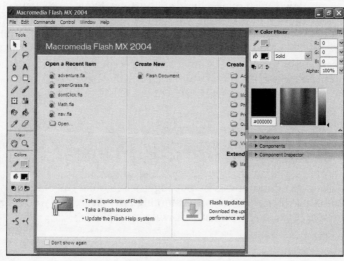

Figure 2-2:
Build a
new Flash
document to
get things
started.

The basic Flash Document project provides the foundation for everything you do to create your game program. From this base document, you can

- ✔ Add buttons, text boxes, and game objects to populate the game interface.
- ✔ Draw and color basic shapes that are the foundation of your games.
- ✔ Move your game's objects around in the game staging area.
- ✔ Control how your objects react over time.
- ✔ Respond to user input from the mouse and the keyboard.
- ✔ Play sounds.
- ✔ Create anything else you typically see in Web-based games.

The other templates simplify the creation of other kinds of programs, including projects optimized for mobile devices and video applications. You can build a game designed to fit on a Pocket PC, a Palm Pilot, or the new generation of cellphones! There's nothing really that fancy about the templates. Everything you can build with them can also be created with a normal Flash document. The templates are simply preset for specific kinds of projects. For example, the Mobile Device templates are designed to be the size of typical PDA and mobile phone screens.

Examining the layout of the Flash environment

As you begin your project, you see a screen like the one shown in Figure 2-3. A Properties Inspector, (bare) Stage, Tools panel, Timeline, and panel stack are at your disposal.

The following sections show how you use each section of the work area.

Stage

Most of the Flash work area is taken by a large rectangle near the center of the screen. This area is the *Stage,* where the action of your game takes place. After you create your games, the user sees only the Stage and the objects that you create bouncing around and interacting on it.

The term *Stage* is from Macromedia's earlier product *Director,* which took a moviemaking analogy to somewhat ridiculous extremes.

Tools panel   Timeline   Stage   Panel stack

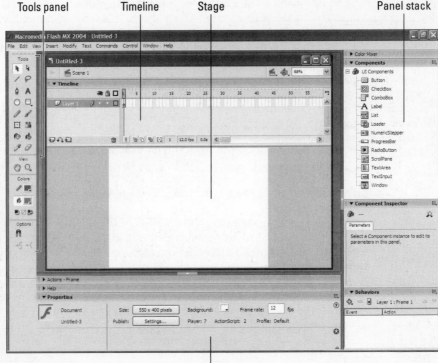

Figure 2-3:
The Flash
MX screen
is divided
into several
major
sections.

Properties Inspector

Properties Inspector

The Properties Inspector box is directly below the Stage. The *Properties Inspector* allows you to change characteristics of the things (such as the buttons, enemy objects, and the player's character) that populate your game. The Properties Inspector also changes automatically to reflect whatever object you're working with.

When the Stage is selected, the Properties Inspector box shows things that you can change about the Stage, such as the size and background color. When you create other objects (space monkeys or whatever) for your games, you use the Properties Inspector to change certain characteristics of these new objects.

Tools panel

The *Tools panel*, which goes along the left side of the screen, features tools for drawing and manipulating basic graphics. You use these tools to create the visual representations of the characters in your game.

Hello, World!

Looking around the interface is nice, but you're here to do some programming! May I suggest that your first program reflect one of the oldest traditions in programming? (Programming has all kinds of tradition and folklore, despite its relatively short time on the scene.) When programmers encounter a new programming environment, they often try it by writing a program that simply says, "Hello, World!" It's a fun tradition, but it also has a practical side. The `Hello World!` program has these benefits:

✔ It's about as simple of a program as you can write.

✔ It provides some kind of feedback (or visible output).

✔ It demonstrates a basic understanding of the mechanics of your programming environment.

There's no point in writing a more complex program until you get down the very essentials. Make sure you can write a minimal program that runs correctly and proves its existence by displaying some output. All other programs will be based on this foundation, so make sure you understand it before you add more meat to the program.

The tools are similar to common painting and drawing programs.

Timeline

The *Timeline* is a grid-like feature at the top of the Flash editor screen. Here, you can work with keyframes and layers to help create and refine your project.

Keyframes

In Flash animation, the Timeline indicates how various elements react over time. As a game programmer, however, you use the Timeline a bit differently, breaking your program into little slices of time called *keyframes*. You repeat each keyframe indefinitely. The timeline for an animation is often thousands of frames long, but most programs take only a few frames because each frame repeats. Instead of relying on the Timeline to control how elements move around on the screen, your code does all the work.

Layers

When you view a typical Flash document, many timelines are stacked on top of each other. Each row of the Timeline represents a different *layer,* which is used to separate parts of the game.

As a programmer, you don't need layers as often as animators need layers. Your code performs most of the features that animators usually generate with layers.

A program by any other name . . .

As a computer programmer, you often name things such as program files, variables, and functions. Keep these rules in mind when creating names for your files and the other elements that you name for your future projects:

✔ **Use meaningful names.** Don't call your file something like `George.fla` or `X.fla` because in a day or two, you won't know what those things mean.

The name should be long enough to be descriptive but not so long that it's tedious to type (or lend itself to typing errors).

✔ **Avoid spaces.** Some operating systems let you use spaces in filenames, but it's a really bad idea. Your Flash programs will eventually end up on the Internet, where it's quite likely they'll be hosted on a Linux or Unix machine. These environments are very fussy about spaces in filenames.

✔ **Carefully capitalize.** Some operating systems care about the *case* (capitalization) of

a filename, and some don't. You don't know what kind of computer will host or run your program after it goes on the Internet. I recommend creating a convention and sticking with it so you don't confuse yourself later.

I prefer *camel-case,* like `helloWorld.fla`. Use lowercase letters everywhere except to *separate* words; use uppercase letters to *start* new words.

✔ **Avoid punctuation.** When you're naming files in a programming environment, be very careful about punctuation and other special characters. These characters often have a special meaning that could cause you problems. For example, the asterisk (*) character is sometimes used as a wildcard character, so don't use it in a filename.

The underscore character — _ — is usually safe, but you should avoid most other special characters, such as $ and #.

Panel stack

The right side of the screen is taken by a series of panels called the *panel stack,* which houses the tools that help you build your games. Figure 2-2 (shown earlier) shows a few panels in the panel stack: specifically, you can see the Color Mixer as well as collapsed forms of three other panels you won't need in this book.

When I show ActionScript programming steps throughout this book, I tell you which elements in the panel stack to use and how to use them.

Writing on the Flash Stage

Writing a `Hello World!` program in Flash is ridiculously easy. In fact, there's no actual programming to it. You can create this simple program with the drawing tools that Flash provides. Follow these steps to say, "Hello" to the world:

1. **Start Flash and click the Flash Document icon in the Create New area.**

   Surprise! A new Flash document appears.

2. **Click the upper-left frame on the Timeline (directly under the number 1).**

   This selects Frame 1, Layer 1 as the starting point for your program.

3. **Click the Text tool (which looks like a capital A) from the Tools panel and then click and drag a rectangle on the Stage where you want your message to go.**

4. **Type your greeting message to the world in the rectangle you created.**

   You can see my message in Figure 2-4.

5. **Highlight your text message to select it.**

6. **Change the text characteristics by using the options you find in the Properties Inspector (along the bottom of the screen).**

   The Properties Inspector panel allows you to modify the text much like you do in a word processor. Play with the text's font, size, and color properties. You can even select and manipulate individual characters or words in a text box. Go crazy and add a few more text boxes to the stage, if you want, to get a feel for all the things you can do with text on the Stage.

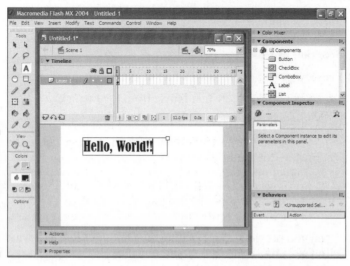

Figure 2-4:
With the
Text tool,
you can
easily write
text onto
the Stage.

7. **Click the Move tool (the black arrow) from the Tools panel; use this tool to select items on the Stage and move them around to your heart's content.**

   When the Move tool is selected, you can simply click objects on the Stage to select them and view their properties, or click and drag them to move them around the Stage.

8. **When you're finished creating, choose File⇨Save to save your `Hello World!` program.**

   The Save dialog box prompts you to choose a folder and name your program.

   The sidebar, "A program by any other name . . ." has naming recommendations.

   Save early, save often. You never know when your computer will be struck by a typhoon or something.

All this text manipulation is fun, but seeing how this little program looks outside the Flash environment or in a Web page (so you can impress your friends and family with your programming prowess, no doubt) is even more fun. The following section puts your Flash program to work!

Testing your program

After you create and save your program, you're ready to run it and see how it works! To view a program, follow these steps:

1. **Make sure the program that you want to test is the current (or only) program in Flash.**

2. **Preview your program with one of these commands:**

   • Choose Control⇨Test Movie from the menu bar.

   • Press Ctrl+Enter.

   If you have experience with Flash Animation, get in the habit of using Ctrl+Enter to preview your Flash game program. (In Flash Animation, pressing only Enter, without the Ctrl key, allows you to preview your animations.) Pressing only Enter can allow you to preview a very simple program (like your `Hello World!` program), but it won't execute code embedded in your programs.

When you preview your creation, you should see a new window pop up with your program inside (something like you see in Figure 2-5). Bask for a moment in the glory of your accomplishment!

Figure 2-5:
The completed **Hello World!** program declaring its birth.

Making a Web page with your creation

If you have access to a Web server, you can publish your work for anyone on the planet to see.

Web page files

To publish your game, choose File⇨Publish from the menu bar. Flash makes a new version of the program for you. Choosing the Publish command generates three different files in the typical publication process. After you publish a program, the folder containing your FLA file contains three related files with these suffixes: `.fla`, `.swf`, and `.html`.

To locate your published game, look in the directory where you saved the Flash file; you should see three other files as well.

.fla

The FLA file is the original Flash program file that was created and saved.

This file is larger than the other two related files. This file contains all the materials necessary for working with the program in Flash. A program file works only in the Flash editor, but you can change it as much as you want.

Think of the FLA file as a photographer's negative. It contains information but isn't useful by itself to the viewer.

.swf

An SWF file is a squeezed version of the program file. Its size is squished (*compressed*) so it can be delivered over the Web. It's created when you publish the program.

Think of the SWF file as a photographic print. It's the completed and compressed version that's useful for the viewer.

Anyone who has a copy of the Flash plug-in (that's nearly everyone) can run your SWF file by clicking it. Users don't need a full-blown copy of Flash to see your program, and they can't change your SWF file.

Usually, you won't make people click an SWF file to play your games. Packaging an SWF onto a Web page is better and easier. This automatically creates an HTML file that you can use.

.html

An HTML file carries the packaged SWF program to the Web. The HTML file is created when you publish the program, along with the SWF file it carries.

Think of the HTML file as the picture frame for your other files. If you wish, you can edit the HTML file with whatever tool you use for editing Web pages.

In this chapter's example, the `helloWorld.html` file is a very simple Web page that has the code necessary to incorporate the `helloWorld.swf` program. If you load this file into your browser (and the appropriate plug-ins are installed), the program runs without the user even knowing that Flash was involved.

If you know HTML, you can modify the resulting page all you want or even copy and paste the `<OBJECT>` and `<EMBED>` tags created by Flash into your own Web pages.

Server requirements

You might also want to make your program visible on the Web.

- ✔ If you want your program to be visible over the Web, you need to
  - Have access to a Web server.
  - Make the program's SWF and HTML files available on that server.
- ✔ If you're writing programs just for fun, you don't need to worry about server stuff.

Adding Buttons

Admittedly, the `Hello World!` program really doesn't do much. It'd be much more interesting to have a program that does something useful. The `Don't Click` program shown in Figures 2-6 and 2-7 is more interesting because the user can control the program, albeit in a very limited way.

Figure 2-6:
I bet you're dying to click that button.

Figure 2-7:
When the player clicks the button, a little window pops up and complains.

3-D buttons

Lines with the right color, shade, and width can make any screen element look three-dimensional. (Computer programs often use this convention to make your buttons look clickable.)

A few changes give your button the appearance of a 3-D button with the light coming from the top-left corner of the screen. For this effect, select the border lines individually with the black arrow Selection tool and change their shade:

1. **Make the top and left borders a brighter shade.**

2. **Make the bottom and right lines a darker shade.**

You can adjust the border width and color by changing the properties in the Properties Inspector (as shown in the figure here).

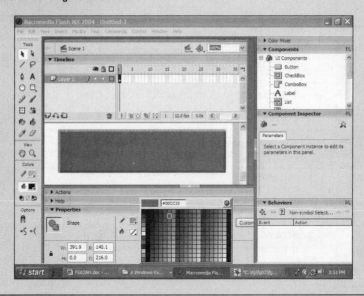

The Don't Click program is really cool because it introduces interactivity. In this example, the program has a button sitting in the middle of the screen:

- Nothing happens until the user clicks the button.

- When the user clicks the button, the user is treated to a lavish display of multimedia extravagance (if you've lavished extravagant multimedia on the program, anyway).

If you're viewing this program at this book's companion Web page, you probably won't see the Ouch!! message. That message goes to a special secret location visible only to programmers (that's you!). I explain the output window in the "Saying Ouch!!" section later in this chapter. Just run the program from within Flash, and everything will work fine.

The Don't Click program demonstrates two critical interactivity features that are covered in the following sections: buttons and pop-up screens.

Building a button

Flash has some built-in button objects, but it's very easy to build your own. Building your own buttons lets you control how your button looks and acts.

Follow these steps to build a button:

1. **Create a new Flash program (if you haven't already created a new program).**

   I show you how to do this earlier in the chapter.

2. **Draw a rectangle on Layer 1 of Frame 1.**

   Make sure that the rectangle isn't touching any text or other drawings on the screen because Flash automatically combines any overlapping objects.

   Buttons don't have to be rectangles, but this example is traditional.

3. **Modify the rectangle's visual characteristics.**

   Change size and color all you want via the Properties Inspector but don't put any text on the rectangle at this point.

4. **Change the rectangle's appearance.**

   Try the steps in the sidebar "3-D buttons."

5. **Select the rectangle.**

   When you're happy with the look of the button, use the black arrow to select it by selecting around the entire rectangle or double-clicking it.

6. **Change your rectangle into a symbol by choosing Convert to Symbol from the Modify menu or by pressing F8.**

   A *symbol* is a generic term for a custom object in Flash. Flash supports three types of symbols. The button is one type of symbol. The other two are movie clips (see Chapter 6) and graphic symbols, which are rarely used in game programming.

   When you create a symbol, you see a dialog box, like Figure 2-8.

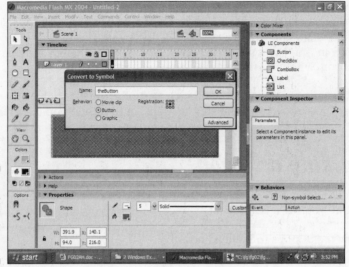

Figure 2-8:
Use Convert
to Symbol
to create
buttons.

Symbol objects are the foundation of all ActionScript programming. The "Symbolically speaking" sidebar describes all three types.

7. Name your button by choosing the Button option in the Convert to Symbol dialog box and then giving your button a name.

For this example, I call mine `theButton`.

Use these rules for button names: Don't use spaces, be careful with capitalization, and don't use any punctuation.

Introducing the Library

After you create your button object, note these two changes:

- **The button looks slightly different onscreen.**
- **You can't select the individual parts of the button.** And, when you select the newly created button, you see it surrounded by a new kind of blue rectangle.

Some very interesting things happen behind the scenes when you create that button. To see what's changed, look in the Library. Choose Library from the Window menu or press Ctrl+L (or F11) to make the Library appear.

Symbolically speaking

ActionScript programming uses three different kinds of symbol objects:

✔ **Button:** Sits still until the user clicks it

Buttons often change their appearance when the mouse is over them or when the mouse clicks them, but they don't move around much.

✔ **Movie clip:** Moves around on the Stage

Chapter 6 shows you how to use movie clips as objects that bounce and crash around onscreen.

✔ **Graphic:** Simple graphic with very few capabilities

Graphic symbols are rarely used in game programming because they're less powerful than buttons and movie clips.

The Library is so important that I'm amazed it isn't a default part of the layout. One of the first things I do when I sit down to a new copy of Flash is set up my own layout:

> ✔ **I make the Library the most prominent element in the right-hand panel.**
>
> ✔ **I minimize all the other panels in the panel stack.**

Note the Save Panel option of the Window menu that you can use to save a particular panel layout. You can then get back to that layout with the Panel Sets option of the Window menu. As you get more comfortable with Flash, you'll probably have your own preferred layout. I suggest that you make the Library easy to reach because you need it all the time for both traditional animation and programming. You'll see your button listed in the Library. You can use the icons at the bottom of the Library to edit or delete the button as well as to look at its properties. More interestingly, you can drag a button from the Library and drop it on the Stage, as shown in Figure 2-9.

This ability to create new buttons indicates a key feature of objects in the Library: They are *definitions* of objects rather than *instances*. It's a subtle but very important difference. I have some students in Macedonia that I teach via a remote connection. If I want to send them some cookies, I probably could, but they'd be crumbled when they got there (the cookies, not the students). Instead, I could send the cookie recipe and have my lab instructor who is already there make the cookies to take into class. Rather than sending actual cookies, I'm sending *instructions*. The instructions can be reused again and again to make cookies, but instructions themselves aren't cookies. (Chewing on the index card won't be nearly as satisfying as a real cookie.)

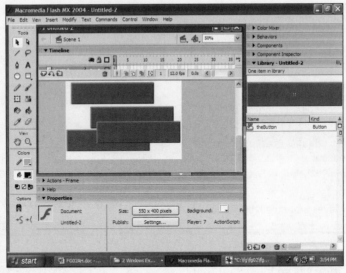

An object in the Library is a definition or recipe for something on the Stage. The object on the Stage is an *instance* of the Library element, just as a cookie is an instance of the recipe definition. This is important in Flash programming because you want all your buttons in a game to look similar. That way, you can design a button one time and reuse it all over your program. If you want to modify the look of your button, you then have to edit it but one time; all the other buttons are immediately modified as well.

Adding state to your button

You can make your buttons even better by applying a *mouseover* effect to them: That is, you can change a button so it looks depressed (pushed down, not saddened) when the mouse is over it or clicks it. (How do you make a button depressed? Don't call, don't write, don't send flowers . . . rim shot, please.) Seriously, Flash has an easy way to add different appearances to a button:

1. **Edit the button.**

   a. Right-click your button in the Library.

   b. Choose Edit from the resulting menu.

   You see a screen much like Figure 2-10. Notice the changes to the Timeline.

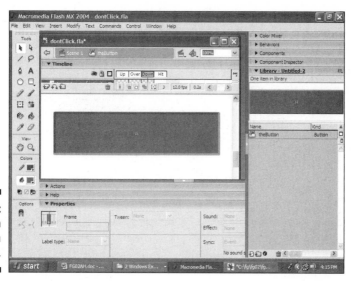

Figure 2-10:
The screen
for editing a
button.

2. Choose a state.

When you edit a button, you have all the normal tools at your disposal,
but you also have a slightly different Timeline. In fact, it's more of an
event line now; it really isn't a timeline at all anymore. The four boxes in
the button editor refer to four different states of a button.

To make your own event line, follow these steps:

a. *Select the second frame in the Timeline (the frame labeled* Over*).*

b. *Insert a new keyframe by either pressing F6 or choosing
   Insert➪Timeline➪Keyframe from the menu system.*

This new frame indicates how the button looks when the mouse is
over it.

3. Modify your button.

Change the button's size or color or any other characteristic of the
button by using the Properties Inspector.

If you want the button to look as if it's been clicked, just change the borders so that the top and left borders are a darker color and the bottom
and right borders are lighter, as described in the "3-D buttons" sidebar,
earlier in this chapter.

4. Give your button another state.

In the same way as creating a standard button, you can create another frame to indicate what the button should look like when the user clicks it: That is, the mouse is over the button, and one of the mouse buttons is being held down. I created three different views for my button by manipulating the border colors.

- *No action:* In the *up* state, the button looks like it's sticking up when it's being left alone.

- *Mouseover:* In the *over* state, all the borders are the same color as the button itself, making the button look as if it's being pressed flat onto the page.

- *Clicked:* In the *down* state, the border colors are set to make the button look as if it has been pressed down into the page.

The fourth frame is special because it is never shown to the user. Instead, you use it to indicate the size of the button's *hot spot* (clickable area) onscreen. By default, you can click the button's visible appearance to activate it. If your button is an odd shape (say, text without a rectangle behind it), the user should be able to click near the text without hitting the text exactly to activate the button. You can draw a rectangle in the Hit frame to indicate what the clickable area will be. With ordinary rectangular buttons, I usually skip this step.

5. **Return to the main program.**

   When you're done modifying the button states, look above the Timeline to see an indicator reading Scene 1. You can click this link to finish editing the button and get back to your main program. If you had any other button instances onscreen, you'll see that they instantly change when you return from the button editor.

6. **Test.**

   Test your new button by running your program. Be sure to save your program first and press Ctrl+Enter to run the program. (***Note:*** Running your program by pressing only Enter doesn't activate the button features. See the section, "Testing your program" earlier in the chapter for a more thorough discussion.) Move your mouse over the button and click it to see all the various button states in action.

Finishing your button

If you've followed this chapter to this point, your button is looking really good now, and your users are going to want to click that puppy. After all, the whole point of a button is to look like it can be clicked. Here are a couple more little flourishes, though, that you can do to make the button act properly: namely, give the button a name and a label.

1. **Return to the main program.**

   Make sure that you're no longer editing the button. You shouldn't see the Up, Over, and Down states in the Timeline. To run this check

   a. *Click* Scene 1 *above the Timeline if you're still in button-editing mode.*

   b. *Make sure that there's only one instance of your button on the Stage.*

2. **Name the instance.**

   a. *Select the button.*

   b. *Set its name to* theButton *in the Properties Inspector by typing the new name in the text box that reads* <instance name>.

This is different than naming the button in the Library. In the Library, you're giving the recipe a name. On the Stage, you give each cookie its own name.

3. **Add text to your button.**

   Buttons often have labels (text for the user) associated with them, so throw some text on top of your button. I've found the best way to guarantee that users will do something is to forbid it, so I placed a text field telling the user not to press the button on top of the button. You can use anything you want for a button's label, including spaces and punctuation.

Adding code to the button

For a button to be useful, you add some behavior to the program so the button does something (besides automatically change its state) when it's clicked.

Follow these steps to breathe life into your button:

1. **Display the Actions panel.**

   The key to code is the Actions panel, usually located near the bottom of the layout. If it isn't visible, press F9 to make it reappear.

Flash MX (as opposed to MX 2004 and later) had a beginner's mode for the Actions panel. Congratulations; you're now an expert. The beginner's mode is extremely frustrating to work with, and there's no real need to use it. Use the menu at the extreme upper-right corner of the Actions panel to use expert mode. Later versions of Flash don't have the beginner's mode, so you won't need to worry about this problem.

The Actions panel is where you write most of your code.

2. **Choose the correct frame and layer.**

   For this example, select Frame 1, Layer 1.

   The Actions panel title bar should read `Actions - Frame`. If the Actions panel title bar reads `Actions - Button`, select the frame in the Timeline before you add any code.

   There are many approaches to writing code in ActionScript. Other books or tutorials show you a different technique, but my technique pays big dividends when you want to build complex and extensible games easily.

   Be absolutely sure you're in the right place when you type this code. I must stress this: The Actions window should read `Actions - Frame`. If it reads `Actions - Button` or something else, your code won't work. To get to the right place, click Frame 1, Layer 1 right before you begin typing the code.

3. **Write some button-handling code.**

   To create a button that responds to mouse input, type the following code *exactly* as it appears here, including spelling and capitalization:

```
// Don't click Me Program
// Demonstrates button clicks

theButton.onRelease = function(){
  trace ("Ouch!!");
} // end enterframe
```

Understanding the code

The code adds some interesting behavior to your button. There's a lot going on here, but it isn't too hard to understand.

Comments

The first two lines of the button code in the preceding steps

```
// Don't click Me Program
// Demonstrates button clicks
```

begin with two forward slashes (//), which indicates a *comment*.

Comments are special text that aren't run by the Flash environment. Even though they are ignored by the computer, comments are important in programming because they explain to other programmers (and you) what's going on. You'll appreciate having comments describing such information as what a program does and who wrote it. I use comments throughout my code.

Why not incorporate text into the button?

You might wonder why I add text to the button after creating it rather than incorporating text into the button itself. The answer has to do with the instance-description problem that I describe earlier in this chapter (in "Introducing the Library"). The text that's associated with a button is an *instance-level* element: That is, each instance of the button has its own label. If you've followed the chapter to this point, I've shown you only how to modify the entire class or definition for all labels in the program. If you try to modify the text on one button, you also change the text on all the buttons in the program. By adding the text as a separate element after you place the button, you get the same effect without much effort.

Building pseudocode for the event

ActionScript is an *event-driven* language: That is, your program is designed to sit around and wait for certain events to occur.

Most game programming involves describing

- ✔ Events that might occur
- ✔ What the computer should do when an event occurs

I recommend writing out the computer's tasks in English before you translate it into the actual programming language. *Pseudocode* is a good way to do this.

Computers are extremely stupid. To get a computer to do something as simple as say, "Ouch!" when a button is clicked, you need to give very explicit instructions in exactly the right form, with exactly the correct spelling and syntax. Be sure that you understand what you want the computer to do. Writing pseudocode shows you the tasks that you can translate as code in the picky language that the computer requires.

In `dontClick`, you're writing code to handle the button-click event. In essence, your code says the following:

```
When the user clicks the button called theButton
  say "Ouch!!"
Stop thinking about the button
```

The logic, written in English, is an example of pseudocode. And this logic happens many times per second while the program is running.

Responding to the button click

The point of having buttons on the screen is to indicate to the user that something will happen when he clicks that button. For that reason, every button you create will have some sort of code attached that does something when the button is clicked.

If you've followed this chapter to this point, you have an instance of the button called `theButton` on your screen. The button has some built-in characteristics, including the ability to recognize certain events. You are doing a number of interesting things when you write this code:

```
theButton.onRelease = function(){
```

You are specifying that the code following this statement will happen when the `onRelease` event of `theButton` occurs. Any button can respond to a number of events, but `onRelease` is the most commonly coded.

Programmers usually make things happen when a button is released (`onRelease`), not when it's pressed. This lets users touch a button without committing to it. The button behavior happens only if the user both presses and releases the mouse over the button. Think of it this way: If you click the `Launch the nuclear missiles` button and then you change your mind, you can move the mouse off the launch button before you release the mouse button, and World War III can be averted.

Saying "Ouch!!"

In the event-handler code, the middle line is the part that pops up this little dialog box reading `Ouch!!`:

```
trace ("Ouch!!");
```

Lots of very interesting things are happening in one little line of code:

✔ **The `trace` statement sends text to an object called the *output window.***

This little window pops up automatically when you use the `trace` statement while testing your program within the Flash environment . If you use your program in a Web page or run the SWF file directly, all the `trace` statements are ignored.

The `trace` function is a programmer's tool. It's a very quick and easy way to send messages to yourself as a programmer, but these messages aren't shown to the program's users. Anything you type in the parentheses behind the word `trace` are copied to the output window, which is visible only in the Flash editor. (*Note:* All the text you send to output should be in double quotes.)

The `trace` line is indented in my code to indicate that it is part of another structure. Flash doesn't care how your code is indented, but it's a very good habit to indent carefully. In a typical program, you usually have code with many layers of structure nested inside each other. Proper indentation can help you keep track of your intentions and prevent mistakes.

✔ **The semicolon indicates the end of the line.**

Almost all your code lines will end with a semicolon. The only common exceptions are

- Lines that end with braces (`{ }`)

- Comment lines (begin with `//`)

Ending the function

In the `dontClick` example program, the last line of code ends the function. The right brace (`}`) is lined up under the line that begins the function to indicate that this brace ends the function. (I usually use a comment character after an ending brace to indicate exactly what I'm ending.)

Stylin'

How you indent and how many spaces you use in indentation are matters of style. Professional software developers are often required to use a particular style, and programming teachers also often have specific style guidelines. There are a number of *style conventions* (writing guidelines) in use.

✔ If you don't have a programming style, I recommend that you use the style that I use in this book. It's straightforward, very typical (can be used in many other programming languages), and produces nice, neat code.

✔ You will sometimes see Flash code written in other styles. For example, the braces in a function might be on their own lines rather than on the same line as the function identifier. The code will work in the same way, regardless of this style nuance. The programmer simply subscribes to a different style convention.

Part II
The Next Steps

The 5th Wave   By Rich Tennant

"We need to pimp our storage system."

In this part . . .

Time to build some sophisticated games. Here you can see how to move data in and out of your programs, master some essential programming techniques, make random numbers, and make text change dynamically onscreen. Just in case anybody's bugging you about how much time you're wasting on games, the big example in this part is highly educational. So there.

Chapter 3 is all about the concept of *state*. You discover how to give your programs multiple personalities, and how to swap between the various states. You finish the part by building an adventure game.

Chapter 4 describes the three moods of text in Flash. You read how to make and use random numbers, how to use conditions to change the way your code behaves, and how to convert various types of data when necessary.

Chapter 5 describes how to make an educational game in some detail. I don't just show you the finished game, but I take you through the process, going from sketches to a finished game. You build a math game that generates random math problems. It just doesn't get any more fun than that!

Chapter 3

Altered States

Computer games often have several scenes. For example, your game might have an introduction screen, a help page, the main game, and pages for winning and losing conditions. Each of these scenes is a *state* (another little tidbit that could be handy if you find yourself magically transported into a computer science cocktail party).

If you follow the instructions in this chapter step by step, you build a simple adventure game. In the process of building the game, I show you how to make a game change according to players' actions.

State of Nonconfusion

The states of an game are like the scenes of a movie. Each movie scene describes a particular environment or situation but all the scenes work together to form the movie.

The ghosts in *Pac-Man* are examples of different states. They look and act differently under different circumstances:

✔ They're tough most of the time.

✔ As soon as you eat the power pills, they run away like little wimps.

The instructions in this chapter demonstrate how to create the adventure game featured in Figures 3-1 through 3-3.

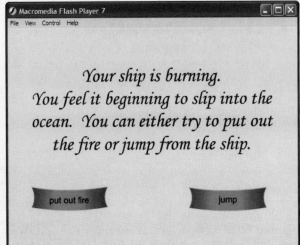

Figure 3-1:
Bad
news . . .

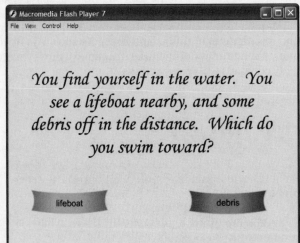

Figure 3-2:
Cool! A
lifeboat!

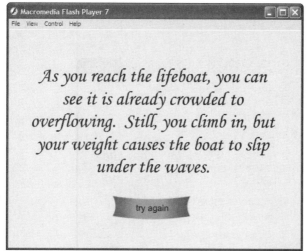

Figure 3-3:
Uh, oh . . .

Adding Keyframes

Think of an adventure game as a series of situations. In each situation, you make a choice that can move you to a new situation (which programmers call a *state*). In an adventure game, the user needs to have the sense of moving around. The same techniques are used in almost all other games to provide instruction screens and also winning/losing conditions.

The Green Grass program shown in Figures 3-4 and 3-5 shows how a very simple game with two states could work.

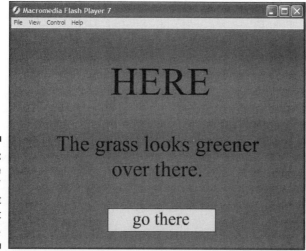

Figure 3-4:
This is the "here" state. I can't wait to get over there.

Figure 3-5:
Now I'm in
the "there"
state. This
could keep
me busy for
quite some
time.

In the Green Grass program, the entire game has two states: The gamer is either in the HERE state or in the THERE state. Each state has a button that allows the player to switch to the other state.

As you can read in Chapter 2, buttons use their own Timeline to handle various states. Most Flash games use the Timeline in a similar way to handle the notion of state. You can specify points on the timeline as *keyframes* (something special happens during that frame). You can read about keyframes in Chapter 2, also.

Building the Green Grass game

The Green Grass game is the simplest example of state-changing that I can think of. Because this technique is used in almost every Flash game, you need to know how to build *multi-state games* (games that support more than one state).

To build the Green Grass game, follow these steps:

1. **Create a new program.**

   Start in Frame 1, Layer 1. (That's where you normally start, anyway.) The first frame is automatically the first keyframe, so you don't need to explicitly make it a keyframe.

2. **Build the HERE page.**

   Place text boxes to indicate the user is "here." See Chapter 2 for details on creating text boxes.

3. **Build the button.**

   Create a rectangle, select it, open the Symbol dialog box (press F8), and convert it to a button. If you wish, you can also modify the button properties.

   Chapter 2 shows you how to build buttons.

4. **Add text to the button.**

   Put the text *over* the button instead of incorporating it *into* the button.

5. **Make the second keyframe.**

   When you're happy with the HERE frame, click Frame 10, Layer 1 in the Timeline. Insert a new keyframe from the Insert menu or by pressing F6.

6. **Add a third keyframe.**

   Insert another keyframe at Frame 20.

   Your Timeline looks like Figure 3-6.

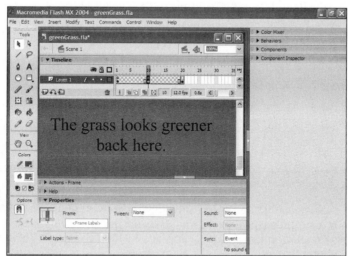

Figure 3-6:
The Timeline now indicates two different states.

You won't really do anything with the keyframe at Frame 20. It just gives you some breathing room that proves useful when you name the frames.

Modifying the second frame

When you create a keyframe in Frame 10 (see the preceding steps), Flash automatically duplicates everything in the first frame. Although they look the same, the objects in Frame 10 are different instances than those in Frame 1, and they can be modified independently.

1. **Modify the text.**

   For this example, select Frame 10 in the Timeline and modify the text in the text boxes.

   Use the black arrow to move or select a text box. Use the Text tool (described in Chapter 2) to modify the text inside the text box.

   When you move between Frames 1 and 10, you see different text.

   Don't incorporate the text into the button. If you incorporate the text directly into the button, you have a problem. Frame 1 and Frame 10 contain different instances of the same button (like two cookies baked from the same recipe). You can't modify an instance. To this point in the book, you've only seen how to change the entire class. If you change the text in one button, you change it in both. My suggestion is to leave text out of the buttons altogether and put a label on top of the button after it's been put onscreen. Your player will never know the difference, and it's a lot easier.

2. **Name the keyframes.**

   Referring to the frames by number gets tedious, so name those frames.

   To give a frame a name

   a. *Select the frame.*

   b. *Look at the Properties window at the bottom of the screen.*

      Indicate a name for the label, as shown in Figure 3-7.

   To create states in this program, name Frame 1 `here` and Frame 10 `there`.

   Frame-name capitalization and spelling are very important. Follow the same rules for naming frames as for naming files: Use no spaces, no punctuation, and camel-case, all of which you can read about in Chapter 2.

3. **Name the buttons.**

   Each button instance can have its own name.

   In the editor, I call the button that lives in the `here` frame `btnGoThere` and the one in the `there` frame `btnGoHere`. It's pretty obvious that `btnGoThere` is the button that goes *there*.

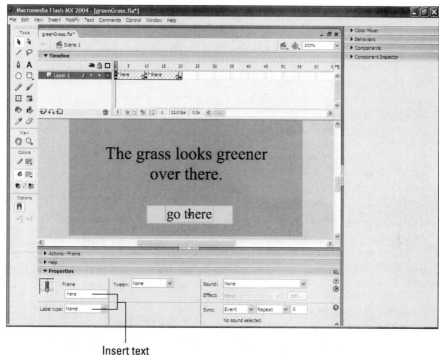

Figure 3-7:
Name the
frame.

Insert text

It might confuse you that `btnGoHere` is in the `there` frame, but it really makes sense when you think about it. The name of the button indicates what the button does, not where it resides. If you're *here,* you want to go *there.* `btnGoThere` is in the `here` frame, and this is the button that takes you *there* — but it can't *be* there. The `btnGoThere` button goes *there* but is located *here.* If you're still puzzled, just look at the program in the Flash editor, and it will probably make sense to you.

Follow these rules for button names:

- Begin buttons names with `btn` so you can easily see that the symbol you just created is a button.

- Make buttons names indicate what they do.

I need it this easy because I get confused easily.

Creating the game animation loop

Games usually are built with an animation loop. Different programming languages have different ways to construct this loop, but the main idea is always the same. The critical parts of the program repeat many times a second, responding to input from the user, manipulating objects onscreen, and displaying the results. Flash has an elegant technique for repeating the code on a particular frame, and this technique is the foundation of ActionScript game programming.

Stopping the train

If you try to run this chapter's example program as soon as you finish building the two states, you get some very strange behavior. The `here` frame shows at first. In less than a second, the `there` frame shows up. `there` is visible for about a second, and `here` comes back. The buttons won't do anything, and the program seems to have a mind of its own. The `here/there` cycle repeats until you stop the program.

A little history lesson is in order. Flash was first an animation tool, and animation is still its first inclination. Animators normally use the Timeline to specify when certain activities happen. In its default setting, Flash shows 12 frames per second (fps). So, before you put any code in the program, Flash assumes that the program is a normal animation. In the example program, it shows Frame 1; then at Frame 10 (almost one second later), it reaches a keyframe. Remember that a keyframe is a hint that something has changed on the Stage, so Flash now displays the new (`there`, in this example) information on the Stage. At Frame 20, there's no more information, so Flash goes back to the beginning and does it all again. This works great for standard, noninteractive animation, but the whole point of computer games is to let the player have some control. Game programmers subvert the Timeline to their own purposes. Rather than letting the Timeline run on its own, programmers prefer to let the program perseverate over and over on one frame until the user somehow indicates it is time to go on. (I know, *perseverate* isn't exactly the most simple word I could have used here, but I like it, and my editors let me get away with it. Go make friends with a dictionary.)

Many games that can last for hours use only two or three keyframes on the Timeline!

To keep a multi-state program looping on only one frame, follow these steps:

1. **Select the frame.**

2. **Type the following script in the Actions panel:**

   ```
   stop();
   ```

   This command stops the default progress of the Timeline. It doesn't actually stop Flash from running, but it continuously repeats the current frame.

Swapping states

After you create a game with multiple states, you need code to switch between the various states.

In this chapter's example, the player switches states in the game by clicking buttons. Each button has code that sends the program to a new keyframe.

Example: here frame

The Actions panel for the `here` frame contains the following code:

```
stop();

btnGoThere.onRelease = function(){
 _root.gotoAndStop("there");
} //end event handler
```

This code first stops the program so that it continually loops through the here frame. It then creates an event handler for the button on this frame. Be sure that you have one button on this frame and that it's named btnGoThere. When that button is clicked, the program goes to a frame called there. The _root keyword indicates that you want to control something (and for the moment only) in the main Flash movie in your program.

The Flash program is a MovieClip object. Throughout this book, I point out a lot more about objects in general, and especially the amazing MovieClip. The MovieClip object has all kinds of built-in characteristics and abilities. You can use code to tell the MovieClip what to do. In this case, when the user clicks a button named btnGoThere, I want the main movie to move to a frame called there and loop that frame indefinitely. The gotoAndStop() command is a built-in feature of MovieClip. The program looks for a frame with the specified name and moves control to that frame.

Example: there frame

The there frame has very similar code:

```
btnGoHere.onRelease = function(){
 _root.gotoAndStop("here");
} // end release
```

The code in the there frame doesn't need the stop() keyword because the only way to get there now is via the button in here, which already tells Flash to stop and repeat the there frame. The button in this frame is btnGoHere, and its job is to send control back to the here frame.

Making a Great Adventure

With text boxes, buttons, and the notion of state, you have all the tools you need to build a great adventure game. To illustrate, I've written a silly little shipwreck adventure that I introduced at the beginning of the chapter (refer to Figures 3-1 through 3-3).

Before you read on, try the shipwreck game yourself. It's at the companion Web site as adventure.html. It isn't any masterpiece of interactive fiction, but it's kind of fun, and I'm going to spoil the game by describing it in the next few pages. You've been warned! Check it out at

www.dummies.com/go/flashgameprogrammingfd1e

Planning your game

It doesn't take long for games to get complicated. You must, therefore, take some time to organize your thoughts before turning on the computer.

Most adventure games begin life as diagrams. Figure 3-8 shows you my diagram for the shipwreck adventure game.

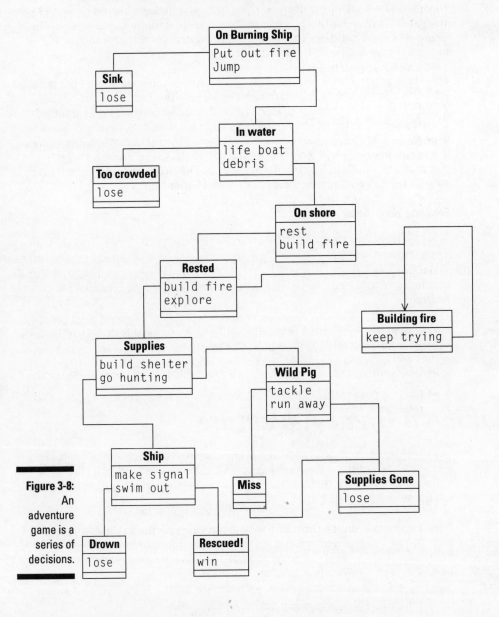

Figure 3-8: An adventure game is a series of decisions.

You can see by looking at the diagram that I've got a devious mind. Building a fire is an endless trap (as you know if you watch those reality shows featuring people on deserted islands). It doesn't matter whether you try to tackle the pig — you lose. There's but one path to the winning situation — and several losing paths.

As small and simple as this game is, thinking it out still took quite some time. The process of planning all the decisions and figuring out how they fit together is a challenge in its own right. You need to have the basic design of the game figured out before you worry too much about exactly how you're going to code it. I did try to keep it organized:

- ✔ **Each decision has a title** as well as one or two possible actions.

- ✔ **All the decisions look pretty much the same.** Each decision has descriptive text and a button or two at the bottom to indicate actions. All use the same font and button styles.

- ✔ **No graphics are needed.** To let the text speak for itself, I decided not to incorporate graphics or sound into this program.

Setting the stage

After you have a plan for your epic game, plan the general layout of your program. The first keyframe is simply an introduction to the game, but it sets the stage (pun intended) for everything that follows. Every page will have a large text box describing the current scene as well as one or two buttons on the bottom.

Make your life easier: Get these big-picture ideas right the first time rather than change them after you write the entire program:

- ✔ Design the first screen well because you duplicate it to make all the others.

- ✔ Choose your fonts so that text boxes and buttons are easy to read and reflect the style of your game.

Building the main text box

When you have your plan in place, you're ready to build the main text box. Follow these steps:

1. **Set up a large text box in the middle of the screen.**

2. **Type some sample text in the text box so you can see how it looks.**

   Choose a font size and color that go well with the theme of your game. Make sure that

   • The font contrasts well with the background color of your game.

   • The type is large enough to be readable.

Building the button

Because buttons are very important in this game, design your buttons so that they contribute to the game's theme.

I wanted my buttons to look nautical, so I created a special ribbon shape.

You can make buttons look like anything you want, but if you want to make buttons like mine, follow these steps:

1. **Build a normal rectangle.**

   Start by drawing a normal rectangle onscreen.

2. **Modify your button shape.**

   Use the black arrow Selection tool (on the Tools palette) to modify your rectangle. When you move the black arrow near one of the sides of the rectangle, note how the cursor changes: This indicates that you can bend that side. You can use a similar trick to move the corners.

3. **Make your shape into a button object.**

   After the button's general shape is right, you can turn it into a button object by pressing F8. You can then add other states as described in Chapter 2.

   I used the Gradient tool in the Color Mixer to get a nice blend of colors. The color mixer is available in the panel stack.

4. **Add other button states if you wish, such as** `over` **or** `down`**.**

   The visual look of your buttons isn't important to the function of your game. You can change it later.

   After you create the button, place a text box over the button so you can add text.

Creating the diagram nodes

After you have the first frame done, give it a name and then add a keyframe. I like to put my keyframes ten frames apart so I can read the labels on the Timeline. Name each keyframe when you build it. Use your diagram for hints, but remember that frame names shouldn't have spaces. To keep things consistent, I recommend copying the frame name onto your diagram as well.

Editing the nodes

Your game state diagram is the key for building the entire game.

Do these steps on each keyframe to make the nodes described in your diagram:

1. **Change the text boxes.**

Change the text for each frame to contain a description of the scene and a the new dilemma facing the player.

2. **Make the needed buttons.**

If the node has two or more choices, drag more button instances from the Library. (Read about the Library in Chapter 1.) Add a text box on top of the new button to give it some text.

3. **Name the buttons.**

Name each button carefully. I like to use a mnemonic name for what the button should do. For example, if the button should go to the `buildFire` frame, call the button something like `btnBuildFire`. This practice makes it easy for you to determine what code should be written for the button..

If you want to line up your buttons with those on other frames, you can use the Onionskin feature of Flash to show lighter versions of other frames behind the frame you're editing. The Onionskin buttons are small icons underneath the Timeline. The most useful icon looks like an outlined square behind a blue square. You can drag selectors on the Timeline to indicate which other frames are visible. This makes it easy to get a consistent look between frames.

Coding the buttons

You could test your program now, but it would run in a straight line under the strict control of the Timeline. Coding gives the player the ability to control his own experience. There is a lot of code in this program, but it's all extremely predictable and repetitive, so it's not terribly difficult. Every button in the program needs code to tell Flash what to do when the user clicks it. All the buttons do the same basic task: Go to a frame and stop there. As an example, Figure 3-9 illustrates the code for my `jump` frame.

The frame occurs when the player jumps into the water near the beginning of the adventure. At this point, he can choose to swim either toward a lifeboat or some debris floating in the water. I created a button for each option, named `btnLifeboat` and `btnDebris`. (Gotta love the logic of mnemonics.) Here's the code for the frame:

```
btnLifeboat.onRelease = function(){
 _root.gotoAndStop("lifeboat");
} // end release

btnDebris.onRelease = function(){
 _root.gotoAndStop("shore");
} // end release
```

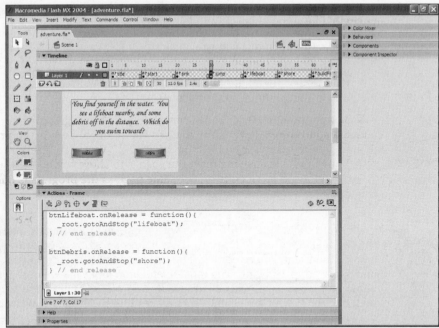

Figure 3-9:
The Flash editor after I write the jump frame.

This code is very much like the code from the Green Grass program earlier in the chapter. Each button has code telling Flash what to do when that button is clicked. In each case, the program's focus shifts to the appropriate state. Every keyframe has code much like this but adjusted to reflect the buttons in that frame as well as the new frames that the buttons indicate.

The very first frame should also have the following line to indicate that program control shouldn't flow along the Timeline but should be controlled by the buttons:

```
stop();
```

You might know about Flash's behavior mechanism, which greatly simplifies this type of coding. Resist the temptation to use this shortcut. You will outgrow the capabilities of the behavior mechanism very quickly. It's very good practice to write the code yourself as well as write it by hand (rather than copying and pasting) so you can get used to the syntax and the flow of programming. If you don't know what Flash behaviors are, that's fine. You won't need them because as you progress through this book, you can do things they can't dream of.

Making the game your own

This book's companion Web site show every line of code for my shipwreck adventure. But the real point is to make your own game. Use mine as a guideline and look at it for ideas or help when you get stuck, but make your own game.

I slightly modified the HTML files containing all the programs in this book: I added a source code listing. You can see every line of code in the program without having to open the file in Flash. Usually, you won't need this for your own games, but because my main purpose is to show you how these programs work, seeing the code on the same page as the program is handy. You can check the code at

```
www.dummies.com/go/flashgameprogrammingfd1e
```

Time to make your own adventure game! To get started, follow these steps:

1. **Start with a diagram.**

   You'll be lost if you don't. Break your story into nodes. Give each node a name, a description, and a list of choices. Each choice should point to another node. (See the earlier section, "Creating the diagram nodes.")

   You can create the diagram on a whiteboard (my all-time favorite programming aid), paper, index cards, crayon on a tablecloth, lipstick on a mirror, or whatever. You can even use a software tool such as Microsoft Visio or open source tools like dia. (I include a copy of this software on the Web site that accompanies this book.) Don't open Flash and start writing without a plan. I tried. I got hopelessly confused. Don't let it happen to you.

2. **Build the first couple of frames, complete with buttons and code, and test them.**

   If your logic is flawed on the first frame, there's no point in writing 15 or 20 more until you figure out what was wrong on the first one.

3. **Extend and modify.**

   After you have things working on the first few frames, you can go crazy. It's pretty easy when you keep your diagram taped to the wall while you work. That's what I did. (You *did* make a diagram, right?)

4. **Embellish the program.**

   You can add graphics to your program. I show you how to do more elaborate graphics, animation, and sound effects in later chapters. You can always come back and embellish your program when you know some other tricks.

5. **Have fun and write a masterpiece!**

Chapter 4

Getting with the Program

Games are really about information. The computer gets information from the user in some form, manipulates that information, and sends information back to the user. In this way, games are just like any other kind of computer programming. (Most "serious" programs, such as databases and spreadsheets, don't feature explosions and sound effects. Hmmm, I wonder whether they'd be more fun if they did.) This chapter shows you a little about how computers work with information and how they make basic decisions based on that information. Along the way, you build programs that roll dice and make decisions.

Different Text for Different Jobs

The first task is to understand how Flash works with information. Games are a lot more fun when they're interactive. Somehow, you need Flash to read text that the user types onto the screen and then change text onscreen while the program runs.

The `greeting` program featured in Figures 4-1 and 4-2 illustrates a basic form of communication between the computer and a human player.

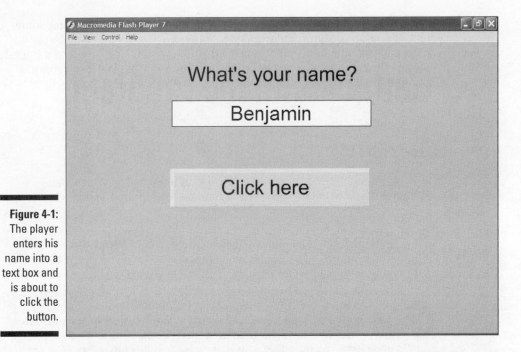

Figure 4-1:
The player
enters his
name into a
text box and
is about to
click the
button.

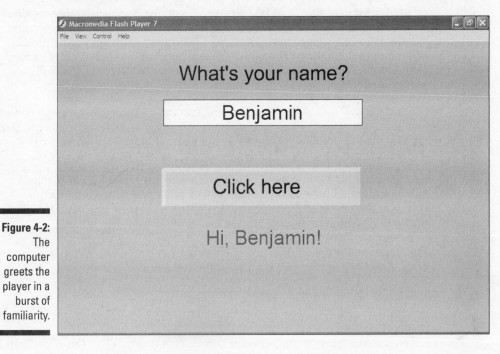

Figure 4-2:
The
computer
greets the
player in a
burst of
familiarity.

The `greeting` program is interesting because you can use it to greet some-one you've never met. The user types text into a specially designated text area, and the button outputs a greeting based on that text. The secret ingredient of this program is the various subspecies of text areas. Flash supports three different types of text areas — static, dynamic, and output — each with different capabilities.

Static text

Static text (such as the ordinary text box that asks, "What's your name?") doesn't change when the program is running. You set up the text when designing the game:

- ✔ The program can't change the value of the text.
- ✔ The user can't change the value of the text.

Static text boxes aren't given names. They usually contain information that's meant to stay onscreen, such as text for labels and button captions. The mouse pointer doesn't change when it hovers over static text, and the user can't copy static text from the screen.

In the `greeting` game, the text area that reads `What's your name?` as well as the button label (`Click here`) are examples of static text.

Dynamic text

In comparison with static text, *dynamic text* can be changed by the program. Although the user can't change a dynamic text field, code inside the program can change its value. Dynamic text boxes can be named, just like buttons. Users can select text in a dynamic text box and also copy values from dynamic text, but users can neither write directly into these boxes nor paste values into them.

Dynamic text is usually used to send *changeable* information to the user. It's often used in games for scorekeeping. In the `greeting` program, the output text box (the one that contains the final greeting) is the only dynamic text box.

Input text

Input text lets the user type a value into the computer. When the user clicks a text field that's indicated as input text, the cursor changes to an I-beam, and the user can type text into the text box. The program can read this text and manipulate it.

Input text is almost always either named or associated with a variable. This chapter shows you how to associate a variable to a text field — a really easy and useful technique. In the `greeting` program, the field where the user types a name is an input text box.

Building the Greeting Program

The `greeting` program is relatively simple to build. The following sections show you how to start by setting up your form with several kinds of text boxes.

Adding text fields to the Stage

The Text tool is used to place text elements on the screen. Use some variants of the Text tool to make the three different types of text fields:

1. **Begin with a new Flash document and make a button.**

   Chapter 2 shows how to start a document as well as how to make a button.

   Your button doesn't have to be as fancy as mine. For a simple program, you don't have to worry about changing button states. Keep it simple at first; then you can add the cosmetic touches later.

2. **Place your first text field on the stage.**

   For the game's label, the top text field should simply read `What's your name?` This field is an ordinary text field, built by simply describing a rectangle on the Stage with the Text tool.

   Static text elements don't need to be named. While the text area is selected, the upper-left corner of the properties tab indicates `Static Text`, and there is no place to indicate the name of the text field.

   Figure 4-3 illustrates the properties available for static text elements.

3. **Create a static text field for input.**

   The user puts text in an input text field. To make one, follow these steps:

   a. *Draw another text element onscreen.*

   b. *In the Properties window, change from Static Text to Input Text (lower left).*

   Figure 4-4 shows some new properties for a text field designated as input text.

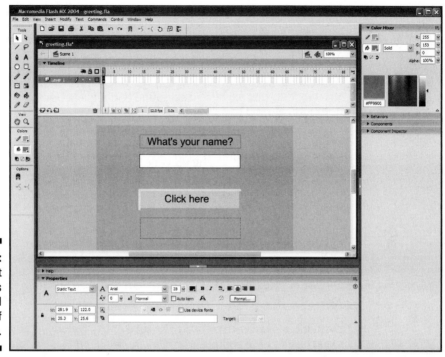

Figure 4-3:
A static text
field has
a limited
number of
properties.

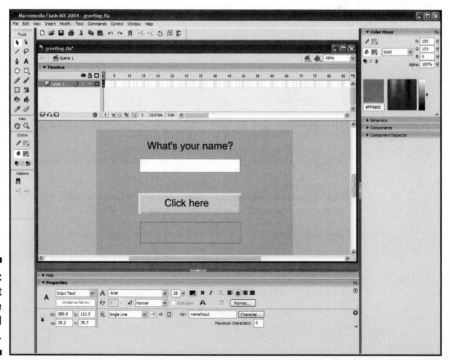

Figure 4-4:
Input text
has some
additional
properties.

The first detail to notice is that input text can have an instance name (like buttons do). Input text can be set to use one or more lines or even to show asterisks for passwords. You can also set a border around input text.

Flash lets you format input text any way you want, but you should provide some hints to the user that the text can be edited. Traditionally, programmers give editable text a white background and a black border. This provides a clue for your users.

The Var field lets you keep track of the contents of the text box in your programs. You'll see more about that in the following section.

Associating variables with text boxes

The interesting characteristic of dynamic and input text boxes is how their values can change. Somehow, the computer needs to keep track of the value inside the text box. That's important because the greeting program transfers information from one text box (the input text field) to another text box (the dynamic text field).

The information is transferred with a special entity called a *variable,* which is a special place in the computer's memory designed to hold information. Flash lets you create a variable and associate it with a dynamic or input text box.

To illustrate how variables and text fields are related, follow these steps:

1. **Select the input text field in the greeting program.**

2. **Assign the input behavior to the field using the Properties Inspector.**

   If the text field isn't already set to Input Text, change it now.

3. **Attach a variable to the field. In the Var field (which lets you associate a variable with the text box), type** nameInput.

   nameInput is the name of a *variable* (a place in the computer's memory that keeps track of the value of this text box).

   Use the normal naming conventions (case-sensitive, no spaces, no punctuation, camel-case) when creating a variable name.

4. **Create a dynamic text field to contain the output.**

   Use the same Text tool used to build other text boxes but set this field to Dynamic Text with the Properties Inspector.

5. **Assign nameOutput to the dynamic text field.**

   Select the dynamic text field and assign the variable nameOutput to it, again using the Var field of the Properties Inspector.

Changing a text box through code

Variables aren't very interesting until you write code. Write code to transfer data between text boxes like this:

1. **Create a button.**

   Build a button and call it `btnGreet`. Make the button as simple or elaborate as you wish, but make sure you turn your symbol into a button, not a movie clip or graphic symbol.

2. **Add the code.**

   Add the following code to the Timeline frame that contains the button:

```
btnGreet.onRelease = function(){
   nameOutput = "Hi, User!";
} // end greet
```

3. **Test the program.**

   Click the button. If all goes well, `Hi, User!` displays in the dynamic text box.

   Here's what's happening: In ActionScript, the equal sign (=) refers to assignment. In this case, you're assigning the value `Hi, User!` to the variable `nameOutput`. The variable `nameOutput` is associated with the dynamic text box. Whenever a program changes the value of `nameOutput`, the associated display onscreen is automatically changed as well.

I read the equal sign as "gets" in ActionScript, so the key line in this code would be read `'nameOutput gets "Hi, User!"'`. This is important because you aren't using the equal sign as it's used in mathematics: that is, to describe equality. I show you how computers say "equal" later in this chapter.

Reading information from an input text box

Variables are useful for storing information. Use a variable to extract information from input fields and also to send information to the user via dynamic text fields.

The `greeting` program should be a little more personable than it is so far. Right now, it always reads `Hi, User!`, but it ignores whatever name the user types into the text field. Modify the code in the frame so that it looks like this:

```
btnGreet.onRelease = function(){
   trace(nameInput)
} // end greet
```

For the preceding code fragment, when the user clicks the button, Flash sends the value of `nameInput` to the output window. (Remember, only the programmer can see things in the output window, but it's very handy for simple tests like this one.) The output window doesn't show the actual text `nameInput` but rather recognizes that `nameInput` is a variable and displays the value associated with that variable (which is whatever was typed into the text box).

Copying data from one text box to another

You can combine input and output to copy the value from one text box to another.

For a better kind of output than the trace window (which the user cannot see), change the button code so it looks like this:

```
btnGreet.onRelease = function(){
    nameOutput = nameInput;
} // end greet
```

Now the program copies whatever value is found in `nameInput` to `nameOutput`. Because both variables are associated with text boxes, the value typed into the input text is copied to the output text.

Combining text with string concatenation

Computer programmers are a fun-loving bunch. One of their favorite tricks is to take a really simple idea and give it a really complicated name. *String concatenation* — one of my favorite examples of this phenomenon — simply means to take two string values and attach them to make a longer string.

The following modification of the `greeting` code shows an example of string concatenation:

```
btnGreet.onRelease = function(){
    nameOutput = "Hello, " + nameInput + "!";
} // end greet
```

Here's how to break down the preceding code block:

- ✔ **If the user types** George **into the input text box, the output box reads** `Hello, George!`
- ✔ **The term** `Hello,` **is a** *literal* **value (something I want to print exactly as I enter it).**
- ✔ **The term** `nameInput` **is a variable name.**

  I don't want Flash to print the variable name (`nameInput`) but rather its value (`George`).
- ✔ **The exclamation point (**`!`**) is another literal value.**

  The quotes designate whether text is literal or a variable name.

Stringing me along

Text in programs is called *strings* because the internal structure used to store text reminded the early programmers of beads on a string. Oddly poetic, and the term has stuck.

Remember these two important rules:

✔ Literal values always go inside quotes, and variable names don't.

✔ Use plus signs to combine the literal and variable values.

Programmers almost always refer to text as *strings.* Now that you're a programmer, you should call text *strings,* too. People will be impressed with you. The plus signs (+) are used to combine string values. Of course, the term *text combining* would be easily understood by nonprogrammers, so programmers invented a more esoteric term for smunching text together, and the term they came up with is a doozie: *string concatenation,* which is the ridiculously complicated term for a simple notion: You combine literal strings with variables using the plus sign.

If anybody asks whether you're gleaning anything from this book, just feign modesty and inconspicuously pepper your conversation with the term *string concatenation.* They'll think you're really smart.

On a Roll: Making Random Numbers

Random numbers are a key part of computer game development. Whenever you want a game to be unpredictable, you need to add an element of randomness. This is done with a *random number generator.* ActionScript has the ability to create random real numbers between 0 and 1. (*Real numbers* are numbers with decimal points, so there are a *lot* of real number values between 0 and 1.) Often, you need to modify this value to get random values within a another specific range.

The `roll` program featured in Figure 4-5 illustrates a program that rolls a standard six-sided die.

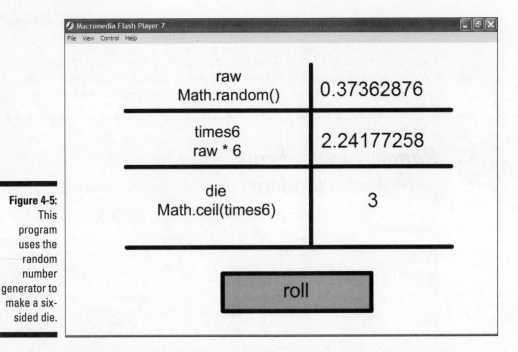

Figure 4-5:
This
program
uses the
random
number
generator to
make a six-
sided die.

For this discussion, just pay attention to the value labeled `die`. Click the button a few times to ensure that the values are what you expect (a random number between 1 and 6 with no decimal values). Unfortunately, ActionScript doesn't have built-in die-rolling capability, so I adjust the 0 to a value (created in the first step) until it's more like a die roll. Here's the full code for the button:

```
// roll
// demonstrates random number, ceil function
// algorithm for rolling a six-sided die
// Andy Harris, 12/04

stop();

btnRoll.onRelease = function(){
  raw = Math.random();
  times6 = raw * 6;
  die = Math.ceil(times6);
} // end roll
```

In the preceding code, the three dynamic text boxes are labeled with the variables they are associated with:

- The top text box is associated with the variable `raw`.

- The middle text box is associated with `times6`.

- The bottom text box is associated with `die`.

Introducing the Math object

Even if you don't love math, it comes in handy time after time when you're writing games. Fortunately, ActionScript has a bunch of great tools that do most of the math for you. They're all collected in something called the `Math` object.

Random acts of randomness with Math.random ( )

In the `roll` game button code, the first line of the code creates a random number and assigns it to the variable `raw`.

Random numbers are generated by the `Math.random()` function. This is a built-in technique for creating random values between 0 and 1 with a long string of decimals.

Numbers containing a decimal point are *real numbers*. Programming languages sometimes have more than one type of real numbers. `Math.random()` returns one of the most common type of numbers, called *floating point* real numbers. Floating point real numbers are often abbreviated as *floats*. (Isn't all this funky vocabulary great? You can concatenate a string but not a float. Try to work *that* into your lunch conversation this week.) `Math.random()` returns a float between 0 and 1.

Click the `roll` button a few times and watch the `raw` text box. The range of values shows that the results are evenly distributed random values.

Computers can't produce truly random values. The values created by the computer are always calculated by a formula, which is by its very nature predictable. However, the pseudo-random values given by `Math.random()` are perfectly suitable for game development.

Getting a 0–5 value

The `Math.random()` function produces a very nice float for the `raw` value, but there aren't any dice with that many decimal points. The goal is to make this thing act more like a die. The trick is to multiply.

The next line of code creates a value in a slightly better range:

```
times6 = raw * 6;
```

The variable `times6` (which is associated with the middle text box) gets the value of `raw` (the top text box) times six. In programming, the asterisk character (*) is usually used to represent multiplication.

Keep clicking the `roll` button and look at the `times6` textbox:

- ✔ The values are now in the 0–5 range, but they're never exactly 0 or 5.
- ✔ The `times6` value is related to the `raw` value, but `times6` reflects a wider range of possible values:
  - When `raw` is very small, `times6` is near 0.
  - When `raw` is larger, `times6` is nearer to 5.

Making a six-sided die

In the `roll` program, the `times6` value is a little better than the `raw` value, but it has two problems:

- ✔ It has all those pesky decimal values.
- ✔ It goes from 0–5, not 1–6.

The `ceiling` function is a simple math trick that solves both problems:

```
die = Math.ceil(times6);
```

In the `roll` game, the `times6` variable is a real number, and most dice display *integers,* which are those numbers that don't have a decimal value. (And you told your math teacher you'd never need to know that.) You need a way to convert a floating point value into an integer.

ActionScript has handy tools to do exactly that:

- ✔ **`Math.round()` rounds a number using the technique you learned in middle school.**
- ✔ **`Math.floor()` goes to the nearest integer lower than the floating point number.** In other words, it always rounds down. It lops off any decimal values and turns the float into an integer.
- ✔ **`Math.ceil()` rounds to the next higher integer.** When you think about it, that's exactly the behavior you want here. If `Math.random()` produces a 0, the die should be the lowest possible value, which is 1. If `raw` is `.99999`, `die` should be 6. `Math.ceil` always rounds up.

Gain from the pain

The hardest part of programming to learn isn't all the esoteric code and syntax. Instead, it's the process of thinking through a problem and applying specific coding concepts to the solution of that problem. Most real programming doesn't happen in a programming language at all! Programmers look for patterns that can be reused and then write these patterns in plain English. After you see a pattern, you can translate it to computer code. Here's the pattern for creating a six-sided die:

1. Get a random 0–1 float.

2. Multiply that number by 6.

3. Go to the next largest integer.

This kind of step-by-step description of a problem is an *algorithm,* which is the key to effective programming. Computer scientists spend their entire careers developing and analyzing algorithms. (Seems dull, but I've been to their holiday parties.)

The next step of algorithm development is to see how an algorithm can be improved. For example, what if you want a 20-sided die or a random number between 65 and 91? (Believe it or not, that last one comes up pretty often.) The algorithm could be improved like this:

1. If you want a random integer between *bottom* and *top,* generate a random float between 0 and 1.

2. Multiply that value by (top to bottom).

3. Use a `floor` method to lop off any decimal values.

4. Add bottom to the result.

After you know what you're going to do, you can look up the programming techniques you need in order to get there.

Keep clicking that `roll` button and watch the relationship between `times6` and `die` until it makes sense.

Making Decisions with Conditions

Computer games usually need to have some sort of decision-making ability: that is, the computer ought to do different things in different situations.

Figures 4-6 and 4-7 illustrate a completely simplistic form of this behavior in a program called `gotSix`.

If you run this program yourself (and you should), it has really odd behavior after it finds its first 6. I show you how to fix that in this chapter.

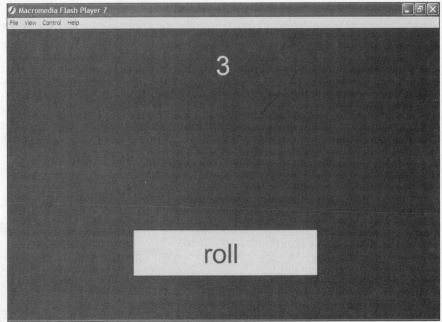

Figure 4-6:
Most of the
time, the
program just
rolls a die . . .

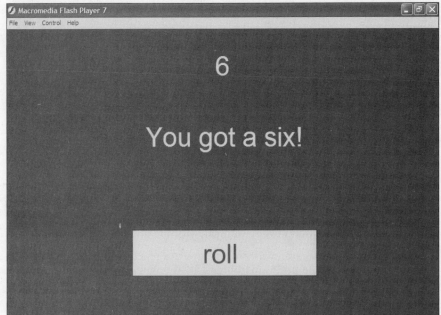

Figure 4-7:
. . . but if you
roll a 6, it
gets very
happy.

The gotSix program has these behaviors:

1. Roll a virtual die.

2. Check the value of that die.

3. If the value is 6, treat the player to a lavish multimedia display. (I'll add the fireworks and dancing pigs later, I promise.)

Although not very exciting, this program lays the groundwork for the behavior of all your computerized opponents.

The following code illustrates a key new programming gem called the if statement:

```
// gotSix
// demonstrates if, conditions
// Andy Harris, 12/04

btnRoll.onRelease = function(){
  //roll a die
  die = Math.ceil(Math.random() * 6);

  //check to see if it's a 6
  if (die == 6){
    output = "You got a six!";
  } // end if
} // end roll
```

Rolling the die

To create a program with the magical discernment of my gotSix program, begin by using the algorithm developed in the roll program.

The following code uses programming tricks to shorten the longer "make a 1–6 die" algorithm into one line:

```
die = Math.ceil(Math.random() * 6);
```

Shortcuts like this can shorten your code. The parentheses are used to indicate what's done first, just like in math.

The code begins at the innermost parenthesis and moves outward to run in this order.

1. Generate a number with Math.random().

2. Multiply that number by six.

3. Perform a `Math.ceil()` function on the resulting value.

   All the work of the `roll` program is condensed on one single line. Nifty, huh?

Checking your 6

The interesting thing about the `gotSix` program is that it differentiates based on the roll. The `if` statement is a great tool specifically designed to let your programs make decisions.

In the `gotSix` button code, you can probably guess what the rest of the code does. It's almost written in English:

```
if (die == 6){
  output = "You got a six!";
} // end if
```

If `die` (that's the variable that contains the randomly rolled die) is equal to the value 6, copy the value `You got a six!` to the `output` variable. This variable is tied to a dynamic text box, so it displays the phrase to the user.

The key to an `if` statement is a *condition,* which is an expression that can be evaluated as `true` or `false`. The action happens only when the condition is `true`.

You see how the `if` statement works if you've ever driven in a car with children. Think of this statement: "If you tease your sister one more time, I'm going to pull this car over."

✔ If I look in the rearview mirror and see sister getting pegged again, the condition is `true`, so I stop the car to play Dad.

✔ If the condition is `false`, we go driving happily along. No loving parental correction is needed.

Building the condition

`if` statements are great, but they use another important programming idea called a *condition.* Conditions are a pretty important part of programming, so you should know how to build them well.

In the `gotSix` program, the condition is `(die == 6)`. Conditions in Action-Script are usually encased in parentheses. Notice also the double equal sign (`==`).

In many languages (including ActionScript), a double equal sign means *equality*. Remember that you should read a single equal sign as *gets* and a double equal sign as *is equal to:*

- ✔ If the variable `die` is equal to the value 6, the program runs any code between the braces (`{ }`). You can put as much code as you want inside the braces, but you should indent each line inside the braces so that you can easily see that the code is part of a special group (that is, code that is executed conditionally).

- ✔ If the condition is `false`, code execution falls to the next line outside the braces. In this particular program, the next line is the end of the program, so nothing else happens.

Conditions are usually *comparisons*. Usually, you'll either compare

- ✔ A variable with a value
- ✔ A variable with another variable

The `gotSix` example uses the equality operator, (`==`) but ActionScript features some other comparison operators, featured in Table 4-1:

Table 4-1	Comparison Operators
Comparison	*Operator*
Equal	==
Not equal	!=
Less than	<
Greater than	>
Less than or equal to	<=
Greater than or equal to	>=

To build an `if` statement, follow these steps:

1. Begin with a condition.

   Decide how you can specify the decision you want by comparing either

   - A variable and a value
   - Two variables

2. **Create an `if` statement around the condition.**

   Building the `if` statement is easy if you've already thought through the condition.

3. **Write the code that should occur when the condition is `true`.**

   Indent all this code. (I usually indent two spaces.)

4. **End the `if` structure.**

   Use the right brace (}) to end the `if` structure.

I align this symbol with the `if` clause to make it clear that this is the end of the structure. I also highly recommend putting a comment indicating what structure you are ending. Remember to use two slashes (//) to indicate that the rest of the line can be ignored by the computer.

In many places, the right brace is used to indicate the end of a structure. If you get into the habit of explaining what you're ending and use proper indentation, you're much less likely to get confused when your programs get more complicated.

Responding to False Conditions

The `if` statement lets you do something if a condition is `true`, but sometimes you want one set of actions to happen if the condition is `true` and something else to happen if the condition is `false`.

Seeing the flaw in `gotSix`

Even well-designed programs sometimes have flaws. If you run the `gotSix` program a few times, you'll probably encounter an odd quirk.

Everything is fine until after you roll your first 6. The program dutifully tells you that a 6 has been rolled. The funny thing happens on the following roll, as shown in Figure 4-8: After rolling a 6, the program appears to report every single roll as a 6.

The program is working perfectly well. Here's the problem: Before you roll the first 6, the `output` variable and its corresponding text field are both blank. The first time you roll a 6, the value of `output` changes to `You got a six!`. If the next roll is a 4, the value of `output` doesn't change, so the text field still reads `You got a six!`.

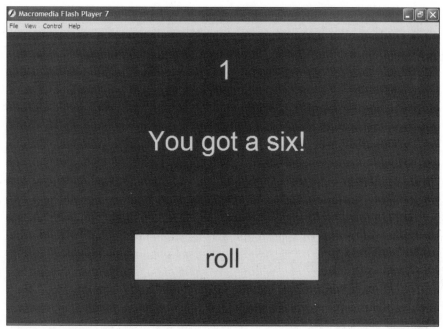

Figure 4-8:
Not a 6!

Using the else clause

A proper form of the gotSix program reports one thing if the player rolls a 6 and something else if the player rolls anything other than a 6.

The sixOrNot program featured in Figure 4-9 shows one way to solve this problem.

The code for the sixOrNot program in Listing 4-1 is only a little different from the rollSix program.

Listing 4-1:   Six or Not

```
// sixOrNot
// demonstrates if-else
// Andy Harris, 12/04

btnRoll.onRelease = function(){
  //roll a die
  die = Math.ceil(Math.random() * 6);

  //check to see if it's a 6
  if (die == 6){
    output = "You got a six!";
```

(continued)

Listing 4-1: *(continued)*

```
  } else {
    output = "That's not a six.";
  } // end if
} // end roll
```

Listing 4-1 features an important new wrinkle. The `if` statement begins just like the one in `gotSix`, but this improved program has an `else` clause. This second batch of program lines executes if the condition is evaluated to `false`. The condition is like a railroad switch, sending the program down one path or the other but never both. Note the indentation: This format helps you see that the various code segments are all part of the `if...else` structure.

This version of the program always reports something back to the user:

- ✔ If the computer rolls a 6, the program says so.
- ✔ If computer rolls a different value, the program sends a different message.

To incorporate an `else` clause, follow these steps:

1. **Begin with a condition.**

   Just like an ordinary `if` statement, the condition is the key to a well-behaved structure. This time, your code does something if the condition is `true` and something else if the condition is `false`.

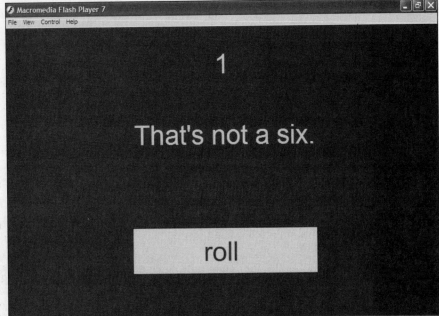

Figure 4-9:
This version
tells you
whether you
got a 6.

2. **Create an `if` statement around the condition.**

3. **Write the code that should occur when the condition is `true`.**

   You often start with an ordinary `if` statement and add the `else` clause later.

4. **Create the `else` clause.**

   The `else` clause contains a right brace, the keyword `else`, and a left brace, like this:

   ```
   } else {
   ```

   I usually put all the elements of the `else` clause on the same line, aligned with the `if` statement. Other programmers sometimes use other styles.

5. **Add the code that should happen when the condition is `false`.**

   Create another set of indented code lines after the `else` clause. This code is enacted when the condition has been evaluated as `false`.

6. **End the `if` structure.**

   I usually align the `if`, `} else {`, and `} //end if` lines vertically, so it's easy to see that they are related.

Making Lots of Decisions

Often, your programs have to make more complicated decisions. For example, maybe you want a different output for every possible die roll. In that case, you need a more sophisticated decision-making mechanism than the basic `if` structure.

The `if` structure is handy because computer programs constantly make decisions based on conditions. The program featured in Figure 4-10 shows another common kind of decision making.

The `binaryDice` program shows a die roll in binary (base 2) notation. Although this is a format that only a computer scientist could love, the program illustrates an important kind of branching situation: Every potential roll has a corresponding value.

The values shown in Figure 4-10 are an example of the binary mathematical system embedded deep into computer hardware. Don't worry if you don't understand how I got these values. If you want to know more, read up on how binary numbers work, including some online tutorials I've written:

www.cs.iupui.edu/~aharris/n241

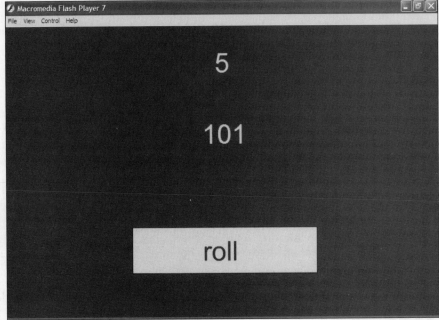

Figure 4-10:
This
program
reports a die
roll in base
2 notation.

This kind of situation comes up pretty often — that is, when you want to check one variable for a number of possible values. Most programming languages provide a special technique called the `switch` to simplify coding this kind of scenario.

The `switch` structure is used in a multiple-branching situation, in which you have one variable with many possible values, as shown in Listing 4-2.

Listing 4-2:   Binary Dice

```
// binaryDice
// demonstrates switch structure
// Andy Harris, 12/04

btnRoll.onRelease = function(){
  //roll a die
  die = Math.ceil(Math.random() * 6);

  switch(die){
    case 1:
      output = "001";
      break;
```

```
        case 2:
           output = "010";
           break;
        case 3:
           output = "011";
           break;
        case 4:
           output = "100";
           break;
        case 5:
           output = "101";
           break;
        case 6:
           output = "110";
           break;
        default:
           output = "problem...";
           break;
     } // end switch
  } // end roll
```

The switch statement begins with an expression (usually a variable name) inside parentheses. The switch statement is followed by a series of case statements:

- ✔ case: The case line ends with a colon (:) and not the typical semicolon (;) character. Each case in the structure indicates a possible value for the variable.

    You can place as many lines of code as you need in each case.

- ✔ break: The break statement indicates the end of a case.

    You can indicate as many cases as you need.

- ✔ default: The default case is used if no other case is true.

    Place a default clause even when you don't think it will ever be needed. This lets you still do something useful even if the unexpected occurs. (I included a default case in this situation. If all goes well, die should always have an integer value between 1 and 6, so the default clause should never occur. There is a big difference between what *should* happen and what *does* happen.)

To create a switch structure, follow these steps:

1. **Begin with an expression you want to evaluate.**

    This is usually a variable, but it could be the results of an expression or function call.

2. **Create the `switch` structure**.

   Use a `switch` statement to begin the structure. The structure uses braces to indicate code is part of the `switch` evaluation.

3. **Follow these steps for each case you want to define:**

   a. *Create a `case`.*

   Each `case` is a specific value that the expression might be equal to. You need to think of all the possible values of the expression and then make a `case` to handle each value you want to test.

   End each `case` line with a colon (not a semicolon, which you use to end most code lines).

   b. *Add code to execute if the `case` is triggered.*

   All code between the colon and the `break` statement happens if the `case` is `true`. Indent the code between the `case` and the next `case` to make this clear.

   c. *Finish the `case` with a `break` statement.*

   Unlike the `if...else` structure, you have to explicitly tell the `switch` structure that you're done and want to exit the structure. The `break` statement does this for you. End each `case` with a `break` statement.

   Sometimes you combine `case`s and don't need the break between them, but those circumstances are relatively unusual. At this stage in your programming career, you can safely assume that all `case`s end with a break.

4. **Create a default clause.**

   The default clause is used if none of the cases are triggered.

   Even if you think you've covered every possible situation, put a default clause in place to handle the unexpected or at least to tell you that something very strange is occurring.

Chapter 5

Making an Interactive Game

Text input/output and random numbers are very useful in games. This chapter shows how you put these ideas together to make an educational game to help children learn basic arithmetic.

This chapter really doesn't introduce a lot of new code. Earlier chapters describe everything you need to build interesting games. Still, the process of building games requires some practice. The focus of this chapter is designing and building a project as well as seeing what to do when the code doesn't work right.

Introducing the Math Game

In Math.fla, my math quiz ties together ideas from some of the earlier chapters in the book. You can easily modify it to suit your own needs. (Maybe you can customize it for the problems your kids are working on in school.)

The math quiz follows these steps:

1. **Begin with the menu displayed in Figure 5-1.**

2. **Choose a problem type.**

   The program presents five problems of the specified type. For each problem, the user

   a. *Receives a randomly generated problem like the one shown in Figure 5-2*

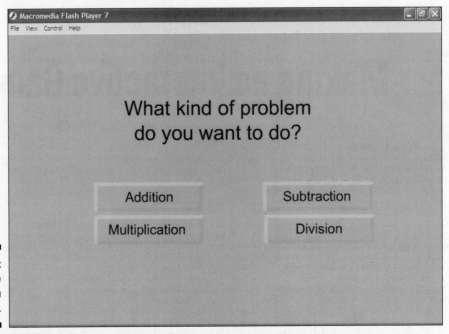

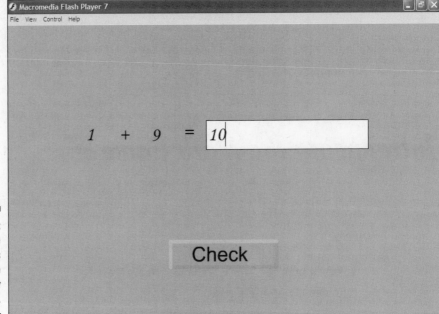

> *b. Types an answer and clicks the Check button to proceed*

Figure 5-3 shows the resulting evaluation.

3. **After five problems of the requested type, the math program returns to the main menu.**

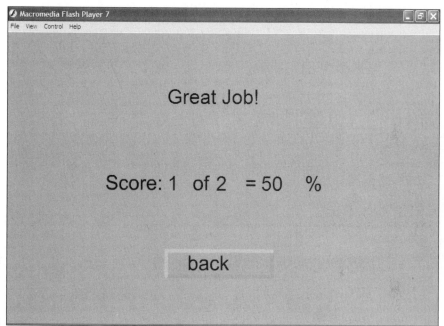

Figure 5-3:
So far, I'm
doing okay.

Making an Adder

With the skills in this chapter, you have enough knowledge to build a simple calculator, like the one displayed in Figure 5-4.

The user interface for this program is very straightforward. It includes two input text boxes, which are tied to the variables X and Y. (I really don't mean anything more specific than *X* and *Y*, so they're okay names for this situation.)

The button named btnAdd should perform these tasks:

1. Takes the input from the two boxes and puts them in variables.

2. Adds the variables.

3. Outputs the result of the addition in a text box tied to the sum variable.

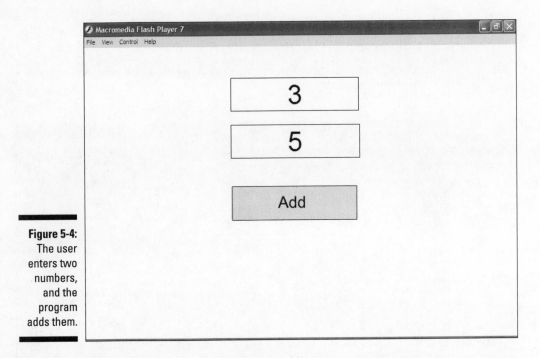

Figure 5-4:
The user enters two numbers, and the program adds them.

The correct code looks like this:

```
// addBetter
// converts variables to integers
// Andy Harris, 12/04

btnAdd.onRelease = function(){
  sum = parseInt(X) + parseInt(Y);
} // end add
```

What's with the parseInt stuff?

You might be wondering why I didn't simply write the function code like this:

```
btnAdd.onRelease = function(){

  sum = X + Y;

} // end add
```

You would expect this simple form to work, but when you run the program, you get surprising results, like the figure here.

The program doesn't work correctly. Fortunately, if you run it a few times, you can find a pattern. *Hint:* If you can identify a problem, it's usually easy to fix. In this case, Flash is confused about what kind of data it's using. Text boxes are designed to handle either text or string data. When you associate a variable with a text box, Flash assumes that you mean a string and thus sets up the memory in the special way associated with text. x and y are both seen by ActionScript as string variables because they come from text boxes.

The following line is surprisingly ambiguous:

```
sum = X + Y;
```

Because ActionScript assumes that x and y are string variables, it dutifully concatenates the two strings. According to this (flawed) logic, 3 + 5 = 35! Somehow, you need to tell ActionScript to interpret x and y as numbers so that the plus sign indicates addition. My addBetter program (see results in the figure here) shows how I correct this defect.

```
// addBetter
// converts variables to
    integers
// Andy Harris, 12/04

btnAdd.onRelease = function(){
  sum = parseInt(X) + parseInt(Y);
} // end add
```

The change in this program is the addition of parseInt(). This statement stands for *parse to integer*. that is, convert the string to an integer number.

By converting x and y to integers, this program eliminates confusion. As integers, the plus sign adds the two values (3 + 5 = 8) instead of concatenating them (3 + 5 = 35).

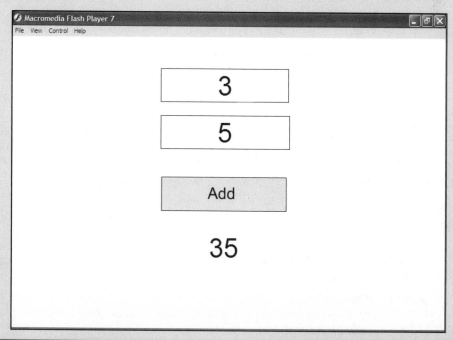

TIP

If variables don't work correctly, try explicitly converting variables into exactly the type you want:

✔ Force the variable myVar to be seen as an integer with this code:

```
myInt = parseInt(myVar);
```

✔ Force the variable myVar to be seen as a floating point number with this code:

```
myFloat = parseFloat(myVar);
```

Building the Visual Design

Creating a game like the Math game doesn't have to be intimidating. Break your design task into smaller segments so you have a clear path through the project. Follow these steps to build your game:

1. **Determine the states your program will have.**

   For example, the preceding Math game example gives the user three major activities. Each of these activities has its own distinctive look:

   a. Choose a type of problem.

   b. Solve a given problem.

   c. See the results of the solution attempt.

   I built the Math game with three keyframes: choose, solve, and report. Each of these frames can be considered a separate page because each does different things.

2. **Sketch the visual layout of each state.**

   Placing the design elements in this program first is important because the various text elements are related to the variables that the game manipulates. Also, the visual design gives you an easy visual template. When you see an input text box, you know you're going to get information from it. When you see a button, you know that it needs to respond to clicking with some code.

REMEMBER

   Before you can write any meaningful code for your Math game, you need to

   • Name your frames.

   • Associate variables with all dynamic and input text fields.

   • Name your buttons.

   In the Math game, the text boxes provide all the action. If you don't map out the variable names to the appropriate text fields, you can't write an interesting program.

3. Identify where elements go.

Start your program on paper. Follow these steps:

a. Diagram the elements you want onscreen.

b. Indicate which variables are associated with each text box.

c. Indicate how the flow moves from one frame to the next.

Throughout the following section, I show you my sketches for the Math game.

4. Write code for each frame.

After the design is done, the code becomes easier to manage because exactly what you need to do becomes more obvious. Each button needs some code attached to it (or it isn't a very interesting button). The button code manipulates the variables designated by the text boxes.

Designing the choose page

Figure 5-5 illustrates my original drawing for the choose screen in the Math game.

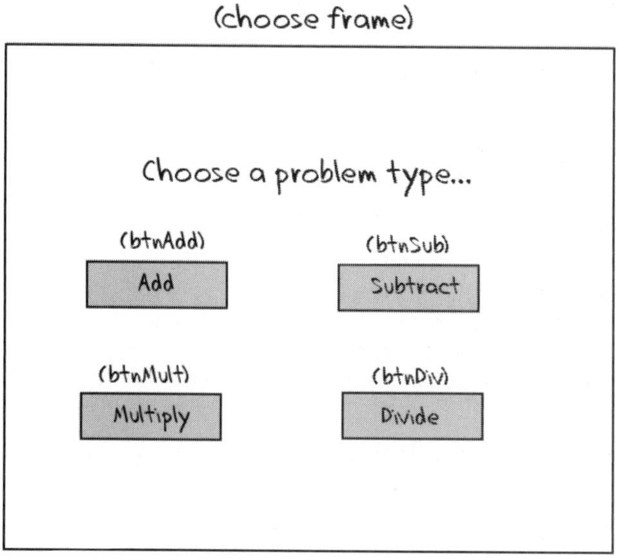

(choose frame)

Choose a problem type...

(btnAdd)
Add

(btnSub)
Subtract

(btnMult)
Multiply

(btnDiv)
Divide

Figure 5-5: My original sketch for the choose screen.

To get started, begin with the choose frame. This frame contains one static text field and four buttons.

Building the program first and then designing it later is tempting. Resist the temptation! Design the entire program on paper or a whiteboard (lipstick on a mirror, spaghetti sauce on the wall, whatever). The point of a sketched design is to see the main ideas while you aren't tied to the details of creating detailed code on the computer. If you use Flash to design your pages before you have a good plan, you will get mired down in details. After you create the design, you can execute the plan in Flash.

To create the choose page, follow these steps:

1. **Begin with a generic button design.**

   You reuse the button for the entire program, so begin by designing one button. You can either

   - Add several button states (as I did in the math example).
   - Create your button now and add the various visual states later.

2. **Make three more copies of the button.**

   After you create your first button, drag three other buttons from the Library onto the Stage.

3. **Make captions for your buttons.**

   Add captions to your buttons as static text boxes.

   Make sure your button labels are *static* text boxes. If you use dynamic or input labels, the mouse pointer turns into a text-editing I-beam, and the user can't click the button in the expected manner.

4. **Name the frame.**

   When you write code that moves between frames, you refer to each frame by its frame name. (You name a frame by entering the name in the Properties window when the frame is selected.)

   This frame lets the user choose a type of problem, so I call the frame choose.

Designing the solve page

On the solve page, there are two activities:

1. The problem is presented to the user.

2. The user enters a guess.

Figure 5-6 shows my diagram for the page.

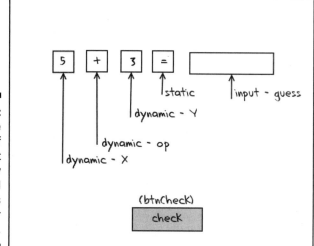

Figure 5-6:
Indicate
the type of
each text
box and any
associated
variables
in your
drawing.

If you account for all the necessary tasks in the diagram, building the page is pretty easy because all the decisions have already been made. Follow these steps for converting the diagram to a working frame:

1. **Create the `solve` page by adding a new keyframe to the main Timeline.**

   Name the frame!

2. **Create dynamic text boxes.**

   For user input, you need a text box for each of these values: X, Y, and op. To create text boxes for the X, Y, and op variables

   a. Set all these text fields to be dynamic.

   b. Associate each text field with the appropriate variable.

3. **Create the input text box for the user's guess.**

   The user's guess goes in an input text box. Follow these steps to create that text box:

   a. Create a text field.

   b. Set the `text` field type to Input.

   c. Associate the text field with the `guess` variable.

If you're using a custom font, associate that font with the text box. Chapter 7 shows you how to use a custom font and ensure that it works properly.

4. **Build labels so the user sees what each text box should contain.**

Each label is simply a static text box.

Flash has a really great feature that make it easy to set up clean user interfaces. The Guides feature shows you little lines around objects that have already been placed on the screen. Turn on the Snap to Guides option in the Modify menu to enable this feature.

5. **Build the button.**

For the Math game, you don't have to make a new button from scratch. Follow these steps:

a. *Drag another instance of the button from the Library onto the Stage.*

b. *Name this new button* btnCheck.

c. *Add a label to* btnCheck *that reads* check.

Designing the report page

This page tallies the results of the last problem and shows the player's current score. Three dynamic text fields are linked to the variables numRight, numTries, and percRight. My diagram for this page is illustrated in Figure 5-7.

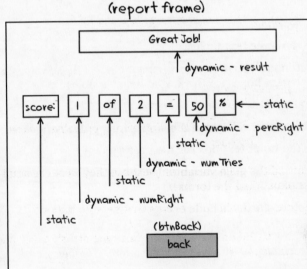

Figure 5-7:
The report page is full of static and dynamic text boxes.

The `report` page is created as a keyframe, much like the two preceding pages:

1. **Add a keyframe called `report`.**

   If you want to easily read the last frame name, add a fourth keyframe. (The name is hard to read on the last frame unless you add another frame later.)

2. **Add dynamic text fields linked to the variables `report`, `numRight`, `numTries`, and `percRight`.**

3. **Add static text labels explaining what's going on.**

   For the `report` page, I arrange the static and dynamic fields so they look like one complete sentence. You can easily create this effect if all fields

   • Use the same font

   • Are aligned neatly

   If they all seem to be on one line, the user cannot tell that it's more than one text field.

4. **Add a button to go back.**

   As usual for creating buttons, follow these steps:

   a. *Drag the button (from the Library) you already created.*

   b. *Give the button a new instance name.*

   c. *Place a static text element on top of the button to make the button's label.*

Coding the Pages

After you set up all the pages of the Math game, you have a strong framework in which to build your code:

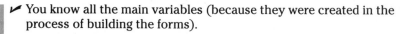

✔ You know all the main variables (because they were created in the process of building the forms).

✔ You know all the main code events that need to happen.

Design programs based on the forms for this type of very basic information-based programming.

After the skeleton is in place, flesh it out with some code.

Coding the choose page

The job of the `choose` page is to let the user decide which type of problem he wants to attempt.

In the Math game, this `choose` page has four buttons. The primary job of the `choose` screen code is to determine which operation the user wants to perform.

The purpose of Listing 5-1 is to send a message to the next screen indicating what type of problem the user wants.

Listing 5-1:   Code in the Math Game, choose Frame

```
// Math Game
// Generates Random Math Problems
// Illustrates text fields, conditions
// basic math
// Andy Harris, 12/04
// code in choose frame

stop();

btnAdd.onRelease = function(){
  _root.op = "+";
  _root.gotoAndStop("solve");
} // end add

btnSub.onRelease = function(){
  _root.op = "-";
  _root.gotoAndStop("solve");
} // end sub

btnMult.onRelease = function(){
  _root.op = "*";
  _root.gotoAndStop("solve");
} // end mult

btnDiv.onRelease = function(){
  _root.op = "/";
  _root.gotoAndStop("solve");
} // end div
```

The following sections show how to build and test the code.

Coding the buttons

All the buttons on this screen work in pretty much the same way, but they all indicate different operations.

Writing efficient code

The Math game is an example of avoiding unnecessary duplication of effort. All four buttons move control to the same frame. It's tempting to have a separate page for each type of problem, but the code on each of these frames would be nearly identical. For efficiency, you should avoid unnecessary duplication whenever possible. My `solve` page can work with any of the problem types: Regardless of the choice, code flows on to the `source` frame.

For each button (`btnAdd`, `btnSub`, `btnMult`, and `btnDiv` on the `choose` page), follow these steps:

1. **Begin your button code with explanatory comments.**

   The more complex your program, the more important comments are. For any program, provide at least

   - The basic purpose of the program

   - Your name

   - The date you wrote the code

2. **Stop the Timeline.**

   Any time your program spans from one frame to another, you should begin Frame 1 with the `stop()` command.

   This directive has two effects:

   - Override Flash's tendency to run through the Timeline

   - Keep code cycling through the current frame until your code moves the program to another frame

3. **Build the `btnAdd` code.**

   When the user clicks the Add button, two events must happen in sequence:

   a. *The program stores the user's choice to work on an addition problem.*

   b. *Flow continues to the `solve` frame.*

   For the Math game, I create a variable called `op` that holds an operation. This button indicates the user wants to do an addition problem, so I store the plus sign character into a special variable called `_root.op`.

Sharing variables across frames

When you break your Flash program into separate frames, note this important side effect: Each frame is actually considered an entirely different program. Any variables created in one frame are destroyed as soon as that frame exits. This is good because it means that you don't have to worry about variables from other parts of the program. Sometimes you want a variable to be shared.

For example, when I create a variable called `_root.op` in the Math game, I'm building a variable that belongs to the entire program, not just the current piece of it. (`_root` stands for the entire program.) With this device, I can transcend the limitations of locally defined variables.

Sometimes you can skip the `_root` indicator, and your variables will still work correctly. I use `_root` only when I think it clarifies things. When it isn't necessary, I don't use it because it can make the code harder to read.

Before you add code to the other buttons, use the following section to check whether the Add button (which is labeled `Addition`) works correctly.

Testing your button code

Test your button code to see whether it's working correctly:

- ✔ **When you run the program, you should be able to click the Add button.**
- ✔ **When you click the button, program control should progress to the `solve` screen.**

    If all is well, the `solve` screen displays a plus sign (which indicates that the user chose an addition problem).

If something went wrong, take a look at the hints you're given:

- ✔ Did an error screen pop up?
- ✔ Did the program move to the next screen?
- ✔ Did the program move to the correct screen but not display the correct character?

Because you've written only a few lines of code so far, figuring out why the code isn't working will be relatively easy. When the code for this button is working correctly, you can use it as a template for the other buttons.

Coding the solve page

The `solve` page of the Math game performs a number of tasks:

1. Generates the problem

2. Presents the problem to the user

3. Accepts the user's guess for the problem

4. Passes control to the `report` page

Listing 5-2 describes the `solve` frame code.

Listing 5-2: Code in the Math Game, solve Frame

```
//Code in solve frame
//From Math.fla

btnCheck.onRelease = function(){
  _root.gotoAndStop("report");
} // end check release

//check operation
switch(op){
  case "+":
    X = Math.ceil(Math.random() * 10);
    Y = Math.ceil(Math.random() * 10);
    _root.correct = X + Y;
    trace(correct);
  break;
  case "-":
    Y = Math.ceil(Math.random() * 10);
    _root.correct = Math.ceil(Math.random() * 10);
    X = _root.correct + Y;
    trace(correct);
  break;
  case "*":
    X = Math.ceil(Math.random() * 10);
    Y = Math.ceil(Math.random() * 10);
    _root.correct = X * Y;
    trace(correct);
  break;
  case "/":
    Y = Math.ceil(Math.random() * 10);
    _root.correct = Math.ceil(Math.random() * 10);
    X = _root.correct * Y;
    trace(correct);
  break;
  default:
    trace("There's a problem here");
  break;
} // end switch
```

To add code to the solve frame, follow these steps:

1. **Code the button.**

   This particular button doesn't do anything but pass control to the next segment, `report`.

   Code that you attach to a button doesn't execute immediately. The code is stored so that it can run whenever the button is pressed.

2. **Create code that executes immediately.**

   Most of the code for this frame should happen as soon as the frame is encountered.

   If you write code directly in the frame (without enclosing it in a function definition), it happens immediately.

3. **Determine the operation type.**

   This code acts differently for each type of operation. The operation that the user wants to perform is stored in the `op` variable. I need to check for four possible values of that variable, so the `switch` structure is the natural tool for the job:

   - The cases I'm concerned with are the four possible values of `op`.

   - I also add a default case even though it shouldn't ever happen.

     Only four operations are available, and my `switch` statement accounts for them all. You don't expect a fifth option to appear, but be ready for it because crazy things can happen when you write real code.

4. **Set up the addition problem.**

   The addition problem is the most basic case, so I set it up first.

   The following is the code fragment pertaining to addition:

   ```
   case "+":
     X = Math.ceil(Math.random() * 10);
     Y = Math.ceil(Math.random() * 10);
     correct = X + Y;
     trace(correct);
   break;
   ```

   I want to create two variables here, `X` and `Y`:

   - Both variables are tied to dynamic text areas, so when I assign values to them, the corresponding text area on the screen changes as well.

- Because I'm designing my program for young children, I want to use single-digit numbers. I use a variant of the die-rolling scheme (see Chapter 4) to build random integers between 1 and 10 for X and for Y.

- I have the computer solve the problem and then place the result in a variable called `correct`. This is useful in the `report` screen so that the computer can determine whether the user's guess is the correct answer.

- I use the `trace` statement to output the correct answer so that I can more easily debug without having to do all the mental math.

5. Write the multiplication code.

Subtraction comes next in the written code, but I recommend performing multiplication here because subtraction requires a minor trick.

The code for multiplication is very similar to the addition code except that the two values are multiplied, not added. The random values are created in exactly the same way as in the addition code:

```
case "*":
   X = Math.ceil(Math.random() * 10);
   Y = Math.ceil(Math.random() * 10);
   correct = X * Y;
   trace(correct);
break;
```

6. Write the sneaky subtraction code.

Because I want to use this game with small children, I must think carefully about the subtraction problems that the program generates. Addition and multiplication are easy because I simply generate two random numbers between 1 and 10. However, if I do that for subtraction, I'll frequently have problems that result in negative numbers. For example, if the computer randomly generates 3 for X and 8 for Y, the difference is –5 (3 – 8). If you're writing a game for an older child, that's fine, but my kids aren't ready for negative numbers.

There are a couple of solutions to this problem, but I came up with an elegant solution. The following code fragment shows my trick for creating problems with only positive answers:

```
case "-":
   Y = Math.ceil(Math.random() * 10);
   correct = Math.ceil(Math.random() * 10);
   X = correct + Y;
   trace(correct);
break;
```

The secret of Easter eggs

Programs (especially games) frequently have little tricks — *Easter eggs* — hidden in them, just like that correct answer `trace` statement. Programmers often use these little tricks to help them debug and test their programs. Many of the Easter eggs in software started as debugging features that programmers put in place, never intending end users to know about them.

Flash has a cool Easter egg. Choose About Flash from the Help menu and then click the tiny trademark symbol right after 2004. I won't tell you what you'll find, but it's worth looking for — and relevant in a book on computer gaming.

Instead of generating X and Y as my two random values, I generate X and `correct` (the correct answer!). Then I reverse-engineer X by adding `correct` to Y:

- The correct answer is guaranteed to be a positive number in the 1–10 range.

- Subtraction problems are in the same range as addition problems.

Sneaky, huh?

7. **Do the dastardly division problem.**

For young kids, you probably want to limit your division problems to avoid remainders. The easy way to do that is to

 a. *Randomly generate X and the correct answer.*

 b. *Derive Y by multiplying X by* `correct`.

More than one way to add

Adding values to variables is very common, so many languages have built-in shortcuts for this kind of situation. In your own code, you can perform the same addition with a line like this:

```
numRight += 1;
```

That line means exactly the same: Add `1` to `numRight`. Because you frequently find yourself incrementing a variable by `1`, there's another shortcut. You can also write the line like this:

```
numRight++;
```

Coding the report page

The `report` page of the Math game has three jobs:

1. Checks the current problem and sees whether the user was correct

2. Reports some statistical information about how many questions the user has answered correctly so far

3. Evaluates the current situation and sends the user to the corresponding frame

   The program's button is a little unusual because it won't always go to the same spot. Most of the time, the button returns the user to the `solve` page to get a new problem. If the user has already solved five problems, the button instead directs the user to the `choose` frame to select a new type of problem.

Listing 5-3 is the code from the `report` frame.

Listing 5-3: Code in Math.fla report Frame

```
//code in report frame
//from Math.fla
//check to see if user is right
if (_root.guess == _root.correct){
  result = "Great Job!";
  numRight++;
} else {
  result =  X + " + " + Y + " = " + correct;
} // end if

//update score
numTries++;
percRight = numRight/numTries * 100;

//back up button goes different places in different
         situations!
btnBack.onRelease = function(){
  if (numTries < 5){
    //create another problem in the same set
    _root.gotoAndStop("solve");
  } else {
    //let user start over
    numRight = 0;
    numTries = 0;
    _root.gotoAndStop("choose");
  } // end if
} // end back release
```

How to make a better language

When computer scientists improved the C language, they called their new language C++. Geddit? It's one better than C! ActionScript is a simplification of C++, so maybe it should be called C++––. (Maybe that's why I'm never asked to name new programming languages.)

Here are the steps for coding the `report` page:

1. **Check the player's math.**

   The first order of business is to see whether the user answered the problem correctly. By the time this frame has been called, the program is aware of two important variables:

   - `correct`: Generated by code in the `solve` frame
   - `guess`: Associated with the text box in which the user typed an answer

   The `report` page checks whether `guess` is equal to `correct` and provides appropriate feedback.

   The condition (`guess == correct`) is a triumph of variable naming. I'm proud of that condition because it's really easy to understand:

   - If `guess` is equal to `correct`, the user answered the problem correctly.
   - If `guess` isn't equal to `correct`, the user answered the problem incorrectly.

   As you get more experienced at naming variables, you can anticipate the conditions in which you use your variables and thus design variable names so that your conditions are easy to understand.

   Code that is written clearly is easier to read and easier to fix.

2. **Inform the user.**

   - *If the user answered correctly,* the program assigns a message to `result`, which is mapped to a dynamic text area.
   - *If the user didn't answer correctly,* the program creates a more helpful message that indicates the correct answer to the assigned problem.

3. **Track the user's progress.**

   The program increments the `numRight` variable with the following code:

```
numRight = numRight + 1;
```

The preceding line performs these tasks:

a. *Retrieves the current value of* `numRight`

b. *Adds* `1` *to the current value*

c. *Stores the new total in* `numRight` *(replacing the original value)*

The sidebar "More than one way to add" shows other ways to increment variables.

When you follow a variable name with two plus signs (++), you tell the computer to add 1 to the variable. Many languages also support the -- and -= operators for quicker subtraction.

4. **Keep some stats.**

The user receives five questions of a given type before being allowed to choose a new question type. The `numTries` variable keeps track of how many questions the user has answered in the current set. Every time the user responds to a question, `numTries` should increase.

`numRight` and `numTries` have these differences:

- The `numRight` variable is incremented only when the user gets a problem correct.

- The value of `numTries` is incremented whenever the code is executed, which is once per problem.

`numRight` divided by `numTries` gives you the player's percent correct as a complicated decimal value. I multiply the percentage by 100 to convert the decimal percentage to a more familiar 0–100 value.

In the report code, all three variables (`numRight`, `numTries`, and `percRight`) are mapped to onscreen dynamic text boxes, so the user can see how he or she is doing.

5. **Move on to another part of the program.**

When the user clicks the button, he goes one of two places:

- *If the user hasn't answered five questions of the current set,* he's given another question in the `solve` frame.

- *If the user has answered at least five questions in the current category,* he's returned to the `choose` frame to pick another type of problem (or more problems of the same type).

The button's multiple personality behavior is determined by a condition inside the button's event handler:

```
//back up button goes different places in different situations!
btnBack.onRelease = function(){
  if (numTries < 5){
    //create another problem in the same set
```

```
    _root.gotoAndStop("solve");
  } else {
    //let user start over
    numRight = 0;
    numTries = 0;
    _root.gotoAndStop("choose");
  } // end if
} // end back release
```

The number of tries determines the behavior of the btnBack button:

- ✔ If the number of tries is less than 5, program control reverts to the solve frame.

- ✔ If the number of tries is 5 or higher (numTries is more than or equal to 5)

    a. Reset the numRight and numTries to 0 (zero).

    b. Move program control to the choose frame.

    This gives the player five fresh tries on another problem set.

Coping with Bugs and Crashes

Don't be discouraged when your program dies an inglorious death.

I'm a pretty experienced programmer, but 90 percent of my programs don't work the first time I test them.

If your program doesn't work correctly, you can fix it. How you make things work depends on what went wrong. Begin by figuring out what kind of problem you're having.

The rest of this chapter shows you some typical types of problems and useful strategies for solving them.

Syntax error

Sometimes when you run your program, the output screen pops up a message (or maybe many messages) that starts with the text **Error**. Figure 5-8 shows such a situation.

This indicates that Flash is confused about your code and doesn't know how to follow your directions. Such an error is a *syntax error*. Your program doesn't run at all under these conditions.

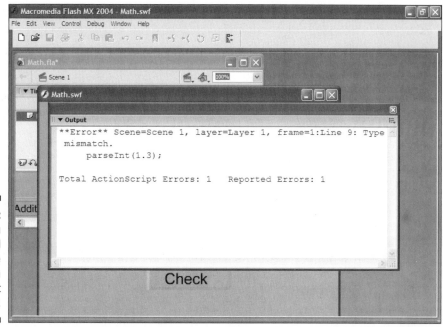

Syntax errors sound pretty bad, but this type of error usually isn't hard to fix: The first thing to do is scroll to the beginning of the error message. Also, make sure the entire error message is visible. Sometimes, the error screen shows up small, and you have to expand it to see the entire error. One mistake often causes others, so only the first error is meaningful. Read the error message, looking for specific clues. Some error messages are worthless, but quite a few actually tell you what is wrong. Pay careful attention to the line number Flash reports. This is the line where Flash noticed the error. That isn't always where the problem is, but it's a good indicator.

Syntax errors are usually caused by typing errors, capitalization errors, misspelling, or incorrect punctuation.

Check the indicated line to find the mistake. In normal reading, you often skip very quickly through text. A syntax error means that some little detail is wrong, and the detail can be *very* small. For example, if you misplace a period for a comma, a numeral one (1) with a lowercase L (l), or one of many similar problems, your code won't work correctly.

Nothing happens at all

Sometimes, you don't have any syntax errors, but your program still doesn't work correctly. In Flash programming, that often indicates that you don't have something named correctly. Check whether your button is responding at all.

In the Math game, you can do that by modifying the btnAdd code so it looks like this:

```
btnAdd.onRelease = function(){
   trace("I got here");
   _root.op = "+";
   _root.gotoAndStop("solve");
} // end add
```

Run the preceding code and watch what happens:

✔ **If the trace statement works, your button code is working.** You have to look at the other code to find the problem.

✔ **If the trace statement never happens, you have a problem with the button or the button code.**

If your button doesn't work, make sure that

✔ **Your button instance (on the Stage, not the one in the Library) is named btnAdd.**

✔ **Your code and the instance name are *exactly* the same, including capitalization.**

For example, if you have a button named btnadd and code for btnAdd.onRelease, the code doesn't execute because Flash thinks you're talking about two totally different buttons.

Statement must appear within onClip event handler

This error is very common among beginning game developers. Check to see that your code is written in the frame context, and not in the button or movie clip context. If you get this error (or some other error you don't understand), look at the title bar of your code window. It should read Actions - Frame. If it reads Actions - Button or Actions - Movie Clip, the code I give you won't work correctly.

You can write code in the button and movie clip contexts, but I find it harder to track down the code when it's in lots of different places. You also have to write code a little bit differently in these other contexts, and certain kinds of code *must* be written in the frame context. For these reasons, I put all the code for the entire book at the frame level. You never need to write code in button or movie clip objects.

The program moves to the score frame, but you don't see the plus sign

Your code assigns the value + to a variable named op. The score frame should have a dynamic text box linked to the variable op. If you don't have such a variable linked to the text box, you won't see any value in it.

Something else is wrong

If the error you encounter doesn't match one of my scenarios, don't panic. You can figure it out. Look for a pattern:

✔ **When does it go wrong?**

Is there a pattern? Does it always blow up, or does it break only part of the time? Can you find a pattern?

✔ **What else is happening?**

What happens immediately before the program breaks? Did it ever work right? Did you make some sort of change to another part of the code that caused this to break? Are you referring to some variable that has somehow changed?

✔ **Can you ever make it work correctly?**

Again, you're looking for a pattern. Can you get back to a version of the program that works correctly?

✔ **Can you isolate the problem?**

Try to determine what section of code made things go wrong. Use comment statements to take out code until you have something working again. Slowly return one line at a time, checking to see whether this line is the one causing problems. Eventually, you can usually track the issue to one or two lines of code, which you can scrutinize or rewrite.

✔ **What's happening with the variables?**

Check to see that your variables contain the values you think they contain. Use trace statements to output the variables and see what they really contain.

✔ **Get help.**

If you can, show your code to somebody else who knows how to program. Even if your friend doesn't know any Flash code, he or she might see something you missed.

Part III
Sprites, or Movie Clips

The 5th Wave   By Rich Tennant

"Ironically, he went out there looking for a 'hot spot'."

In this part . . .

Game programmers have long used a theoretical concept called a *sprite* as the foundation of action games. Flash doesn't have a built-in sprite object, but it does have an object called the *movie clip* that makes a dandy foundation for sprites. In this part, you see the basics of building sprite-based games. You can build pretty much any 2-D game after you know how to build and use sprites.

Chapter 6 shows you how to make a very basic sprite as well as how to move it around onscreen. After an object can move, it can go places it shouldn't, so I show you several strategies for dealing with screen boundaries. You also discover how to replace the mouse cursor with any symbol you want.

Chapter 7 helps you build the mother of all arcade games: *Pong*. Once again, I take you through the process and describe how to build the game rather than simply dissecting the completed game.

Chapter 6

Introducing Sprites and Movie Clips

- -

In This Chapter

▶ Using movie clips to make sprites

▶ Moving things onscreen

▶ Dealing with boundaries

▶ Following the mouse

- -

Most games have certain things in common. Games usually involve various objects moving around onscreen crashing into each other. Game programmers usually call these objects *sprites*. In this chapter, I tell you all about sprites, how they relate to the `MovieClip` object built into Flash, and how to make sprites move around onscreen.

Building a Sprite

As a programmer, patterns are your friend. When you can spot a pattern, you can usually take advantage of it to make programming easier.

Early game programmers noticed that games often involved little things moving around onscreen and crashing into each other. They named these little elements *sprites*.

Even today, most 2-D game designs use sprites:

✔ *Pac-Man:* The ghosts and the yellow Pac-Man are sprites.

✔ *Civilization III:* Each unit (settlers, soldiers, elephants) is a sprite.

✔ *Diablo II:* The player and the monsters are sprites.

✔ *Asteroids:* The ship and the space rocks are sprites.

In general, anything in a computer game that moves is a sprite.

Making a movie clip

A sprite is a conceptual framework that programmers use to think about game objects.

Few programming languages actually have sprites built into them. Usually, game programmers begin by creating sprites that they can manipulate.

In Flash, a built-in object called the `MovieClip` is a dandy foundation for sprites.

To begin making a sprite, build a ball and turn it into a movie clip object. Later, you can add code to the movie clip to make your sprite move around and bounce into stuff.

To make your first movie clip sprite, follow these steps:

1. **Create a new project in Flash.**

   Try new ideas on a clean palette.

2. **Draw a circle in the center of the Stage, using the Oval tool.**

   The sidebar, "Making a ball that looks 3-D" shows you how to make your circle look like a ball.

3. **Convert your circle to a movie clip object.**

   To convert the drawing to a movie clip, select the circle and then either

   • Choose Modify⇨Convert to Symbol.

   • Press F8.

   This part of creating movie clips is like building buttons, but the following step is different.

   The dialog box for creating a movie clip is shown in Figure 6-1.

TIP

Making a ball that looks 3-D

A *radial gradient* gives a circle a 3-D appearance. Follow these steps:

1. **Choose Radial from the Color Mixer panel.**

2. **Choose two colors for the gradient.**

   Radial gradients place the first color in the center of a selection. The second color is used on the edges of the selection. Use a radial gradient to simulate the highlights of a ball. If you want your circle to look like a blue sphere, for example, choose white as the first color and a dark blue as the second color.

3. **Apply the gradient you just created to the circle.**

Use the Paint Bucket tool to apply your gradient to the circle. If you choose white and dark blue, your circle has a white highlight in the center and dark blue borders. The white area in the center makes the 2-D ball look like a 3-D sphere with a highlight. Experiment by placing the gradient in various parts of the circle.

The black border on the circle defeats the illusion of a 3-D object. To delete the border, select it and press Delete. See the result in the figure.

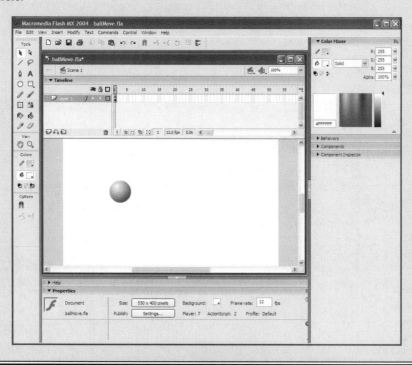

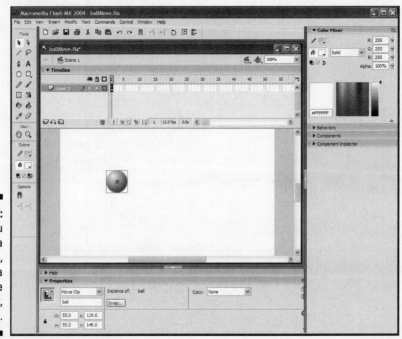

Figure 6-1:
Name your
new movie
clip. Be sure
to create a
movie clip,
not a button.

4. **Name your ball.**

   In the Convert to Symbol dialog box, give your object a name. I call mine
   `ball` — not inspiring, but easy to remember.

   Choose the Movie Clip selection, not Button or Graphic.

   See the result in Figure 6-2.

Figure 6-2:
When you
select a
movie clip,
you see a
rectangle
around it,
not shading.

The movie clip is the most common type of symbol you create for games.

If it doesn't appear by default, open the Advanced options and select Export for ActionScript (from the Linkage section; refer to Figure 6-1). (Chapter 8 explains why exporting for ActionScript is necessary.)

After you convert your drawing to a movie clip, the object looks like the one in Figure 6-2, with a rectangle around it. The ball is now a movie clip object, and you can treat it like a sprite.

When you create a sprite, the center of the screen becomes a special point called the *registration point.* When sprites move and rotate, they rotate around the registration point. Be sure that the registration point is near the center of your sprite. If this point isn't near your object's center of gravity, the rotation doesn't look natural.

It's alive! Adding motion to your movie clip

The following steps breathe some life into a movie clip sprite:

1. **Move your sprite to a suitable starting position.**

   In this first example, the sprite moves to the right. Drag your ball to the left-hand edge of the Stage so it has plenty of room to move.

2. **Name the sprite.**

   In the Properties box, you see a text box that reads something like `<instance name>`. Type **ball** into that box to name this particular instance `ball`.

   You might think you already named this thing `ball`, and in a sense you did. The object in the Library is a plan for making `ball` objects, and the one on the screen is an instance of the `ball` object. (See the recipe and cookie analogy from Chapter 2 for more on the relationship between Library objects and instances on the Stage.) When you have only one instance of a particular object, it's typical (at least in ActionScript) to give the Library object and the instance the same name.

3. **Select the appropriate frame.**

   To select a code context, click Frame 1, Layer 1 in the Timeline.

4. **Open the Actions panel.**

   If the Actions panel isn't already open, bring it up by pressing F9.

5. **Get in the Actions - Frame mode.**

   Be sure the title bar above the Actions panel reads `Actions - Frame`. If it reads `Actions - Movie Clip` (or something else), the code in the following step doesn't work correctly.

If your code doesn't work, read this!

How you write code depends on whether that code is attached to a frame or a movie clip. I find the distinction to be confusing and unnecessary, so I write all my code in frames. If code from this book doesn't work correctly, make sure that you typed it into a frame context, not a movie clip or button. Determine the context by looking at the Actions panel. It should always read `Actions - Frame`, never `Actions - Movie Clip`.

---

6. **Write code to move your sprite.**

   For the ball example, type the following code into the Actions panel:

   ```
   //from ballMove.fla
   ball.onEnterFrame = function(){
     ball._x += 5;
   } // end function
   ```

7. **Test your code by pressing Ctrl+Enter and seeing what happens.**

   With this example, your ball slowly moves across the screen to the right. With the current code, it leaves the screen altogether and keeps on going forever. Figure 6-3 shows the ball's behavior. I added the arrow so you can see what the ball does.

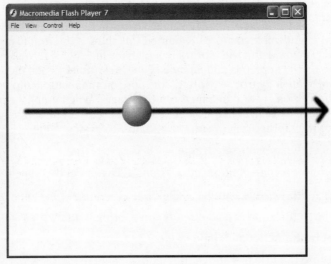

Figure 6-3: The ball moves slowly to the right and eventually leaves the screen.

Understanding the code

The code in the Actions window is really the secret to the power of ActionScript. Each little piece adds something. When you can decipher this little segment of code, you can add a few more things to it and animate anything. (Insert mad scientist laughter here — "Muhahahah!")

ball.onEnterFrame is a special element called an event handler. (In Chapters 2 and 3, the onClick event of the button object is another event handler.) Movie clip objects have a special set of events.

In movie clip objects, the EnterFrame event is especially powerful because you can indicate instructions that are meant to happen many times. By placing code in the EnterFrame event, you ensure that code happens several times per second. If that code modifies an object that's visible onscreen (as the ballMove code described here does), the movie clip looks animated:

✔ Only one frame is in the moveBall program, so that frame repeats indefinitely at the indicated frame rate. (By default, this rate is 12 frames per second [fps].)

✔ Any code you place in the EnterFrame event happens each time the program *enters the frame.* (Oooooh, I get it!)

ball._x is really sneaky and powerful. The ball is a movie clip object. This type of object already has a bunch of characteristics built in. These characteristics of an object are its *properties*.

Most of the movie clip object's built-in properties begin with an underscore. ball._x and ball._y indicate the position of an object called ball on the screen:

✔ y measures vertical position (height).

✔ x measures horizontal position (width).

ball._x += 5 When you change the value of an object's properties, those changes are often reflected onscreen. In the Flash coordinate system, changing the _x property of the ball object moves it in the left–right axis. The += operator means *add 5 to this property.* If the ball begins all the way to the left of the stage, its original _x value can be 0 (zero). The first time the program reaches this code, it increments ball._x by 5, giving it a new value of 5. This moves the ball five pixels (screen dots) to the right. The next frame increases x by another five pixels. Because the code is repeated 12 times per second, the ball appears to move smoothly and slowly from left to right. To make the ball move faster, add a larger number. To make the ball move right to left, add a negative number to ball._x.

} // end function indicates the end of the function. (Braces usually indicate code that is grouped together).

Basic objects

Object has a special meaning in the programming world. In general, an object is a self-contained combination of code and data. Objects are designed to interact with the user, the environment, and each other.

If you're *really* technical, you can say that ActionScript isn't truly an object-oriented language. Programming geeks might describe ActionScript as an *object-based language* because it doesn't meet all the formal requirements of an object-oriented language. But ActionScript's support for objects is good enough to do some interesting things.

Don't Object to Objects

Game programming is a lot easier if you use a modern programming scheme called *object-oriented programming* (OOP). ActionScript lets you look at movie clip elements as objects.

The sidebar "Basic objects" covers the background of object-oriented programming. You can also read in Chapter 13 how to create your own custom objects.

I use a variation of object-oriented programming throughout this book. It's a gentle introduction to the principles of object-oriented programming but not quite as strict or powerful as the more complete implementations of the technique. I cover object-oriented programming more in Chapter 13 as you see there how to build your own custom movie clip objects.

Properties

Properties are an object's characteristics, such as its size, color, and position. (In the `ballMove` example, `_x` is a property of the `ball` object.)

Properties are like adjectives in human languages.

Properties have the following characteristics:

- ✔ You can modify an object by assigning new values to its properties.
- ✔ You can read an object's properties as if they were variables.
- ✔ An object can have built-in properties.

Special functions

Methods and *events* are special functions attached to an object. They both are used to describe actions associated with an object.

Methods are like verbs in human languages: Methods describe actions. Events are triggers that automatically happen. Here's a true real-life example: My kids' guinea pig has a built-in squeak event that triggers every time the refrigerator opens.

The big difference between methods and events in Flash is how they're started. After they start, methods and events behave the same way.

Methods

Methods are functions that must be called explicitly in your code.

Methods don't happen automatically. If you want something to happen automatically, the function must be an event. You can't make new events. There are just a few, and they're already built into Flash. The only two event handlers you need in this book are `onEnterFrame()` and `onRelease()`.

I show examples of methods later in this chapter. For almost every remaining program in this book, your sprites will have methods named `move()` and `checkBoundaries()`. These are behaviors that a well-trained sprite object should know how to perform.

Events

Events are functions that happen automatically when another specific activity occurs. After an event starts, it behaves like a method.

Most events begin with the keyword `on`. The most common events in ActionScript are

- The `onRelease()` event of the button object
- The `onEnterFrame()` event of the movie clip object

Flash treats events and methods strangely

Flash combines events and methods in a way that is reasonably easy to program but not typical of all object-oriented languages. The "events and methods are basically the same thing" concept works fine for Flash, but if you move on to another object-oriented language, you'll see that other techniques are more common.

Characteristics

A well-organized object-oriented system has the following characteristics.

Inheritance

Inheritance lets objects be made from other objects.

For example, if you make a `mammal` object, you could give it characteristics common to all mammals (fur, live-bearing, warm-blooded). If you make a new animal object based on `mammal`, the new object already has the characteristics of the parent object type. You have to worry about only those characteristics that differentiate a type of mammal: For example, some mammals have hooves, and some have paws.

ActionScript supports a limited form of inheritance.

Inheritance is important in ActionScript because you base all kinds of objects in the `MovieClip` class, such as the `ball` object in the `ball00P` program.

In `ball00P`, as soon as `ball` becomes a movie clip, you instantly inherit all the characteristics of a movie clip, including

- `_x` and `_y` properties
- The ability to recognize an `onEnterFrame()` event

Encapsulation

Encapsulation lets programs and data break into chunks to hide detail. ActionScript encourages encapsulation with function and object entities.

Encapsulation makes your programs easier to write and easier to follow. Remember song sheets from camp? They feature the chorus the first time you sing it. After that, the sheet reads *Chorus* instead of repeating the lyrics.

Polymorphism

Polymorphism lets objects adapt to different conditions.

Polymorphism lets you

- Build objects with different starting values
- Adapt the behavior of an object's methods for the current circumstances

Making a Well-Behaved Object

A moving ball can be created using object-oriented techniques. The object-oriented approach pays off as your sprites get more complicated because each object keeps track of the variables that control its own behavior.

Listing 6-1 looks quite different than the code in `ballMove`.

Listing 6-1: Object-Oriented Moving Ball

```
//from ballOOP.fla
//demonstrates turning ballMove into an Object-oriented
           program

ball.dx = 5;
ball.dy = 5;

ball.onEnterFrame = function(){
  ball.move();
  ball.checkBoundaries();
} // end enterFrame

ball.move = function(){
  ball._x += ball.dx;
  ball._y += ball.dy;
} // end move

ball.checkBoundaries = function(){
  //do nothing for now
} // end
```

In Listing 6-1, the boundary-checking routine is empty. For now, it's a placeholder. Later in the chapter, I show examples of boundary checking. Each example plugs into the `checkBoundaries` method in Listing 6-1.

The code in Listing 6-1 does most of the same things as the `ballMove` program featured at the beginning of this chapter, but this object-oriented version has some very nice advantages.

Adding dx and dy properties

The `dx` and `dy` properties let you manipulate motion in a flexible way. These properties determine how the ball's position properties should change each frame.

Position values

An object's horizontal (left-to-right) and vertical (top-to-bottom) positions are separate properties that combine to find its exact position onscreen:

- **Horizontal position** (current side-to-side position on the Stage) is determined by the object's built-in _x property.

  _x is the current horizontal position (position from left to right).

- **Horizontal motion** (change in side-to-side position) is determined by the custom dx property.

  dx is the change of the horizontal position (how much the object will move left or right in the current cycle).

- **Vertical position** (top onscreen) is determined by the object's built-in _y property.

  y is the current vertical position (position from top to bottom).

- **Vertical motion** (change in top-to-bottom position) is determined by the custom dy property.

  dy is the change of the vertical position (how much the object moves up or down in the current cycle).

In dx and dy, think of the *d* as the *difference* in position. (Scientists and mathematicians might think of *d* as the *delta,* or *rate of change.*)

The _x and _y properties are built-in properties of the movie clip object. Remember that Flash tends to begin all built-in properties with the underscore character. I added dx and dy myself, so they do not begin with an underscore character. Even though dx and dy are not built into movie clip objects, you'll find them so useful that you will add them to nearly every moving object in your games.

Position changes

The dx and dy properties don't do their jobs automatically. The code in the move method uses these properties to move the ball.

To add dx and dy properties to a sprite, start by writing code before the onEnterFrame code:

- The ball.dx and ball.dy values are new properties of the ball object.
- If you create a variable attached to an object such as ball.dx, you're creating the dx property of the ball object.

```
//ballOOP
//demonstrates turning ballMove into an Object-oriented
          program

ball.dx = 5;
ball.dy = 5;
```

This code creates the properties dx and dy, adds them to the ball sprite, and sets the initial value of both properties to 5. Because the code occurs outside any function definition, it happens immediately when the program runs.

Building the onEnterFrame event

The code beginning ball.onEnterFrame = function(){ is an event handler that indicates what should happen every time the current frame is activated.

I moved most of the actual code out of this function. Instead, I replace the original code with references to two new methods of the ball object.

Even if you don't know exactly how these methods work, you have to admire the clarity of the following code:

```
//from ballOOP.fla
ball.onEnterFrame = function(){
   ball.move();
   ball.checkBoundaries();
} // end enterFrame
```

Even if you don't know anything about programming, you can easily guess what this code is supposed to do: When the ball enters the frame, it should move and check for boundaries.

The enterFrame event is a triumph of encapsulation. It shows the cool thing about encapsulation. In this function, I just want to know what the ball is supposed to do. I don't really care *how* it does these things, just that it does them. Describe the big picture here. Each of the main things that needs to be done gets its own method.

Moving the ball OOP-style

I created a new method for the ball object in much the way I created the onEnterFrame() event. Here's the move code:

```
//from ballOOP.fla
ball.move = function(){
  ball._x += ball.dx;
  ball._y += ball.dy;
} // end move
```

In the move method, I added ball.dx to ball._x and ball.dy to ball._y. However, this function is much more profound than it might appear at first glance:

- ✔ **It isn't simply a function.** It's attached to the ball object, so it's now technically a method of that object.

- ✔ **The function is more adaptable.** In the moveBall program, I always changed x by positive (+) 5, moving the ball five pixels to the right each frame.

In this version of the program, the ball is moved by the values of the dx and dy properties. This means that your code can manipulate these variables to change the speed and direction of the ball:

- ✔ **You can change dx and dy to change the speed and direction of your sprite:**

  - • If you give dx a large positive value, the ball races across the screen from left to right.

  - • If you give dx a negative value, the ball goes from right to left.

- ✔ **If you know high-school geometry, the dy value might surprise you:**

  - • Computer screens are drawn from top to bottom, so y is 0 at the top and increases as you move down the screen.

  - • In geometry, y values of 0 usually are at the bottom of the graph and increase upward.

Figure 6-4 shows the coordinate system as Flash sees it.

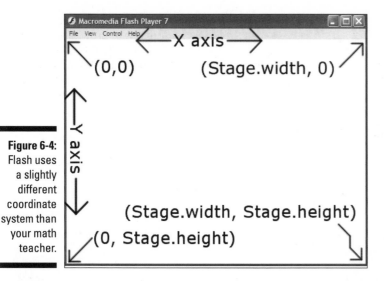

Figure 6-4:
Flash uses
a slightly
different
coordinate
system than
your math
teacher.

To see dx, dy, and Flash's upside-down geometry, grab the ball00P.fla file from the Web site (www.dummies.com/go/flashgameprogrammingfd1e) and mess around with the values of ball.dx and ball.dy:

✔ Watch what happens when you change these values.

✔ See whether you can make the ball move in any direction you wish simply by changing the values of the dx and dy properties.

In ActionScript, the main difference between events and methods is how they're called by ActionScript:

✔ **Events** are automatically called when they occur. All events in this book begin with the phrase on.

✔ **Methods** must be called *explicitly* in your code. Methods do not begin with the keyword on.

  • In the preceding ball00P code, I explicitly call the move() and checkboundaries() methods. It is not necessary to call the onEnterFrame() method because it happens automatically when the frame cycles.

  • If you create a function called onEnterFrame(), ActionScript automatically knows that function is an event and calls any code in that method when the appropriate trigger occurs.

Overcoming Your Boundaries

Boundary checking might sound like a self-help program, but it's actually an important part of game programming. Just like children and pets, when you let sprites loose, they encounter borders sooner or later. You must "teach" sprites what to do when they try to go out of bounds.

Sprites don't learn from timeout chairs or a newspaper swatted across the nose. Believe me, I've tried.

Boundary effects

Whenever you move an object onscreen, you need to anticipate the potential boundaries of the Stage.

In the preceding section, if you run the `ball00P` program, the ball moves until it reaches an edge of the Stage. When the ball gets to the edge of the Stage, it continues moseying along. If you haven't stopped the program, the ball is still wandering in the empty space off-Stage. This is probably not what you want in your games.

In the gaming world, when an object hits the edge of the screen, it can react in a number of ways.

The following programs extend the basic `ball00P` program by adding different code in the `checkBoundaries()` method.

The following code fragments don't show all the code in the programs. Most of the code in these programs is the same as the code in `ball00P`. I just show you how to change `checkBoundaries()` for different boundary effects.

Wrapping around the screen

One common effect is to wrap the sprite around the screen, much like the word-wrap feature of a word processor.

- ✔ If the object disappears off the left-hand side of the screen, it appears on the right-hand side.
- ✔ If the object disappears off the bottom, it shows up at the top.

This behavior can simulate a much larger area than the actual screen. *Asteroids* is the classic example. The wrapping effect is one of the easiest to achieve. Figure 6-5 shows a ball wrapping around the screen. (The arrows aren't in the actual program; I added them to show how the ball moves.)

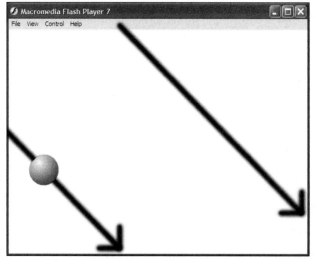

Figure 6-5:
If the ball
leaves the
screen, it
reappears
on the
opposite
side.

The wrapping behavior is achieved by Listing 6-2 in `checkBoundaries()`.

Listing 6-2: Wrap Demo

```
//from wrapDemo.fla
ball.checkBoundaries = function(){
  //wrap demo

  //ball leaves right side
  if (ball._x > Stage.width){
    ball._x = 0;
  } // end if

  //ball leaves left side
  if (ball._x < 0){
    ball._x = Stage.width;
  } // end if

  //ball leaves bottom of stage
  if (ball._y > Stage.height){
    ball._y = 0;
  } // end if

  //ball leaves top of stage
  if (ball._y < 0){
    ball._y = Stage.height;
  } // end if

} // end checkboundaries
```

In Listing 6-2, the `checkBoundaries()` method uses `if` statements to check the ball's horizontal (width) and vertical (height) positions in relationship to the Stage.

Coordinate values

In Listing 6-2, the horizontal and vertical position of the ball is determined by the `x` and `y` coordinate values:

✔ **x coordinate value (horizontal position)**

- `0` is the left edge of the Stage.
- `Stage.width` (the width of the Stage in pixels) is the right edge of the Stage.

✔ **y coordinate value (vertical position)**

- `0` is the top edge of the Stage.
- `Stage.height` (the height of the stage in pixels) is the bottom edge of the Stage.

`Stage.width` and `Stage.height` don't follow the same naming conventions as the movie clip object. The sidebar "Strangeness on the Stage" shows you the important differences.

Code process

In `wrapDemo`, the code checks the ball's position against `stage` properties in a series of `if` statements:

1. **The first two `if` statements check whether the ball is too far left or right of the Stage.**

   ✔ The first `if` statement checks whether the ball's `x` property is greater than the `stage width` property:

   - *If the ball's x property is greater than the* `stage width` *property, the ball is about to move off the right side of the Stage.*

     In that case, the next line of code triggers. The ball's `x` property changes to `0` (zipping it over to the left side of the Stage).

   - *If the ball's x property isn't greater than the* `stage width` *property, the program skips the next line of code.*

   ✔ The second `if` statement checks whether the ball's `x` property is less than `0`:

   - *If the ball's x property is less than* `0`, *the ball is off the left side of the Stage.*

TECHNICAL STUFF

Strangeness on the Stage

`Stage.width` and `Stage.height` have some surprising characteristics. To start, the term `Stage` is capitalized. `Stage` is the name of the built-in Flash object that describes the Stage. Built-in objects usually begin with a capital letter in Flash (and in many other object-oriented languages). Just like movie clips and buttons, it has properties you can look at and manipulate:

✔ The `width` property shows the width of the Stage.

✔ The `height` property shows the height of the Stage.

For your program to work correctly, you must capitalize each property correctly:

✔ `Stage.width` is the width of the `Stage` object.

✔ `stage.width` (all lowercase) is the width of the undefined `stage` object. If you refer to `stage.width` rather than `Stage.width`, your program will not work properly.

✔ The built-in properties of Stage don't begin with an underscore.

The `width` and `height` properties of the movie clip objects begin with underscore characters, but the similar properties in the `Stage` object do not. Thanks for that pointless inconsistency, Macromedia.

In that case, the next line of code triggers. The ball's x property changes to `Stage.width` (zipping it over to the right side of the Stage).

- *If the ball's x property isn't less than 0, the program skips the next line of code.*

2. **The next two `if` statements check whether the ball is too far above or below the Stage.**

   These statements compare the y property with the `stage height` and 0.

Keeping the ball on the Stage

When you run the `wrapDemo` program, the ball gets halfway off the screen before anything happens. That's because the ball's x and y coordinates are based on the *registration point* of the ball, which is usually at the center. If you want to make the jump to the other side of the screen as soon as it touches the screen, you need to adjust for the width of the ball.

The following variation of `wrapDemo` makes the ball wrap without appearing to leave the Stage:

What size is the Stage?

Even if you know the Stage's exact width and height, it's better to test against `Stage.width` and `Stage.height` than the exact numbers:

✔ Someone might change the Stage size (if your program is run as a standalone SWF file, for example).

✔ Whenever possible, make your code easy to read. It's easy to look at the code and guess that `Stage.width` means the width of the stage; `500` doesn't have an obvious meaning.

```
if (ball._x > Stage.width - (ball._width/2)){
  ball._x = ball._width/2;
} // end if
```

I think wrapping looks better if you let the ball partially leave the screen. I show how to keep the entire ball onscreen in the other boundary examples because I think balls that bounce off the screen should not appear to halfway leave the screen.

Stopping at the border

If you're creating a stop behavior, the object isn't allowed to leave the screen when it reaches the border.

Depending on the needs of your game, you might make the object either

✔ Stop completely (stop moving both horizontally and vertically)

✔ Slide along the side of the screen until it hits a corner or changes direction:

  • *If the object reaches the left or right border,* you can let the y value change so the object can move up or down.

  • *If the object reaches the top or bottom border,* you can let the x value change so the object can move left or right.

In some games (such as a racing game), the object might incur damage. Chapter 10 shows you how to keep track of damage.

Having the ball stop at the screen border is not difficult. Figure 6-6 shows one way to achieve this effect.

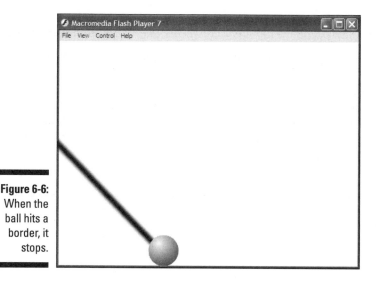

Figure 6-6:
When the
ball hits a
border, it
stops.

The general structure for this effect is similar to the wrapping code, as the
checkBoundaries code in Listing 6-3 shows. (Listing 6-3 shows only the function that changed. The rest of the code is exactly like the ball00P code
shown earlier in Listing 6-1.)

Listing 6-3: Stop Demo

```
//from stopDemo.fla
ball.checkBoundaries = function(){
   //stop demo - stop as soon as ball encounters edge
   //keep ball entirely on stage

   //ball leaves right side
   if (ball._x > Stage.width - (ball._width/2)){
      ball.dx = 0;
      ball.dy = 0;
   } // end if

   //ball leaves left side
   if (ball._x < ball._width/2){
      ball.dx = 0;
      ball.dy = 0;
   } // end if

   //ball leaves bottom of stage
   if (ball._y > Stage.height - (ball._height/2)){
      ball.dx = 0;
      ball.dy = 0;
   } // end if
```

(continued)

Listing 6-3 *(continued)*

```
//ball leaves top of stage
if (ball._y < ball._height/2){
  ball.dx = 0;
  ball.dy = 0;
} // end if

} // end checkboundaries
```

There is a critical difference between Listing 6-3 and the code for wrapping. In Listing 6-3, when the ball hits an edge, I set its dx and dy values to 0. This means that the ball's difference in x should be 0 (it should move 0 pixels in the x axis), and dy is 0 (indicating 0 motion in y). The move() method is called 12 times per second, but each time it's called, the program doesn't add anything to the ball's x and y positions. The ball is paralyzed.

Mathematically manipulating dx and dy is the key to 2-D game programming. These manipulations let you

✔ Speed an object by giving it larger values of dx and dy.

✔ Slow it by giving the dx and dy properties smaller values.

✔ Reverse the direction of an object by inverting the values of dx and dy.

Bouncing off the walls

Sometimes, objects simply bounce off the walls. (This happens in the *Pong* game.)

This leads to the technique for bouncing an object off the Stage boundaries. Figure 6-7 shows what this might look like; I added the arrows to show the ball motion. (I recommend running the program yourself to see the action.)

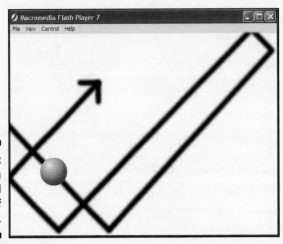

Figure 6-7:
This version of the ball bounces off all the walls.

To produce the bouncing effect, make another small modification of the `ballOOP` program:

✔ Invert the value of `dx` each time the ball hits a vertical (left or right) wall.

✔ Invert the value of `dy` each time the ball hits a horizontal (top or bottom) wall.

The code in Listing 6-4 shows exactly how to duplicate this effect.

Listing 6-4: Bounce Demo

```
//from bounceDemo.fla
ball.checkBoundaries = function(){
  //bounce demo - bounce off walls
  //keep ball entirely on stage

  //ball leaves right side
  if (ball._x > Stage.width - (ball._width/2)){
    ball.dx = -ball.dx;
  } // end if

  //ball leaves left side
  if (ball._x < ball._width/2){
    ball.dx = -ball.dx;
  } // end if

  //ball leaves bottom of stage
  if (ball._y > Stage.height - (ball._height/2)){
    ball.dy = -ball.dy;
  } // end if

  //ball leaves top of stage
  if (ball._y < ball._height/2){
    ball.dy = -ball.dy;
  } // end if

} // end checkboundaries
```

Here's how the `bounceDemo` code works for horizontal position:

Because the following code is called in an `onEnterFrame` method, it repeats indefinitely:

1. **The current value of a sprite's dx indicates whether it's moving to the right or the left.**

   • If `dx` is a positive value, adding `dx` to `_x` moves the object to the right.

   • If `dx` is a negative value, adding `dx` to `_x` moves the object to the left.

   For example, if `dx` is 5 (the default value), the program keeps adding 5 to the ball's x until the ball hits the right-hand wall.

2. **When the object hits the right wall, its (positive) dx gets its inverse value (and then becomes negative).**

   The program keeps adding –5 to the ball's x position.

   This makes the ball move toward the left until it hits the left-hand wall.

3. **When x hits the left wall, the now-negative dx is inverted again, returning the value to a positive value.**

   If the ball's dx is –5, it becomes 5 (positive five) after it hits the left-hand wall.

A similar process handles dy to set the vertical position. If dy is non-zero, the following steps repeat indefinitely (again because the code is placed in an enterFrame method):

1. The object moves vertically up or down until it hits the top or bottom border.

2. When the object hits one of the borders, the value of dy inverts.

3. The object goes in the opposite direction until it hits the other border.

Ignoring borders

Once in a while, a game allows objects to move outside the visual area. You can achieve this effect by simply omitting the boundary checking statements. Be careful of this effect because it can result in the user losing control of the out-of-sight object. You can see examples of this effect in the space games in Chapter 12.

I once wrote an air traffic control simulator that simulated a much larger area than the screen showed. The player reads "radio" messages and locates planes before they became visible. The player still has information about the whereabouts of the objects even though they're not visible.

Combinations

You can use different kinds of boundary checking in a game for either

✔ Different objects

✔ Different properties of an object

Most games use more than one boundary behavior:

✔ *Civilization* **uses different boundary-checking strategies for horizontal and vertical position:**

   • The characters can wrap across the left and right borders.

- Traffic can't cross the top and bottom borders.

This turns the map into a cylinder, which is close enough to a globe shape to simulate a planet in the game.

✔ *Pong* **uses different boundaries for paddles and balls:**

- Paddles stop at the edge of the screen.

- The ball bounces off the top and bottom walls (and the paddles), but it ignores the left and right borders (and then resets the ball position).

Making a Cursor

One very interesting difference between game programming and mainstream programming is the mouse cursor:

✔ **Cursor:** In traditional programming, it's considered very rude to mess with the mouse cursor unless you change it to one of a number of well-understood icons (an hourglass or a crosshairs icon, for example). Users know what these icons mean and don't want to be surprised.

✔ **Pointer:** In game programming, it's very common to change the mouse pointer and even to hide it. You often want the user to forget he's using a computer.

You can replace the familiar mouse pointer with whatever other object you want. The `customCursor` program featured in Figure 6-8 shows exactly how to convert the mouse to some other symbol.

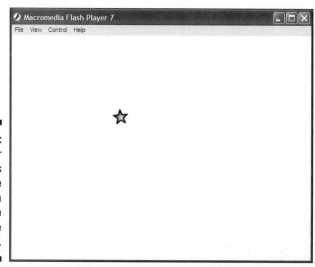

Figure 6-8:
This star moves around the screen as a substitute mouse pointer.

In this example, as long as the mouse is over the Stage:

✔ The normal mouse pointer is hidden.

✔ A star takes the place of the normal mouse pointer.

This substitute mouse is a very common device in Flash games. Here's how it's done:

1. **Create a new Flash document.**

   Chapter 2 shows you how to create a new document.

2. **Build a shape to be the new pointer.**

   The sidebar "Some pointers about pointers" has tips for making a great mouse pointer.

3. **Convert your shape to a movie clip and export it to ActionScript.**

   Give our new symbol a name that describes its shape or purpose.

4. **Name your pointer instance on the Stage.**

   Because you have only one pointer, you can name the visible version the same thing as the object in the Library.

5. **Hide the mouse pointer.**

   When your program first runs, it should turn off the normal mouse pointer so that your custom pointer appears instead. To accomplish this, use `Mouse.hide()`. Flash has a built-in object called `Mouse`, which has a very handy method called `hide()`. Hiding the mouse is something that should be done on the initial run of the game, so it's good to write an initialization method that handles this as well as other startup housekeeping activities.

   Write the following code in Frame 1, Layer 1:

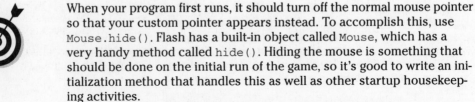

```
//customCursor
//demonstrates how to turn any movie clip into
//a custom cursor

init();

function init(){
  Mouse.hide();
} // end init
```

Some pointers about pointers

You can use any shape as a pointer. Here are some tips for making a good pointer shape:

✔ **Smaller shapes usually are best.**

The pointer shouldn't hog the entire screen. It's used to indicate position on the rest of the screen.

✔ **If you need precision (for example, to press small buttons on the screen), use a shape with an obvious point (such as an arrow or a pointing finger).**

The registration point of your shape becomes the actual hot spot of the new pointer.

The preceding code has two sections:

- A series of comments explaining what's going on

- A call to the `init()` function

  When the frame is first encountered, any code in `init()` runs. (The code in `init()` simply hides the mouse.)

6. Build an `enterFrame` event handler for the pointer.

The pointer needs to check several times per second for the mouse's position and move accordingly. The `enterFrame` event is perfect for this.

`enterFrame` code happens many times per second, but code called from the frame (like the `init()` function) happens only once (when the program encounters the frame).

Your event handler looks something like this:

```
star.onEnterFrame = function(){
  //get star's X and Y values from mouse's X and Y values
} // end enterFrame
```

I put a comment inside the preceding code explaining how I intend to move the star. Presumably, there's some way to retrieve the mouse's x and y values. If I can retrieve those values, I can move the star there, making it act like a mouse cursor.

7. Follow that mouse pointer!

Flash's `Mouse` object doesn't have the same x and y properties as movie clip objects, so follow this step carefully. (The sidebar "Where's the mouse?" explains how the `Mouse` object differs from a movie clip.)

Where's the mouse?

When I discovered that Flash had a `Mouse` object, I figured it would have some kind of x and y properties just like the movie clip objects. I was surprised to find that Flash doesn't do it that way. Instead, each movie clip has the ability to determine where the mouse pointer is in relationship to its own position. Movie clips store this info in the `_xmouse` and `_ymouse` properties.

In my example, you can't use the `star` movie clip to determine the position of the mouse pointer because the star's position changes with the mouse. However, the entire program is a movie clip object, and the program has all the properties of ordinary movie clips. That means you can access all the properties of the main movie by referring to it as `_root`.

For the `customCursor` program, use the special keyword `_root` to refer to the entire program's properties. Armed with this knowledge, you can now fill in the `enterFrame` code, like my following example (change *star* to the name of your pointer):

```
star.onEnterFrame = function(){
  //get star's X and Y values from mouse's X and Y values
  star._x = _root._xmouse;
  star._y = _root._ymouse;
} // end enterFrame
```

8. **Test your program.**

   You should be able to wiggle the mouse around and watch the custom pointer follow it around perfectly.

Chapter 7

Won't Be Long 'Til You Write Pong

*I*t was the mid-1970s. I was a young teenager, hanging out at a pizza parlor with my family. We had been there many times, but this time, something new was in the joint. The pinball game that had stood in the corner for years was replaced by this strange new game, played on a black-and-white TV screen! I watched people playing this marvel, and I wondered how on Earth it could work.

Of course, the game was *Pong*. At the time, I knew it was something big. Now, of course, the game seems very simple although it's still a lot of fun. *Pong* was a big hit partially because of its simplicity. (*Pong* was actually the second video arcade game released. The first, *Spacewar,* was more sophisticated, but it didn't do well. It was just too far from anyone's experience.)

The simplicity of the game made it simple to program as well as simple to learn. Still, the basic concepts of that very basic game remain the foundation of all 2-D video games even today. As a foundation, there are objects onscreen, some of which move on their own as well as some that move by player control. The objects move according to some sort of predictable logic, and when they collide with each other, interesting things happen.

The things that made *Pong* so successful back when I had a bad complexion are the same things that make it a great game for beginners to program. If you can build a *Pong*-type game, you can extrapolate the same ideas into much more complicated projects.

Building the Game Plan

Figure 7-1 shows a variation of *Pong* I wrote for this book:

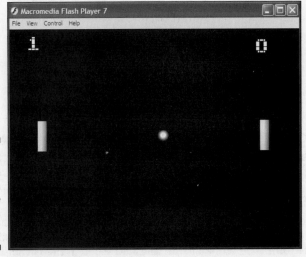

Figure 7-1:
My version
of *Pong* lets
you play
against the
computer.

Play this game from this book's companion Web site to see how it works
(www.dummies.com/go/flashgameprogrammingfd1e). In this chapter, I
show you the techniques used to build just about any 2-D arcade game. At
the end of the chapter, I show you how to put these concepts together to
build your own version of *Pong*. Cool, huh?

If you can bounce a ball around onscreen and make objects follow the mouse,
you're halfway to completing your own Pong game. (Chapter 6 shows those
skills.)

Font troubles

When you open `pong.fla` in Flash, you might get an error stating that a font is not available. That
happens because I used a custom font called `arcade.ttf` in this application. I included a copy
of the `arcade` font on the companion Web site.

> www.dummies.com/go/flashgameprogrammingfd1e

If you want to see the font in the Flash editor, install `arcade.ttf` onto your system. If you don't
install this font, the game will still play just fine, but you need to choose another font. See the section "Adding scorekeeping text fields" later in this chapter for information on using custom fonts
in your Flash applications.

Building any game has a series of steps:

1. Visualize the result.

2. Write down — in words — how you want the game to work.

3. Plan for incremental steps to build your game.

4. Build the game one component at a time.

5. Check each component as you build.

6. Review. Periodically check against your original plans.

I show you in the rest of this chapter how to build the Pong game from nothing. The process is what really matters because there's very little new programming to learn. I start with a blank screen and continually add new components.

As you look through the process, you see lots of little code fragments in the book. In this chapter, I show only those things that have been added or changed from previous incarnations of the program. If you want to see any code in its current context, look at the HTML version of each program as it appears on the Web site that accompanies this book. I provide the complete code listing to the Web page containing the example, including a description of where each code snippet is in the Timeline. Of course, I also provide the original FLA file for you to examine as well. (The file types are described in Chapter 2.)

The first step of game development is to build a plan for the game.

Your game plan should clearly state your goals in plain language.

The following example is my plan for the Pong game:

- ✔ **I intend to build a clone of the classic arcade game *Pong*.**
- ✔ **My game will run on a Web page.**
- ✔ **The user can control the left-hand paddle by moving the mouse.**

  The player paddle follows the mouse paddle's y value but remains constant in x.

- ✔ **The opponent paddle generally follows the ball but will have some sort of lag built in, thus making it possible for the human player to win.**

  It should be possible to adjust the lag for different skill levels.

- ✔ **The ball will bounce off the top and bottom walls; if the ball passes either paddle, the other player scores 1 point.**
- ✔ **Whenever a point is scored, the ball is reset heading directly away from the paddle of the player who just scored.**
- ✔ **Whichever player first accumulates 3 points wins the game.**

✔ **Whether the player wins or loses, he's taken to an appropriate screen and given an opportunity to restart the game.**

✔ **The ball bounces off the paddles in a way that gives the players some control of the direction.**

- If the ball hits a paddle near the center, the ball returns perpendicular to the paddle.

- The farther from the center the ball hits, the more extreme its return angle is.

✔ **The visual style of the game should balance a retro and modern feel.**

- The screen is black, with 1980s-style fonts for score and titles.

- The ball and paddles should stand out a little by using grayscale gradients.

- No color is used in the game.

The most common game programming error is failing to write a detailed plan like the one in this section. If you can just sit down and write code that works without a plan, hey — I'm happy for you. However, when your code doesn't work, you probably needed either a plan or a better plan. Think of it this way: You don't pull out a map every time you drive to work, but you likely do use a map any time you go someplace that you haven't visited before. Game programming is about visiting new, interesting places. If you write and follow directions, you enjoy the trip a lot more.

Following the Mouse with the Player Paddle

The first milestone is really important because it sets up the rest of the program. I decided the first thing I wanted to tackle was the player behavior. In the overall game plan, the player paddle should follow the mouse. This requires a number of steps:

1. **Start a new Flash document in the normal way.**

   Write a few comments in the Frame 1, Layer 1 code window, reminding yourself what the program should do and when you started it.

2. **Build a rectangle that will become the player paddle.**

   To produce the look I wanted, I play around with the linear gradient. My paddle seems to be lit from the left and slightly up.

   Whenever you use gradients to simulate 3-D lighting effects, make all objects in the scene appear to be lit from the same source. Inconsistent lighting distracts the player even if he can't identify what is wrong.

Making molehills out of a mountain

Writing a game plan like the one I presented in the previous section can be more difficult than it seems because

- ✔ Taking an idea as seemingly simple as *Pong* and breaking it down into the smallest component tasks is challenging.

- ✔ After you see all the small steps, it's easy to be intimidated by the size and complexity of what first seemed to be a very simple project. I often look at several steps, wondering how in the world I'm going to implement them.

Don't build your game randomly. You can build very complex programs if you are systematic about your process:

- ✔ Figure out a strategy for writing the parts you plan.

- ✔ Tackle new things one at a time.

Here's my order of attack for the Pong game:

1. Put a player paddle onscreen that can follow the mouse.

2. Add the ball and give it the ability to bounce off the walls.

3. Make the ball bounce off the player paddle in a simple way and then make a more advanced version of the ball-paddle collision.

4. Add a simple opponent paddle with proper ball-rebounding behavior.

5. Improve the opponent's behavior to be more lifelike.

6. Add scorekeeping and game-winning mechanisms.

7. Work in advanced features such as sound effects, difficulty levels, and *power-ups* (special bonuses that give the user temporary abilities when hit).

Although each of these steps is still potentially challenging, I turn a mountain into a series of small hills. There are other completely correct paths to writing this game, but this is the strategy I chose because I think each step builds nicely on the preceding steps. I like having a lot of little goals because I can celebrate when I reach each one. For example, each time I reach a program milestone, I like to go play with the kids for a few minutes. (That is, unless I'm programming at two in the morning. My wife frowns at waking the kids just so I can play with them.)

3. **Turn the paddle into a movie clip object.**

   Name your new object `paddle` and make it available for ActionScript coding with the usual Convert to Symbol technique.

4. **Name the instance of the paddle `player`.**

   Use the Instance Name text box in the Properties panel to name the specific paddle on the screen `player`.

   Because you'll have another paddle on the screen named `opp` (for *opponent*), you need to tell them apart.

5. **Add an `enterFrame` event handler to the player.**

   You want the ball to follow the mouse every time the mouse moves.

To do this, you need code that checks the mouse position several times per second. The `enterFrame` event is perfect for this, so add the following code to Frame 1, Layer 1:

```
//from paddle.fla
player.onEnterFrame = function(){
  //player paddle follows mouse's y value
} // end enterFrame
```

This code sets up the event handler. The comment explains what you intend to do.

Comments are ignored by Flash, but they're one of the most important parts of programming. You need to know exactly what you want to do.

6. Have the player paddle follow the mouse's y.

The player paddle can use a variant of the custom cursor idea! The paddle is different, though, because it always keeps the same x value and simply matches y values with the mouse.

The code in the player's `enterFrame` function looks like this:

```
//from paddle.fla
player.onEnterFrame = function(){
  //player paddle follows mouse's y value
  player._y = _root._ymouse;
} // end enterFrame
```

7. Hide the mouse cursor.

The paddle follows the y value of the mouse if you did everything correctly so far, but the normal mouse cursor is distracting.

Build an `init()` function to hide the mouse in the `customCursor` program in Chapter 6:

```
//from paddle.fla
init();
function init(){
  //turn off the mouse pointer
  Mouse.hide();
} // end init
```

You'll add other code to the `init` function later as you have more objects to initialize, so the `init` function is a good thing to have around.

8. Test and refine your code.

Try it out. Check whether it works. If something goes wrong, take a look at the error message that pops up, which is at least somewhat helpful. If that doesn't work, look again at the code. Even little things like misplaced commas and misspellings can cause big problems. When your code is working, do a little happy dance.

Celebrate your small victories!

Figure 7-2 shows the program with the paddle following the mouse.

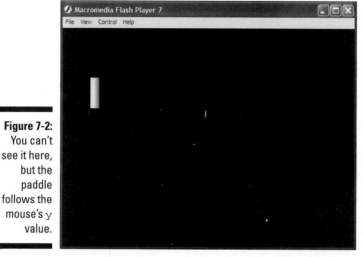

Figure 7-2:
You can't
see it here,
but the
paddle
follows the
mouse's y
value.

Adding the Bouncing Ball

The next milestone on the game plan list is to add a ball.

The first iteration of the ball should be able to interact with the walls. At first, I just let it pass right through the paddle. These steps build a ball that moves on its own and bounces off the walls:

1. **Create a circle that will become the ball.**

   I use a radial gradient to give my ball a 3-D appearance. If you use gradients to simulate texture, the light should appear to come from a consistent source.

2. **Turn the ball into a movie clip by pressing F8.**

   I recommend using the same name (in this case, `ball`) for

   - The movie clip
   - The instance (using the text area on the Properties tab)

3. Give the ball some default properties.

The best place to do this is in the `init()` function. Modify `init()` so it looks like this:

```
//from paddleball.fla
function init(){
  //turn off the mouse pointer
  Mouse.hide();

  //initialize ball speed
  ball.dx = 15;
  ball.dy = 5;
} // end init
```

The new feature in this section comprises the `ball.dx` and `ball.dy` properties. I give the ball `dx` and `dy` properties just like the ones in all the earlier ball programs.

4. Add an `enterFrame` event handler to the ball with the following code:

```
//from paddleball.fla
ball.onEnterFrame = function(){
  ball.move();
  ball.checkBoundaries();
  ball.checkPaddles();
} // end enterFrame
```

Through the miracle of encapsulation, I turn the event handler into a to-do list for the program. Anything the ball needs to do each frame is delegated from this event. Of course, this implies that the ball has those three methods (`move`, `checkBoundaries`, and `checkPaddles`). It doesn't yet have those methods, but it won't be long before it does.

5. Add a `move()` method to the ball.

I told you it wouldn't be long! The `move` method moves the ball according to its current values of `dx` and `dy`. It should look like this:

```
//from paddleball.fla
ball.move = function(){
  ball._x += ball.dx;
  ball._y += ball.dy;
} // end move
```

This `move` method is the same one I describe in Chapter 6.

Any object that you move around onscreen in your games probably has a `move()` method very much like this.

6. Add a `checkBoundaries()` method to the ball.

This `checkBoundaries` is similar in structure to the ones used in the various boundary demos from Chapter 6:

```
//from paddleball.fla
ball.checkBoundaries = function(){
  //bounce off top and bottom walls
  if (ball._y < 0){
    ball.dy = -ball.dy;
  } // end if

  if (ball._y > Stage.height){
    ball.dy = -ball.dy;
  } // end if

  //if past left of screen, opponent scores
  //wrap for now
  if (ball._x < 0){
    trace("Opponent Scores");
    ball._x = Stage.width;
  } // end if

  //if past right of stage, player scores,
  //bounce for now
  if (ball._x > Stage.width){
    trace ("Player scores");
    ball.dx = -ball.dx;
  } // end if
} // end checkboundaries
```

The ball simply bounces off the top and bottom walls. The left and right walls are a little different because they eventually lead to scoring opportunities. For now, simply put `trace` statements to indicate that the human or computer player would score in this situation. I had the ball wrap if the opponent scores and bounce if the player scores, so in either case, the ball returns to the human player. Later in the section, "Adding a Scorekeeping Mechanism," I set up more sophisticated behavior. Here, the main goal is to get the ball back in play.

7. Add a `checkPaddles()` method to the ball.

The purpose of this method is to detect collisions between the paddle and the ball. The movie clip comes with a very handy method for checking

TIP

Recognizing programming patterns

Whenever you move any kind of object onscreen, you're likely to give it the same general methods. Learn to recognize patterns so that when your plan reads *build a moving object,* you know that it needs dx and dy properties, a move() method, and some mechanism for dealing with walls. The goal is to build a series of patterns in your mind. When you think *bounce the ball off the wall,* the pattern should guide you to a standard wall-bouncing technique (by inverting dx or dy).

whether two movie clips have collided: `hitTest()`. Because the paddle is inherited from the movie clip object, it inherits this useful behavior.

The following code checks whether the ball has hit the player paddle:

```
//from paddleball.fla
ball.checkPaddles = function(){
  //check to see if ball touches paddle
  if (ball.hitTest(player)){
    //simply bounce off for now
    ball.dx = -ball.dx;
  } // end if
} // end checkPaddles
```

The `hitTest()` method can be used in a couple of ways. The form shown in this code accepts one parameter, which is another movie clip.

- *If the two movie clip objects touch or overlap,* the `hitTest()` method returns the value `true`.

- *If the two movie clip objects don't touch,* the `hitTest()` method returns the value `false`.

For now, if the ball hits the paddle, it simply bounces off the paddle as if the paddle were a wall.

8. Test and save the program.

Make sure that everything is working correctly before you proceed to improving the paddle-ball collision.

Building a Better Bounce

In my Pong, the key to winning the game is how exactly the ball and paddle collide.

In most forms of *Pong* (and its cousin *Breakout*), the user controls the ball by hitting it with different parts of the paddle:

✔ If the ball hits a paddle in the center of the paddle, it bounces perpendicular to the paddle — that is, straight to the right in a perfect horizontal trajectory.

In most implementations of *Pong,* the angle at which the ball hits the paddle (the angle of incidence) doesn't matter. The angle at which the ball leaves the paddle (the angle of reflection) is determined entirely by the relative position of the ball and the paddle at the moment of impact.

✔ As the impact point moves farther toward the ends of the paddle, the angle at which the ball leaves the paddle becomes more extreme.

The diagram in Figure 7-3 shows my plan for paddle-ball collisions.

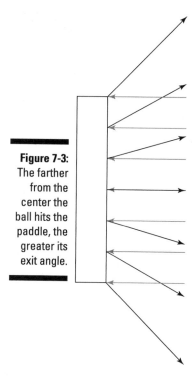

Figure 7-3:
The farther from the center the ball hits the paddle, the greater its exit angle.

Risk has its rewards

More risk, more reward is an important principle in game design. Safe play should lead to small rewards. Make the player take some risks to get the perfect shot or the bonus points. This makes the game more interesting and rewarding for the player.

Here's how the risk-rewards principle works in the Pong game:

- ✔ If a player hits the ball in the center of the paddle, he is very unlikely to miss, but the ball sent to the opponent is
  - • Extremely predictable (low risk)
  - • Easily returned (bad)
- ✔ If the human player wants to get the ball past the computer opponent (after there actually is an opponent), he must use the riskier high-deflection shots at the edges of the paddle:
  - • If you aim just a corner of the paddle at the ball, you stand a great chance of missing the ball altogether (high risk).
  - • If you hit that difficult shot, you can set up a very difficult shot for the computer player to return (good).

Many ways to bounce a ball

There are many other ways to handle the collision between a paddle and a ball. For example, you could consider the ball's incoming angle, or you could calculate the relative motion of the two objects. I chose the angle approach because

✔ It's simpler than the other techniques to implement.

✔ It's pretty typical of early *Pong* games (because it's easy to do).

✔ It still gives a pretty good level of control to the player.

I usually start with the simplest approach I can think of and then embellish that plan after it's working well.

Load the `paddleBounce` program from this book's companion Web site (`www.dummies.com/go/flashgameprogrammingfd1e`) and play around with it a little bit to see how the ball bounces off the paddle as described in the preceding section. This program looks just like the last one when it isn't moving, so I won't provide a screen shot. You need to play the game to see the difference.

Refining the bounce

The only new element of `paddleBounce` comprises

▌ ✔ Some refinements in the `checkPaddles()` method

▌ ✔ A new function called `getDy()`

Listing 7-1 shows the new code in `paddleBounce`. The complete code is on the companion Web site.

Listing 7-1: New Code for Paddle Bounce

```
//from paddleBounce.fla
ball.checkPaddles = function(){
  //check to see if ball touches paddle
  if (ball.hitTest(player)){
    //simply bounce off for now
    ball.dx = -ball.dx;
    ball.dy = getDy(player);
  } // end if
} // end checkPaddles

function getDy(paddle){
  //determines dy based on where ball hits paddle.
```

```
//relY is relative Y of ball to paddle
relY = ball._y - paddle._y;
//trace relY

//relPerc is relY / height of paddle
//will range from -.5 to +.5
relPerc = relY / paddle._height;
//trace (relPerc);

//new DY ranges from -15 to +15
newDy = relPerc * 30;
//trace (newDy);
return newDy;

} // end getDy
```

The `checkPaddles()` routine is easy to understand:

- ✔ It inverts the ball's `dx` property.
- ✔ It delegates the handling of `dy` to the `getDy()` function.

Getting a new dy value

The real secret to the `paddleBounce` program is the `getDy()` function. It works, but it's hard to see from the code how I got there. This is where programming becomes an arcane art.

There are many ways to produce the type of behavior you're looking for here. I chose a mathematical approach. It's actually very flexible and really not hard to understand after you understand the trick.

Table 7-1 summarizes how the ball and paddle should interact.

Table 7-1		Determining Bouncing Behavior		
paddle._y	*ball._y*	*relY* *paddle._y – ball._y*	*relPerc* *relY / paddle._height*	*newDy* *relPerc * 30*
100	70	−25	−.5	−15
100	80	−20	−.4	−12
100	90	−10	−.2	−6
100	100	0	0	0

(continued)

Table 7-1 (continued)

paddle._y	ball._y	relY paddle._y – ball._y	relPerc relY / paddle._height	newDy relPerc * 30
100	110	10	.2	6
100	120	20	.4	12
100	130	25	.5	15

The key to producing this chart is to think of the results you're looking for:

- ✔ **If the ball hits the paddle squarely in the middle, the new dy value should be 0, meaning no change in y or a completely horizontal path.**

- ✔ **If the ball hits the top edge of the paddle, dy should be a large negative number. I set it to –15, which is a pretty steep angle.**

  This makes the ball move sharply upward on every frame.

- ✔ **If the ball hits the bottom of the paddle, it should have a large positive dy component of 15.**

  This makes the ball move downward a large amount in each frame.

What I had to do was figure out

- ✔ Where the ball is in relation to the paddle

- ✔ How to convert the ball-paddle relationship to the range of numbers I need (in this case, +15 to –15)

To figure out the appropriate formula, use the following steps:

1. **Identify the information you have.**

   The only tools I really have are the characteristics of the paddle and the ball, but that's quite a bit. The relevant details are `ball._y`, `paddle._y`, and `paddle._height`.

2. **Determine the resulting information you want.**

   I want a formula that gives me –15 when the ball is at the top of the paddle, 0 when the ball is at the center of the paddle, and +15 when the ball is at the bottom of the paddle.

3. **Make some test cases to make your life easier.**

   I want to write formulas that work for any arbitrary paddle size and position onscreen. However, I'm going to set up a set of test cases that simplify the math. I'm presuming that the paddle is 50 pixels tall. The paddle's y position (which is at the center of the paddle) is 100.

I test for

- Extreme cases (where the paddle's position is at the top and bottom of the paddle)

- A predictable center point (where the ball and paddle have the same y values)

- Some predictable points in between the center and the extremes

4. **Begin to translate the information you start with to something more useful.**

   In this collision algorithm, the actual position of the ball and the paddle don't matter. You need their position in relation to each other. If you subtract `ball._y` from `paddle._y`, you should get a value between –25 and 25 if the paddle is 50 pixels tall. I call this value `relY`, for *relative y*.

5. **Normalize the value to be more universal.**

   The –25 to +25 range isn't bad as a beginning point, but I need the values to be in a different range. The easiest way to get to an arbitrary range is to start with something more universal. If you divide the –25 to +25 value by the height of the paddle (which I'm presuming to be 50 for this example), the result is a ratio between –.5 and +.5. I call this value `relPerc`, for *relative percentage*.

6. **Multiply the relative percentage to some constant to get exactly what you want.**

   For the final `dy` value, I'm looking for values between –15 and +15. If I multiply `relPerc` by 30, I get values in exactly the range I want.

The code for the `getDy()` function shows that it simply carries out the operations I determined in my chart. Here's one other interesting thing about `getDy()`: It is built to accept a movie clip as a parameter. Right now, the only paddle in the game is the player paddle, so that's the one I sent to the program. In the following section, I add an opponent. You'll see there that I can apply the same function to the other paddle without having to rewrite the code.

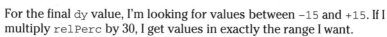

There's a fancy name for this . . .

If you're handy with a spreadsheet (such as Microsoft Excel), you can use it to work up this type of chart that converts one range of numbers to another range that you need. The process described here is a variation of a mathematical operation called *linear regression analysis*, which is a technique for predicting values of functions that can be defined as straight lines. If you want more information, look up linear regression in any statistics book.

Adding a Computer Opponent

One of the most appealing aspects of computer games is the ability to play games when a human opponent is unavailable. Computer opponents are sometimes called *AI* (for Artificial Intelligence). There is an art form behind creating computer opponents. A good AI has the following characteristics:

✔ **It's easy to beat.** Players want to win most of the time. If you give them an opponent that never loses, they lose hope and stop playing the game.

✔ **It isn't *too* easy to beat.** An opponent that's a total pushover is no fun, either. If it doesn't put up much of a fight, the user loses interest.

✔ **It can be adapted to various player abilities.** As the player's skill improves, the AI should become better so that the game continues to be challenging.

✔ **It should suspend disbelief.** Games are like stories. If a user is supposed to face some sort of robot, it should act like a robot, with logical, pre- dictable behavior. If the game is about outwitting a psychopath, the opponent's behavior should be much less predictable. If the game is about beating the stock market, the market and the other traders should reflect an actual stock market. The AI needs to support the story the player is being wrapped inside.

Take a look at `basicOpp`, as shown in Figure 7-4. It's the `paddleBounce` pro- gram with a computer opponent thrown into the mix.

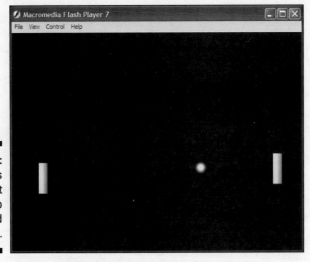

Figure 7-4: Now there's an evil robot paddle to contend with.

The AI for this robot paddle is quite good. In fact, it's perfect, and that's the problem: It never misses. That won't be very fun for the user. Later in this chapter, I show you how to make the paddle a little more human.

To add the basic opponent, follow these steps:

1. **Begin with the `paddleBounce` program.**

2. **Display the Library if it isn't already open.**

   Press F11 to display the Library panel.

3. **Drag a new paddle onto the screen.**

   The paddle is the movie clip in the Library. You can have more than one copy of a movie clip on the Stage at once, and that's exactly what you want to do here. Drag the second movie clip near the right-hand side of the Stage, where the opponent will live.

4. **Name this new paddle `opp`, using the text box in the Properties panel.**

   This changes the name of the paddle instance.

   You can have two instances of the same object with different names. In the code, you give these two objects different behavior even though they start from the same movie clip.

5. **Add an `enterFrame` event handler to the opponent.**

   Type the following code into Frame, 1 Layer 1 in an appropriate place:

   ```
   //from basicOpp.fla
   opp.onEnterFrame = function(){
      opp._y = ball._y;
   } // end function
   ```

   Because this function is an `enterFrame` event handler, it occurs repeatedly. During each cycle of the game, the opponent's y property is set equal to the ball's y property. The opponent always has the same y property as the ball, so the opponent can never miss.

   If you try the `basicOpponent` game, you'll face a perfect computer opponent. No matter how devious your deflection, the opponent always defends and returns.

6. **Teach the ball to bounce off the opponent paddle.**

   This is quite easy because you laid the groundwork in the preceding segment.

Change the code in the `ball.checkPaddles` method so it looks like this:

```
//from basicOpp.fla
ball.checkPaddles = function(){
  //check to see if ball touches paddle
  if (ball.hitTest(player)){
    //simply bounce off for now
    ball.dx = -ball.dx;
    ball.dy = getDy(player);
  } // end if

  if (ball.hitTest(opp)){
    ball.dx = -ball.dx;
    ball.dy = getDy(opp);
  } // end if
} // end checkPaddles
```

I added a section in the preceding code to check whether the ball hit the opponent. This code is almost identical to the code checking for a player hit. The only difference is that I send the `opp` paddle the `getDy()` function. If the ball hits `opp`, the new value for `ball.dy` should be based on the relationship between the ball and the `opp` paddle.

The extra work involved in setting up a generic function to handle ball-paddle collisions really pays off because

- ✔ You don't have to go through the headache of figuring out how to make the ball collide with this new paddle.
- ✔ If you change how balls and paddles collide, you have to change the code in only one place.

Building Artificial Stupidity

The basic opponent described in the preceding section is very good at playing Pong. Too good, in fact. Human players get bored quickly playing against an infallible opponent.

The key to artificial opponents isn't to make the AI perfect but rather to make it imitate human behavior in a believable way.

The opponent can't be perfect. It needs weaknesses for the human player to learn and exploit. (Check any monster movie for verification of this fact.) The problem with the `basicOpp` AI is that it has perfect reflexes.

The following example gives the opponent a variable reflex.

In the earlier example, the opponent paddle doesn't have a `dy` value (neither does the player paddle). Instead, both paddles blindly follow the `y` value of some other object. (The player paddle gets its `y` from the mouse, and the opponent gets its `y` from the ball.)

My plan for creating a more loveable opponent works like this:

Each time through the loop

✔ **Check whether the ball is above or below the `opp` paddle.**

This can be done by comparing `ball._y` with `paddle._y`.

- *If the ball is above the paddle,* set the paddle's `dy` to a negative value.

- *If the ball is below the paddle,* set the paddle's `dy` to a positive value.

✔ **The magnitude of `paddle.dy` is the paddle's speed.**

- *Set a large value to* `paddle.dy` *for a very good opponent.*

- *Set a low value to* `paddle.dy` *for a slow, ineffective opponent.*

The maximum expected `dy` for the ball is 15, so the ball can move a maximum of 15 pixels in the y axis each frame:

✔ If the paddle's `dy` is set to +/-15, it should keep up with the paddle almost all the time.

✔ If the paddle's `dy` value is set to 5, the opponent can keep up with the ball on relatively flat trajectories but is outclassed when the ball's `dy` is larger than 5. The opponent paddle will appear to be extremely slow, and the human player can beat the computer easily by propelling the ball at high trajectories.

The paddle's speed can be set to give varying levels of AI and difficulty.

Play against the `artStupid` program. The game is more entertaining when the opponent is challenging but not unbeatable. You can see what happens when you change the `opp.speed` variable value.

To make a more fallible computer opponent, follow these steps:

1. **Begin with the `basicOpponent` program.**

2. **Add a `speed` property to the `opp` object.**

    This is done in the `init()` function. Change that function so it looks like Listing 7-2.

Listing 7-2: Artificial Stupidity

```
//from artStupid.fla
function init(){
  //turn off the mouse pointer
  Mouse.hide();

  //initialize ball speed
  ball.dx = 15;
  ball.dy = 5;

  //opp speed is opponent speed
  //determines max dy for opponent.
  //15 is nearly flawless
  //0 is dead
  opp.speed = 10;

} // end init
```

In the `init` function, I set `opp.speed` to `10`, which is good but not hard to beat. Change `opp.speed` to larger and smaller values for a demonstration of how the algorithm works.

`opp.speed` is always a positive value. I'll add or subtract this value to make the opponent move up or down.

3. **Change the opponent paddle's motion by updating the `paddle.onEnterFrame()` method:**

```
//from artStupid.fla
opp.onEnterFrame = function(){
  //check to see if ball is above or below opp
  if (ball._y < opp._y){
    //move opp up
    opp.dy = - opp.speed;
  } else {
    //move opp down
    opp.dy = opp.speed;
  } // end if

  opp._y += opp.dy;

} // end function
```

The opponent's code can be summarized like this:

- *If the ball is above the opponent paddle*, set `opp.dy` to negative `opp.speed`.

  This increases the paddle by `opp.speed` units each frame.

- *If the ball is below (or equal to) the opponent paddle*, set `opp.dy` to `opp.speed`.

  This moves down `opp.speed` units each frame.

Adding a Scorekeeping Mechanism

The Pong game needs a scorekeeping system to be a complete game.

The game needs to

✔ Keep score

✔ Determine whether the player wins or loses

Adding scorekeeping text fields

It won't matter what the score is if you don't report the score to the user. Use dynamic text fields to display the player and opponent scores, as in Figure 7-5:

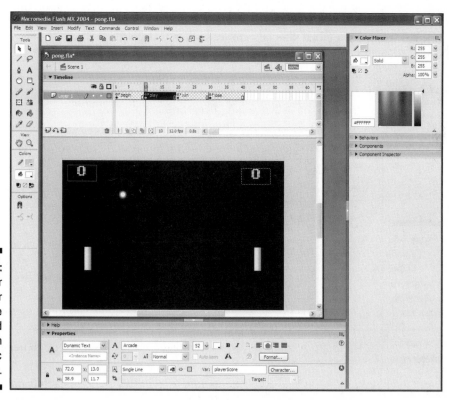

Figure 7-5: The user and player scores are displayed with dynamic text fields.

To add scores, follow these steps:

1. **Create a dynamic text field for player score.**

   Place this near the player paddle. Let the position of the field indicate its meaning so you don't have to write anything else onscreen. This example game benefits from a spare, simplistic design, so I don't want any unnecessary labels onscreen.

2. **Choose an appropriate font.**

   The characters should be relatively large and easy to read.

   Fonts are a great way to jazz up your programs. I did a search for free fonts and found a really cool font called *Arcade* by Jakob Fischer. Check out his site (`www.pizzadude.dk`) for more wonderful fonts. If you want to see the font in Flash, you'll need to install it on your computer.

3. **Specify the characters to embed.**

   If you use a custom font, Flash usually includes only the visible characters onscreen. The initial value of the score is 0.

   To embed special characters in a text field:

   a. Select the text area.

   b. Click the Character button to embed characters.

   c. Add the uppercase characters and the numerals, as in Figure 7-6.

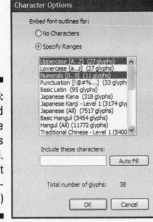

Figure 7-6:
Embed all the characters you need. (Flash won't do it automatically.)

4. **Assign a variable to the text field.**

   The text field near the player paddle should be associated with the variable `playerScore`. Associate the variable by typing **playerScore** in the `var` text field of the Properties window.

5. **Build the opponent score field.**

   You can copy and paste the player score field to create the opponent's score field. To make the new field attach to the opponent's score

   a. *Move the opponent score toward the opponent paddle.*

   b. *Set the associated variable to* `oppScore`.

Add the scorekeeping code

Think through the mechanism for scoring:

✔ You need to know what condition indicates the player has scored.

✔ You also need to know what condition indicates the opponent has scored.

The `artStupid` version of Pong already has placeholder code that traces a report to the screen when any player scores.

Now it's time to implement code to

✔ Increment the score when somebody has made a point

✔ Check whether the player has won or lost the game

To add scorekeeping code, follow these steps:

1. **Initialize the scores in the `init()` function.**

   Add the following code to `init()`:

   ```
   //from pong.fla
   //reset scores
   playerScore = 0;
   oppScore = 0;
   ```

   This code resets both scores to `0`. It ensures that whenever the game begins, both the player and the opponent have a score of `0`.

2. **Update the score code in the `ball.checkBoundaries()` method.**

   The code should now read like Listing 7-3. The complete code is on the companion Web site:

   ```
   www.dummies.com/go/flashgameprogrammingfd1e
   ```

Listing 7-3: Pong

```
//from pong.fla
//if past left of screen, opponent scores
if (ball._x < 0){
  //trace("Opponent Scores");
  oppScore++;

  //opponent serves
  ball._x = opp._x - 50;
  ball._y = opp_y;
  ball.dy = 0;

} // end if

//if past right of stage, player scores,
if (ball._x > Stage.width){
  //trace ("Player scores");
  playerScore++;

  //player serves
  ball._x = player._x + 50;
  ball._y = player._y;
  ball.dy =0;
} // end if
```

It's easy to add basic scorekeeping functionality. Simply add a line to

- Increment `oppScore` when the ball gets past the player's border.

- Increment `playerScore` when the ball passes the opponent's edge.

The two score variables are attached to dynamic text fields, so the text onscreen automatically changes to reflect the new score.

In both cases, set up a cleaner serving situation so the ball gets back in play in a sensible way. The new "serving" mechanism moves the ball in front of the paddle that just scored, heading toward the other paddle.

3. **Test your program.**

Play against the computer for a while and let it score. Make sure the onscreen mechanism is incrementing correctly.

To make it easier to see what happens when you score, temporarily set the `ball.speed` to a low value in the `init()` function. This way, you can score more easily and see what happens.

Many game programmers leave little triggers in their games to allow themselves to quickly access a part of the game for testing without playing through the entire game.

This is one origin of the cheat codes, or *Easter eggs,* that hard-core gamers enjoy. The publishing houses caught onto the potential of this; secret bonus features are now built into most games. These features are often "leaked" after the game has been out for a while, presumably to renew interest in the game and keep it selling.

Add starting, winning, and losing states

To call a game complete, the user must be able to win or lose. Otherwise, it isn't much fun. The easiest way to do this in Flash is to make different frames on the Timeline represent different states.

The Adventure game in Chapter 3 shows how to build a game with multiple states.

To add introduction, winning, and losing screens to your program

1. **Modify the game so it begins with a splash screen, as shown in Figure 7-7.**

   Read about splash screens in the upcoming section, "Making other states."

Figure 7-7:
Now when the program starts, the user is treated to a startup screen.

2. **When the user clicks the button, the program goes to the usual play screen.**

3. Winning or losing the game leads to other states.

- *If the user wins,* he is taken to the elaborate Win screen, as shown in Figure 7-8.

Figure 7-8: If the user wins, he sees a (not so) colorful display.

- *If the user loses,* he sees another terse but relevant message, as shown in Figure 7-9.

Figure 7-9: The Lose screen is very much like the Win screen.

These screens are very much alike in this program, but they don't have to be. The mechanism here lets you jump control to any other part of the program. The new frame can be a static frame like I've made in this program, but it could also be an elaborate animation, another game, or even another Flash file.

Making other states

Previously in this chapter, the Pong program existed in just one frame. It's time to do some surgery on the Timeline. To add other states, follow these steps:

1. **Select Frame 10, Layer 1 in the Timeline.**

2. **Choose Insert⇨Timeline⇨Keyframe.**

   A new duplicate of Frame 1 appears in Frame 10.

3. **Go to Frame 20, Layer 1 in the Timeline.**

4. **Choose Insert⇨Timeline⇨Blank Keyframe.**

   This creates a new keyframe without any movie clips in it. Frame 20 is used for the winning state. It will have a much simpler interface than the game, so I don't want to copy the paddles and ball from the first frame.

5. **Insert a static text field into Frame 20:**

   a. Set the font and font size to create the effect you want.

   Titles should be large, but instructions can be smaller.

   b. Set the text to read Win! *or something else appropriate for the winning situation.*

6. **Build a button in Frame 20.**

   The button can be made any way you want, as long as it

   • Is a button object

   • Reads something like Click to Play

   To make a button, follow these steps:

   a. Build an object with normal drawing tools.

   b. Press F8 to convert the drawing object to a button.

   c. Select the button on the Stage and name the button instance btnPlay.

   If you have text in or on the button, make sure it's static text so the mouse cursor doesn't change to an edit cursor when the mouse is over the button.

7. **Go to Frame 30, Layer 1 in the Timeline.**

8. Choose Insert➪Timeline➪Keyframe.

This frame handles the losing condition.

This frame is almost identical to the winning frame, so inserting a keyframe (as opposed to a blank keyframe) duplicates the last keyframe created. This can be a very handy timesaver.

9. Go to Frame 40, Layer 1 in the Timeline.

10. Choose Insert➪Timeline➪Frame.

This last frame doesn't need to be a keyframe. In fact, it doesn't need to be there at all. I put it in so that when you label the frames in the next step, you can read all the frame labels in the Timeline.

11. Modify the text field in Frame 30 so it reads Lose! **(or whatever losing message you want to use).**

12. Label the keyframes according to the following table:

Frame	Label
0	begin
10	play
20	win
30	lose

You name a frame in the same place you name buttons and movie clip objects:

a. Select the frame in the Timeline.

b. Type the name on the Properties tab.

13. Build the begin frame.

You currently have two complete sets of paddles and ball: one in the begin frame, and one in play. You don't need them both, so follow these steps to delete the sprites where they are not needed:

a. Select all the elements on the begin frame by dragging the mouse around them and pressing Delete.

b. Go to the win frame and select all the elements there.

c. Copy the screen objects from the win frame.

d. Return to the begin frame and paste the elements you just copied.

e. Modify the text box in begin to be some sort of greeting.

This greeting screen is commonly called a *splash screen*. Many programs have them, especially Flash programs. The main purpose of a splash screen is to keep the user's attention while your program loads media elements in the background. The Pong game (and most games in this book) are written so efficiently that there's no noticeable lag in the game-loading process. For this game, the splash screen is nice because the player can get situated before the game begins.

Adding code to handle states

At this stage of development, your program should have four keyframes:

- ✔ The begin, win, and lose frames all have a text field and a button.
- ✔ The play frame contains the paddles and ball from the Pong game.

Examining the code window of each frame shows that the code is now out of date. There is code only in Frame 1, Layer 1, and that code refers to objects that aren't in that frame (the paddles and ball). Fortunately, you can easily move the code around and add the missing pieces.

Setting up the start and play frames

Follow these steps to get the start and play frames working correctly:

1. **Copy the code from the start frame. Follow these steps:**

   a. *Save your work.*

      If something goes wrong in the following steps, you need a backup.

   b. *Go to the start frame and open the cod- editing pane.*

   c. *Select all the code in the Actions panel and copy it.*

   d. *Move to the play frame and look at the editor again.*

You shouldn't have any code in the play frame yet. If there's code, make sure you're really in the right place (the Actions panel of the play frame).

   e. *Paste all the Pong code into this text editor.*

2. **Clear the code in the start frame.**

   Be *extremely* careful. Make sure you have code in the code window of the play frame before deleting the code in the start frame.

3. **Add some comments to the begin frame.**

   The begin frame needs some simple code to make it wait until the user clicks the button and then advance to the play frame when the button is clicked. Add the following code to the begin frame.

```
//Pong
//By Andy Harris
//For Flash Game Programming for Dummies
//March '05
//Most code in "play" frame
```

In the first frame of the program, I added a few comments about the entire program. It's customary to put similar comments in the most easily accessible code area of your program. In this case, I add it to the code in the `begin` frame. Of course, change the comments to reflect your own name — it's your program now!

 4. Add a `stop` command to the `begin` frame.

```
stop();
```

In the `play` frame, the first executable line is `stop();`. This command stops Flash from moving beyond the first frame. It wasn't necessary when the Pong game contained only one frame, but now if you don't stop the program, the `begin` frame shows up for a little less than a second and then moves directly to the game, which also shows for a second, followed by the `lose` and `win` frames. Flash defaults to animation mode. Use the `stop()` function to turn off this default behavior. Your code will control the user's movement along the Timeline.

 5. Add button code to the `begin` frame.

Of course, the purpose for the button is to let the user begin the game when he is ready to do so. Make sure that your button's instance name is `btnPlay` and add the following code to the `begin` frame's code window:

```
//from pong.fla
btnPlay.onRelease = function(){
  _root.gotoAndStop("play");
} // end button
```

The preceding code tells Flash to move to the `play` frame when the user clicks the button. Because it uses the `gotoAndStop` directive, the other frames don't need the `stop()` command. Flash simply goes to the frame directed and loops it until some code makes it move to another frame.

 6. Duplicate the button code.

The `win` and `lose` frames have buttons identical to the one in the `begin` frame. These other buttons also have the same behavior. Any time the user clicks any of these buttons, he should be sent to the `play` frame.

The code for these frames (which is identical in `win` and `lose`) shows one more interesting feature:

```
//from pong.fla
Mouse.show();

btnPlay.onRelease = function(){
  _root.gotoAndStop("play");
} // end button
```

In the preceding code, the `Mouse.show()` method reveals the mouse. The `Mouse.hide` command you put in `init()` hides the mouse at the beginning of the `play` frame. Now that a button is onscreen, it's only fair to give the mouse back to the user so he can actually click the play button.

Modify the scorekeeping code

Follow these steps to move focus to the winning and losing states:

1. **Modify the opponent score code.**

   After your program has a way to handle winning and losing conditions, you need to change your code so that these conditions are tested. Begin by modifying the segment of `ball.checkBoundaries()` that checks whether the opponent has scored. Modify that code so it looks like this:

   ```
   //from pong.fla
   //if past left of screen, opponent scores
   if (ball._x < 0){
     trace("Opponent Scores");
     oppScore++;
     //check for opponent win
     if (oppScore >= 3){
       gotoAndStop("lose");
     } // endif
     //opponent serves
     ball._x = opp._x - 50;
     ball._y = opp_y;
     ball.dy = 0;

   } // end if
   ```

   Immediately after incrementing the opponent score, test whether the opponent score is greater than the maximum score. In this case, I'm still testing the program, so I want to play very short games. I set the maximum score to 3. Of course, you'll probably want longer games when you release the final version of the code.

If the opponent score is now larger than or equal to 3, program control gets diverted to the lose frame. The rest of the code simulates the opponent serving. The ball is placed near the opponent paddle and is served horizontally.

2. **Modify the player score code.**

Make a very similar set of modifications to the code that checks for player scores:

```
//from pong.fla
//if past right of stage, player scores,
if (ball._x > Stage.width){
  trace ("Player scores");
  playerScore++;
  if (playerScore >= 3){
    gotoAndStop("win");
  } // end if
  //player serves
  ball._x = player._x + 50;
  ball._y = player._y;
  ball.dy =0;
} // end if
```

The preceding code is much like the opponent code, except this time, the code checks whether playerScore is past the maximum score. If the player has scored enough points

- Program control goes to the win frame.

- The player wins the game.

3. **Test your program to ensure it's working correctly.**

If you can port yourself back to 1972, you can use your new programming abilities to write Pong yourself and make a *lot* of money. Say hi to Nolan Bushnell for me!

Part IV
Getting Control of the Situation

"Amy surfs the Web a lot, so for protection, we installed several filtering programs that allow only approved sites through. Which of those nine sites are you looking at now, Amy?"

In this part . . .

1 show you how to let the user control sprites to make more interesting games. This part leads to a complete arcade game with sound, keyboard input, user-controlled sprites, computer-controlled monsters, collisions, and scorekeeping.

Chapter 8 shows how to work with audio files to add cool sound effects to your games. You also discover how to use the keyboard to get precise control of your characters.

Chapter 9 looks at how Flash movie clip objects relate to sprites and also how to make interesting animated sprites. With this knowledge, your characters can look however you want, and they can walk, mosey, or saunter around the screen under user or computer control.

Chapter 10 outlines the design process of another complete game. The Monster Traffic game sports all the features you'd expect in an '80s-style arcade game. Plus, it has really loud and annoying sound effects!

Chapter 8

Keyboard Input and Audio Output

· ·

In This Chapter

▶ An overview of the Monster Traffic game

▶ Responding to arrow key input

▶ Importing audio files

▶ Playing sounds on demand

· ·

Games (like all programs) require input and output. In this chapter, I introduce an input technique and an output technique that are both vital to games. Flash games often rely on the keyboard (including arrow keys) for input. Here you can discover techniques to read the keyboard and respond to various kinds of keyboard input. Sound is also critical to games. You will often use sound effects to communicate important ideas to the player as well as add atmosphere to the game experience.

Introducing the Monster Traffic Game

In the next few chapters, I show you how to build a complete 2-D arcade game. I show you how to do this by building a fun game called Monster Traffic. The introduction screen to this game is shown in Figure 8-1.

A screen shot can't do this game justice. You need to play the game to see what it does. Although it isn't brilliant, the game has a lot of features you won't see by looking at this book. For example, the monster is animated, moving its head from side to side while chasing the car. The car also spits out little puffs of smoke and wobbles a little bit as it drives. The instruction screen shown in Figure 8-2 lays out the premise of the game and the game controls.

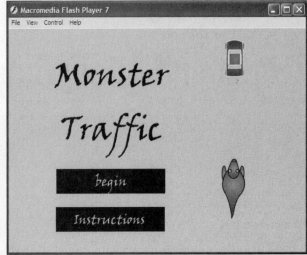

Figure 8-1:
The little
monster and
car chase
each other
before the
game starts.

Figure 8-2:
Even very
simple
games
benefit
greatly
from an
instruction
screen.

The user plays the part of a monster, who is stuck in some sort of parking lot. (Maybe he's at a monster sale at the mall.) The monster can warn away cars (and earn points) by blasting the cars with his fireballs. If a car hits the monster, his health decreases. The actual game is shown in Figure 8-3.

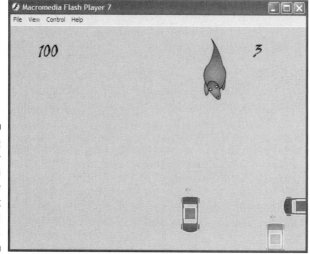

Figure 8-3:
The player
(monster)
tries to fry
cars without
getting
dinged.

The monster and the cars all *wrap* around the screen (leave one side of the screen and return on the other). The fireball disappears after it leaves the screen. Eventually, the monster is (sigh) defeated. When the game is over, the score is shown in a screen like Figure 8-4.

Figure 8-4:
The cars
eventually
win, but
it was a
good run.

Monster Traffic has a few features you might not have seen before. You control the monster by pressing the arrow keys, and pressing the spacebar makes the monster shoot a fireball. All the sprites, which are animated, can move in the eight primary directions.

The game also features sound effects. The fireball erupts from the monster with a whooshing sound; you hear crashes when cars bonk into the monster; and (my personal favorite) when you hit the cars with a fireball, a car alarm goes off.

The game is used to highlight a number of new technical features, including more sprite character animation, moving in a particular direction, detecting key strokes, and working with audio.

In this chapter, I describe how to respond to keyboard input as well as how to attach audio files to a Flash program and play them on demand.

Responding to the Keyboard

The keyboard is a very popular input device, especially the arrow keys. The `keyboardDemo` program shown in Figure 8-5 shows two ways to get information from the keyboard.

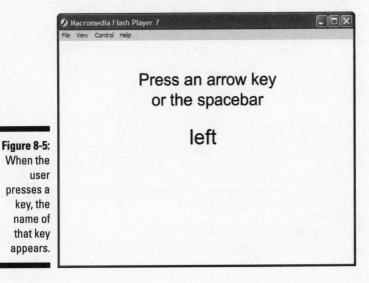

Figure 8-5:
When the user presses a key, the name of that key appears.

Other ways to read the keys

Other techniques are more frequently used in nongaming applications, in which the timing of each keystroke is less important than the sequence of strokes. For example, you could have keyboard input that simply tells you what key was pressed last or keeps track of all the recent keystrokes in a special memory area called a *buffer*.

Trolling for key presses

The most useful technique to get keystroke information in game programming is *hardware polling*. In this system, a binary value indicates whether a particular key is pressed.

Games use hardware polling because games often need immediate responses.

Examining keyboard input

My demo program shows the keyboard polling technique in the most simple form that I could think of.

My code features two dynamic text areas, linked to variables called `output` and `lastPressed`.

The code in Listing 8-1 is in Frame 1, Layer 1.

Listing 8-1:   Keyboard Demo

```
//keyboardDemo

_root.onEnterFrame = function(){

  output = "";
  if(Key.isDown(Key.LEFT)){
    output = "left";
  } // end if

  if(Key.isDown(Key.RIGHT)){
    output = "right";
  } // end if

  if(Key.isDown(Key.UP)){
```

```
        output = "up";
    } // end if

    if(Key.isDown(Key.DOWN)){
        output = "down";
    } // end if

    if(Key.isDown(Key.SPACE)){
        output = "space";
    } // end if

    if(Key.isDown(65)){
        output = "A";
    } // end if

    lastPressed = String.fromCharCode(Key.getAscii());
} // end function
```

Working with the Key object

The code relies on a special object built into Flash called the Key object. This object contains information and methods pertaining to the keyboard. Look up the Key object in the ActionScript dictionary for some ideas about what this object can do.

Computers assign specific numeric codes to each key on the keyboard. If you need the code for any particular key, you can look it up in the Flash online help. You can easily access Help by pressing F1 anywhere in the editor. Look for the ActionScript Language Reference section. (That's how I found the code for the A key, which is 65.) Many of the special keys, including the arrows, spacebar, Shift, and Ctrl keys, have special named values called constants. You can also look these up in the online Help if you need them. Most arcade games simply use the keys that I use in this program: the arrows and the spacebar. Their special names are pretty easy to guess: Key.DOWN, Key.UP, Key.SPACE, and so on.

Make a test program for new ideas

Before you add keyboard testing procedures to existing programs, be smart and build a test program like mine first to make sure you know what's going on.

When you first test a new idea like keyboard handling, test your concept in isolated code because

✔ If you mess things up, you don't want to break code that was working.

✔ Existing code can have complexities that get in the way of seeing a new idea.

Why trap for ordinary keys?

It makes sense that game programs frequently make use of special keys like the arrow keys, spacebar, and function keys, but you should also know how to trap for other keys as well.

Games that use the keyboard and the mouse at the same time don't usually use the arrow keys because the arrows are placed at the right-hand side of the keyboard. If you use your left hand to control the arrow keys and your right hand to control the mouse (as right-handed players tend to do), your body is forced in an uncomfortable position to the right of the screen. Many action games use the W, A, S, and D keys as alternative arrows because they can be comfortably controlled with the left hand.

In particular, I'm interested in the `Key.isDown()` method, which

1. Accepts the code for a particular key on the keyboard
2. Returns a binary (`true` or `false`) value based on the status of that key

For example, the following code fragment determines whether the spacebar is being pressed:

```
if(Key.isDown(Key.SPACE)){
  output = "space";
} // end if
```

The preceding code fragment performs these tasks:

1. **Checks whether the spacebar is down.**

   The `Key.isDown` call either

   - Returns `true` if the spacebar is pressed
   - Returns `false` if the spacebar isn't pressed

2. **If the spacebar is pressed, the `output` variable is assigned the value `space`.**

   Because `output` is tied to a dynamic text area, the screen displays `space`, indicating that the spacebar is pressed.

3. **Lather, rinse, and repeat.**

   Because this code happens inside an `enterFrame()` event, it happens many times per second.

The good news about the keyboard polling technique is that it lets you determine exactly when a key was pressed and released. For games, this is a critical feature. However, this approach can be tedious because you have to write an if statement for each key press you want to trap for. Sometimes all you need to know is what key was pressed most recently. The following line shows how to get this information:

```
lastPressed = String.fromCharCode(Key.getAscii());
```

The `Key.getAscii()` method returns a numeric code for the last key pressed.

A common format for text files in computers and on the Internet, *ASCII* (American Standard Code for Information Interchange) uses alphabetic, numeric, or special character represented with a 7-bit binary number (a string of seven 0s or 1s); there are 128 possible characters. Modern computers have often switched to another form called UTF (for Unicode Transformation Format), but the most common form (UTF-8) is nearly identical to the ASCII standard I describe here.

The ASCII code returned by `Key.getAscii()` and the key code used in the `Key.isDown()` method are related numeric codes, but they aren't the same, especially on international keyboards:

- The key code usually refers to the *physical location* of a key on the keyboard.
- The ASCII value refers to the *character encoding* that appears onscreen in most applications when that key is pressed.

The ASCII code returned by `Key.getAscii()` isn't very useful on its own (unless you happen to speak ASCII), but fortunately, ActionScript has a built-in function for converting from ASCII to a more readable format. The `String.fromCharCode()` method takes an ASCII value and converts it into a text character.

These two techniques are used in different circumstances:

- **Use `Key.isDown()` when**
  - You know which keys should be pressed.
  - You want a different specific action for each key.

  In most gaming environments, you use the `Key.isDown()` technique.

- **Use `Key.getAscii()` when**
  - The user can press any key on the keyboard.
  - You just want to know which key was pressed most recently.

Adding a keyboard handler

To add keyboard input handling to your programs, make a plan:

1. **Consider which keys will do what.**

   Make sure you decide what should happen when the user presses a certain key.

   If you aren't using one of the keys with a constant, look up the key codes you need in the online Help and jot them down before you start writing code.

2. **Decide which keyboard approach you will use:**

   - If you need to check for any key on the keyboard, the `Key.getAscii()` function usually is best.

   - In most other gaming applications, the `Key.isDown()` technique is preferable.

3. **Determine which event handler will hold the code.**

   In the techniques I've shown you, keyboard handling isn't its own event but is instead checked inside some other event handler. Because keyboard events can happen pretty frequently, they often go inside an `onEnterFrame()` method:

   - If the input refers to a particular object, you probably want to associate the keyboard inputs to that object's `enterFrame` event, so it's easier to find the code later. In general, place all code associated with an object in one of that object's methods.

   - If it doesn't really matter (as in this example), you can put it in the `onEnterFrame()` method of the main movie clip (_root).

4. **Write a Key.isDown() condition for each key.**

   Use a simple `if` structure to test for any of the keystrokes you expect.

   The keyboard demo program ignores any keys you don't explicitly test for.

Adding Sounds

Sound effects have always been a critical part of arcade games. The early machines were incapable of anything but the most rudimentary sound effects. Flash's background as an animation tool gives you really wonderful audio capabilities. You can prepare your game with several preloaded sound effects that play on whatever cue you want. You can use many different types of existing sounds or create and mix your own. Audio can support a game tremendously by setting the stage, adding humor, building tension, indicating when key events occur, and providing help to the user.

Figure 8-6 shows a very simple program that demonstrates Flash sound effects at their simplest.

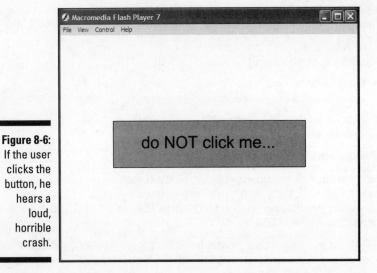

Figure 8-6:
If the user clicks the button, he hears a loud, horrible crash.

If you're testing the programs for this book in a library or other public computing facility, you should really wear headphones unless you enjoy irritating everyone around you. (Of course, it would be fun to write a program that causes all kinds of screeching and crashing when the next person sits at the computer — not that I'm suggesting you do this. I've never written anything like that in a public library. Honest.)

The program uses a button and the code in the following sections.

How Flash sound works

Flash animation and programming handle audio differently:

✔ **Animation:** In animation, you incorporate a sound by importing it into the program and dragging it to the Stage. Sounds frequently take up many frames because sounds are inherently *time dependent* (that is, they happen over some specified range of time). In animation, this is fine —

and even desired — because you frequently want to synchronize various animations to specific parts of the sound. In fact, many animations begin with sound and add the other elements to match the sound.

✔ **Game programming:** In game programming, you want your sound effects to be queued in the background, ready to be triggered. In a game, everything is triggered by game events (not completely scripted according to a timeline). Game sounds must follow the same convention.

Flash has a construct called a Sound object. This is an object in the same general vein as the Stage object and the Mouse object. It is a construct that lets you treat some entity as a variable with properties and methods. However, unlike Stage and Mouse, you actually create the Sound object. And you can have many of them, one for each sound effect you want to use in your project.

Getting sound effects

Getting sound effects for your games is really easy. Flash accepts the very common WAV and MP3 audio formats. Thousands of audio files in these formats are available from sound effects CDs, Web sites, and commercial services.

Of course, just because it's technically easy to obtain sound effects, don't overlook important legal and ethical concerns. As with any kind of intellectual property, you shouldn't use sound effects that someone else has created without getting his/her permission.

Here are several ways to approach intellectual property problems.

Get the author's permission

If you can identify the original author of a work, you can always write to him and seek permission to use his work.

I've found that people are generous if you're willing to give them credit, especially if your project is free or educational.

Use a commercial medium

You can find numerous sound effects collections in both

✔ **Digital formats (formats intended for computer use)**

✔ **Traditional audio formats (audio CDs, LPs, and tapes)**

Check your local public library for sound effects collections.

Extensive sound effects collections can be expensive, but here are some less-expensive alternatives:

✔ I've found very cost-efficient sound effects collections with thousands of sound effects. And although the quality of the sounds on cheaper collections can be uneven, you can often either find what you're looking for or something close.

Of course, you get what you pay for. The sound effects in the commercial collections are often of much better quality and usually cover much more specific kinds of sounds.

✔ Look for *royalty-free* audio effects, so you don't have to deal with licensing issues.

Create your own sound effects

You can make passable sound effects without a huge amount of talent, equipment, or software. I've recorded plenty of good audio with ordinary desktop microphones and freeware audio software. *Audacity* is a very powerful open source audio editor. This program lets you do many of the things the professionals do, including noise reduction, effects filtering, combining and reversing samples, and lots more. Check this book's companion Web site for a link:

Check this book's companion Web site for a link to Audacity:

    www.dummies.com/go/flashgameprogrammingfd1e

Creating your own sound effects has two major advantages:

✔ You won't get into copyright trouble because you're creating an original sound. (If your sound incorporates samples from somebody else's protected work, copyright protection laws might still apply.)

✔ You can make the sound exactly what you want.

Considering audio compression

Who doesn't hate games that seem to take hours to download? When this happens, the author has typically included large audio files that really slow the start of the game because they must be downloaded to the client before the game can start.

Sound files use lots of memory, so audio compression is a necessity. The sidebar "I want my MP3" briefly describes the popular MP3 compression scheme.

I want my MP3

One second of uncompressed CD-quality audio (44 kHz, 32-bit sample rate) is about the same file size as 78 pages of text. (That's why you almost never see uncompressed high-quality audio on the Internet. It simply takes too much time to download.)

The easiest path to a small audio file is a shorter recording time. Even short uncompressed recordings are usually too large to distribute on the Internet, so compression is a virtual necessity. A couple of techniques are used to make an audio file smaller:

✔ Any digital audio tool can save a sound in ways that trade audio quality for file size. Whenever you edit or create a digital audio file, you can lower the *sampling rate* (number of samples per second) or lower the *bit depth* (precision of each sample) to get a smaller file. The tradeoff, however, is a less-clear sound.

✔ The MP3 file format throws away data that the human ear is less capable of perceiving.

When you incorporate a sound file into Flash, it nearly always does some of this compression for you. The sidebar "Controlling your own sounds" shows how to turn off the compression and use your own.

You need to know that Flash's automatic audio compression is happening because the automatic compression sometimes creates problems. I find Flash to be overzealous in its audio compression. It frequently makes the audio files very difficult to hear. If I'm careful, I can achieve a better sound at the same file size by doing my own compression and telling Flash to simply use the file as I provide it.

Start with high-quality audio when possible. You'll almost always lose some audio quality in the compression process, but you can usually control the process so that

✔ The loss in quality isn't noticeable.

✔ The resulting game is small enough to download quickly.

Importing a sound into Flash

To use a sound in a Flash application, you must import it. Follow these steps:

1. Identify the sound.

Find the sound file you want to use:

a. Get a local copy of the sound.

Make sure the sound file is on your own machine, not online or on some other medium.

   b. Put the sound file in a directory with the other resources you're using for the current project.

If you want to edit your audio file, do it before you import it into Flash. After Flash gets hold of the file, you have less control of it.

2. Import the sound via File➪Import➪Import to Library.

Import to the *Library,* not the *Stage.* (Stage-based audio is much harder to control programmatically.)

3. Select the file you want to import from the Import to Library dialog box.

You can choose more than one audio file at a time by using the Ctrl key while selecting filenames.

4. Open the Library, if it isn't already visible (press F11).

The only way to see whether your file is loaded is through the Library panel:

   • You see a WAV or MP3 form of the file when you select it.

   • You can preview the file with the small Play icon in the Library.

When you listen to a file in the Library, you don't hear how the user will hear it. Most files are compressed in the preview process and lose some quality when you create the final SWF file. The sidebar, "Controlling your own sounds" shows you how to preview and control the final sound.

5. Set the linkage properties for the sound. Follow these steps:

   a. Right-click the sound in the Library.

   b. Choose Linkage from the contextual menu that appears.

   A dialog box like Figure 8-7 appears.

Figure 8-7:
If you
don't set
the linkage
correctly,
you can't
hear your
sound
effects.

Linkage Properties

Identifier: crash.wav

AS 2.0 Class:

Linkage: ☑ Export for ActionScript
☐ Export for runtime sharing
☐ Import for runtime sharing
☑ Export in first frame

URL:

OK

Cancel

c. Select the Export for ActionScript check box.

This automatically enables the Export in First Frame check box.

Flash automatically adds anything it sees on the Stage to the final SWF file. However, if a sound file (or any other element) is in the Library but not on the Stage, Flash doesn't incorporate that element into the final SWF file. The linkage directive informs Flash that the audio file will be used even though it isn't currently on the Stage and also that it should be included with the file.

If your sound effects don't work, make sure you've set the linkage properties.

6. Tune up the audio compression.

Flash almost always compresses audio files. An automatic algorithm tries to find the best compromise between audio quality and download time.

I'm rarely happy with the results of Flash's automatic compression. To specify your own compression properties, see the sidebar, "Controlling your own sounds."

7. Create a `Sound` object in your code.

When you have a sound in the Library, you need to attach it explicitly to a software `Sound` object. Create a `Sound` object with code like this:

```
sndCrash = new Sound();
```

You repeat this code for every sound you import into the Library. Give each sound a name that you can remember.

8. Attach the Library sound to the `Sound` object.

The following line makes the connection between the `Sound` object and the file in the Library:

```
sndCrash.attachSound("crash.wav");
```

The text inside the parentheses is the name of the audio element in the Library (*not* the filename of a particular file). As you add a file to the Library, the sound effect's default name is the filename. This technique doesn't connect to the file system but refers only to sound already loaded into the Flash environment. This lets you package all the sounds in the SWF file without having to send separate files for all the sound effects.

9. Play the sound, using the `Sound.start()` method.

For example, the following code plays the crash sound:

```
sndCrash.start();
```

If you want to play the sound in response to a button click, for example, place the `start()` call in the button's `onRelease()` event.

Controlling your own sounds

Monkeying around with Flash's audio compression is pretty easy:

1. **Right-click the sound file in the Library.**

2. **Choose Properties from the contextual menu.**

   You see a dialog box like the following figure.

✔ If you leave the compression setting to Default, Flash decides how to compress the sound. When you run the program, you usually lose too much quality.

✔ If you switch the compression type to MP3, you can play with the compression rates yourself and often produce both decent sound and effective compression.

After you change the compression options, you can click the Test button to hear how your audio effect sounds.

Tests take longer to compile when you choose better compression. (Every time you test a program, Flash rebuilds the sound file at the quality you request.) To keep compile times reasonable, use a weaker algorithm while testing your programs.

✔ Switch to a better (but slower) algorithm for your final build.

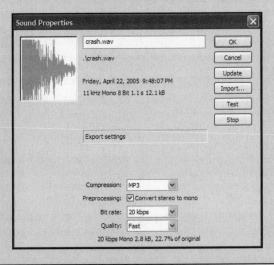

Incorporating sound into your programs

Typically, you break your sound coding into three steps:

1. Gather and configure the sounds in the Flash editor.

2. Write initialization code to set up the Sound objects.

3. Play the sounds in response to events in the game.

Listing 8-2 shows how the soundDemo ties all these ideas together.

Listing 8-2:   Sound Demo

```
//soundDemo
//illustrates how to add code-driven sound to
//games
//Andy Harris, 4/05

//assumes a file called "crash.wav" has been loaded into
         library
//with link settings changed to "export for actionscript"

init();

function init(){
  //create a sound object
  sndCrash = new Sound();
  sndCrash.attachSound("crash.wav");
} // end init

btnCrash.onRelease = function(){
  sndCrash.start();
} // end
```

If you have many sounds, initialize them all in the init() method. (I often immediately play a sound to ensure it's working before I move the sound's start code to another place.)

Getting the most from your sounds

Sound is important, but it can be tricky to work with. Any resource that makes your game larger needs to have an adequate payoff. Here are the most important things to remember when working with sound files in Flash:

✔ **Don't use long songs.** Background music can dramatically lengthen your game's download time, and it gets annoying quickly. Many people turn off background music, so don't use it unless it's really important to your game.

If you need music, look for short loops of music that can be repeated. Audio in Flash games is better used with either special effects or instruction and splash screens.

✔ **Import MP3 files.** If you're pretty handy with audio, you might want to do your own MP3 conversions. If you load an MP3 file directly into Flash, the Use Imported MP3 Quality check box of the Properties dialog box is activated. This setting means

• You do all your tweaking in your audio tool.

• Flash plays your file at the settings you mandate.

If you don't enable the Use Imported MP3 Quality check box, Flash tries to optimize your already optimized MP3 file (and often makes a mess of things).

✔ **Flash doesn't love all rates and settings.** If Flash doesn't accept an MP3 file or plays a file too quickly or too slowly, Flash probably doesn't interpret the settings correctly. I recommend these settings as a starting place:

- 24 kHz works pretty well for music.

- You can probably get away with 11 kHz or less for spoken words.

If your audio file does not sound right, re-encode the file at a speed that Flash is more comfortable with.

✔ **Test audio with headphones or high-quality speakers.** Concentrating on audio quality and stereo effects is much easier if you can hear sounds clearly — and hear little else.

Headphones might make your roommates happier.

✔ **Go mono.** Unless the user is wearing headphones, mono is probably just as good as stereo and cuts the loading time in half.

You can create stereo effects from mono sound with the `Sound.setPan()` method (available via online help). You can make the sound louder in the left speaker if the object is nearer the left, and so on.

✔ **Dynamically adjust the volume.** You can adjust the volume of a sound effect through code. Look up the `Sound.setVolume()` method to see how you can dynamically modify sound to make objects sound closer or farther away.

✔ **Remove sounds during testing.** Those sounds that add so much to a game while you're playing it can drive you nutty when you're testing a game. They can lead to divorce if your spouse is in the room the five-millionth time you've played that agonizing death scream as you try to fix some bug. Sound effects also slow your testing because Flash has to compress the audio file each time you test the program. Save your sound effects work for late in the project or at least get them working and temporarily comment them out while you work on other parts of your project.

✔ **Make it quiet.** You can use the `Sound.stop()` method to make a sound stop. This is an easy way to turn off background music.

✔ **Combine sounds.** You can play several audio clips at once. This might be an interesting way to combine sounds for some good effects. Some developers have even built basic music generators using nothing more than the skills described in this chapter and a few buttons.

Chapter 9

It's Alive! Animating Your Sprites

Games aren't much fun without some kind of motion. The two main kinds of sprite animation are

✔ Changing how a sprite appears onscreen

✔ Changing its position

I show you both forms of animation in this chapter.

Creating Animated Sprites

Flash includes some very powerful tools for creating animations inside your games. You can add visual appeal to your games in many ways. For example, some objects should rotate to point whichever direction they travel, which requires both visual and programming elements. You also might want to add animation effects to your sprites so they appear to walk, sway, jump, or whatever else they do (sashay? mosey? amble?). You use a variation of Flash's built-in animations for these effects.

Building a shape

Although you can use other drawing tools to create your images, the drawing features in Flash are well worth learning because

✔ They're an easy, powerful way to build any kind of image you want.

✔ These images are already optimized to work within Flash, so they're more efficient (smaller files and animate with less work).

Walk like a monster, wobble like a car

When you play the Monster Traffic game, some small animations add a lot to the game:

- The monster's head and tail sway from side to side while he walks.

- The cars wobble and spew out exhaust fumes.

These elements aren't critical to a game, but they're a wonderful way to add detail. In this case, I use animation to emphasize the cartoon-like flavor of the game. Although I'm certainly no artist,

the drawing and animation tools available to a Flash programmer make creating fun graphics easy. This figure shows several frames of the monster up close so you can see his many moods.

The central body remains constant, but the head and tail sway while the feet move. When all these frames are shown within one second, they give a reasonable illusion of a walking monster. In your games, you'll build something else, but the techniques in this chapter work for drawing anything.

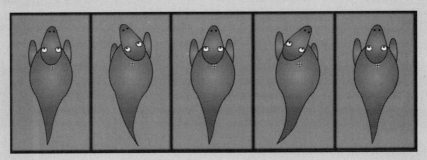

With a little practice, you can build any shape you want with Flash. For example, here's how I built the basic teardrop body shape of the monster.

To build the next few screen shots, I created a simple Flash animation. (If you want to look directly at that animation to see the process of building this shape, look at buildShape.swf on this book's companion Web site: www. dummies.com/go/flashgameprogrammingfd1e).

1. **Begin with a blank movie clip.**

   Although you can draw simple shapes on the Stage and then convert them to movie clips later, more complex movie clips are much easier to build if you choose Insert➪New Symbol from the Flash main menu.

2. **Zoom in tight.**

Flash uses a vector-drawing technique that scales very well. When you build a sprite, increase the magnification so you can clearly see what you're doing. You can then make the sprite smaller when you place it on the screen.

3. **Use basic shapes.**

Flash gives you many powerful drawing tools, but I really like starting with a basic rectangle. When you combine it with Flash's powerful deformation features, you can make any shape you want. Figure 9-1 shows my basic rectangle.

Figure 9-1:
The basic rectangle is the starting point for any shape in Flash.

A basic
rectangle

Make your image large when you're starting. Flash uses vector drawing, so you can resize your work later without losing any resolution.

4. **Consider gradient fills.**

I love using gradient fills because they're an easy way to get a 3-D look in images. In this case, I choose a green radial gradient to look like the back of a green monster. Start by getting the gradient in place. You can modify it later. Check out Chapter 6 for information on using gradient fills.

5. **Deform the points and lines.**

You can modify any shape by using the black selection arrow:

a. *Move the selection arrow near a corner or edge of your shape.*

If you're near a corner, a small corner cursor appears; near an edge, a curve cursor appears.

b. *Drag the corner or edge.*

The shape changes; you can move the corner or "bend" the edge.

You can move the corners and bend the sides to build a body shape.

In Figure 9-2, I deform the top and sides of my rectangle to build a bullet shape.

Figure 9-2:
The top and
sides curve
out to make
a rounded
shape.

Deforming
the top and
sides

In Figures 9-3 and 9-4, I move one of the bottom corners of the original rectangle to form the tail.

Beginning
the tail

Figure 9-3:
Move one
corner to
begin
creating
the tail.

Completing
the tail drag

Figure 9-4:
The tail
corner is
in place.

I clean up the nearby edges to make the corners disappear.

6. Add new vertices if needed.

By using this Flash technique, moving the vertices of your original shape is easy. If you want to have more vertices, you might need to add them yourself.

For example, I want some convex curves near the tail to give it a more convincing shape, but I don't have enough vertices in the original rectangle. (Okay, I do, but it would have been a very awkward transformation.) Simply draw a line intersecting any of the segments where you want new vertices to appear, as shown in Figure 9-5.

Adding new
vertices

Figure 9-5:
Create new
vertices by
adding a
temporary
line.

7. Continue transforming with the new vertices.

Figure 9-6 shows the tail being formed with the new vertices. If I bend the sides below the new line, everything above the line stays in place.

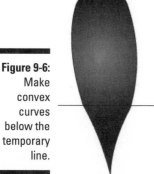

Building
convex
sections

Figure 9-6:
Make
convex
curves
below the
temporary
line.

8. Remove the temporary line.

You can select the temporary line and delete it, and the underlying image stays intact.

You probably need to tweak the new vertices and line segments a little to hide the vertices if you want an organic rounded shape (like this monster body).

9. **Adjust the gradient as necessary.**

The Fill Transform tool resides on the toolbar right below the paint-brush icon. When this tool is selected, you can change the size and rotation of a gradient fill. I use this tool in Figure 9-7 to fix the gradient so it looks more like what I want.

Removing
the line and
transforming
the gradient

Figure 9-7:
Remove the
temporary
line and
modify the
gradient fill.

Building an animated sprite

After you know how to build a basic shape using Flash's built-in tools, building a more complex animated sprite image is no big stretch.

I made a Flash document called `buildShape.fla` (available on the companion Web site) showing the animated sprites before adding any code to them:

✔ Run that file to see the sprites moving.

✔ Look at the FLA file and dissect the sprites (by double-clicking them to see their underlying structure).

To build something as complicated as the monster and cars, follow these steps:

1. **Begin with a new movie clip.**

Animated sprites often use multiple frames and layers, but the finished movie clip occupies only one frame and one layer in the actual movie.

TIP

To avoid confusion, make a separate workspace for your sprite by choosing Insert➪New Symbol from the main menu.

2. **Work in layers.**

   In actual Flash games, I rarely take advantage of the layers in the Timeline because programming code can do most of the same things. However, when using Flash as a drawing and animating tool (as you're doing *inside* the sprite objects), layers are very useful indeed. Figure 9-8 shows the various layers of the monster object.

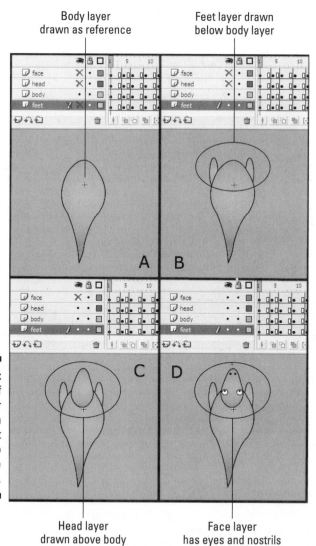

Body layer
drawn as reference

Feet layer drawn
below body layer

Head layer
drawn above body

Face layer
has eyes and nostrils

Figure 9-8:
The parts of the monster are in different frames to facilitate animation.

3. **Orient your image facing up.**

The animation scheme later in this chapter assumes that the default orientation of each object is facing toward the top of the screen. This makes the math easier when you make your sprites move in other directions.

4. **Add other frames for animation.**

The movie clip is like a movie within a movie. Although the primary program is often halted at one frame, a movie clip residing on a frame can have its own Timeline and can progress along that Timeline. This makes animations quite easy. At the default 12 frames per second (fps) frame rate, 12 frames equal 1 second of animation. If you want an animation to cycle every second, you can build a 12-frame animation in the sprite's Timeline. For my example, I broke the monster's Timeline into five segments. I start with the head facing forward, then left, then forward, and then back. This sequence is shown in Figure 9-9.

Figure 9-9:
The monster walks via animation on the Timeline.

The easiest way to get this effect is to create new keyframes in Frames 4, 7, 10, and 13 after drawing the image in Frame 1. Add these keyframes in every layer of your drawing. Now you can modify each layer of each frame independently by using the Free Transform tool (located under the Pencil tool on the main toolbar). Because each body part is isolated, you can manipulate them all independently for exactly the look you want. For more detailed animation, simply add more keyframes.

5. **Repeat animation for other objects.**

In my Monster Traffic game, I have three main sprites. (The cars are all the same except for color.) For the animated flame effect, I simply create a radial gradient with what seemed like flame colors to me and drew a lot of small circles on the screen. I built five frames with different circle placements. Although it looks corny now, when it's moving across the screen with appropriate sound effects, the rapidly changing fireball looks surprisingly convincing. To add a cartoon-like effect to the cars, I made all the shapes rounded and moved the original shape slightly from side to side in each frame. I also added small exhaust circles (just like the fireballs).

Moving a Sprite under Computer Control

The Monster Traffic game has three different kinds of sprites: the cars, the monster, and the fireball. All the sprites work in similar but not identical ways. The car moves in a randomly chosen but constant speed and direction. If you design the code that handles car motion carefully, you can reuse the code for the other objects. The carMove program does exactly that. The program begins with the monster and car sprites defined and on the Stage. The next several examples refer to that program, which you can see in its entirety on the book's companion Web site.

To see any of my graphics up close, follow these steps:

1. **Open the original FLA file.**

2. **Double-click a movie clip object to edit it.**

   • Use the Zoom command on the Stage to look closely at the object.

   • Move throughout the Timeline to see how it changes over time.

   • Hide and show any layer by clicking the eyeball icon next to it.

General plan for moving sprites

For most arcade games, you'll want to be able to move any sprite. Here's one procedure for moving a sprite:

To move any sprite using this technique

1. **Create the sprite movie clip.**

   Make sure that the sprite's default position points north (up). It's better to create an empty sprite and then build all its layers and keyframes. You can then back out to the main Timeline to manipulate the sprite as a completed entity.

Name both the sprite in the Library and any instances of that sprite on the Stage.

2. **Initialize the sprite in the program's `init` method:**

   • Set appropriate values for `dir` and `speed` properties.

   • Position the sprite by setting its `_x` and `_y` properties.

3. **Be sure that your program has `turn()` and `move()` functions.**

   The following functions are handy for moving and turning your sprites. Use mine at first; then modify them to behave as you want.

4. **Turn the sprite with the `turn(*spriteName*)` function, where *spriteName* is the name of your sprite instance on the stage.**

   The `turn()` function translates direction and speed to `dx` and `dy` properties. The `turn()` function needs to be called every time that speed or direction changes. This might be only one time if the sprite isn't meant to change speed or direction, or it might be in the sprite's `enterFrame()` event if the sprite is meant to change speed and direction throughout the game.

   The `carMove` code shows the `turn()` function in full.

5. **Move the sprite using the `move(*spriteName*)` function, where *spriteName* is the name of the sprite instance on the Stage.**

   The `move()` function moves the sprite object on the Stage and sets its visual orientation correctly.

   The `move()` method should usually be called from the sprite's `enterFrame()` event because you usually want to be able to move the sprite on every frame.

As an example of sprite motion, the following high-level code sets up a car sprite going north at a speed of 5 pixels per frame (ppf):

```
init();
function init(){
  //randomly position car
  car._x = Stage.width / 2;
  car._y = Stage.height;
  car.dir = NORTH;
  car.speed = 5;
} // end init

car.onEnterFrame = function(){
  turn(car);
  move(car);
} // end car enterFrame
```

This code presumes the existence of two new functions, turn() and move(), which I introduce in the appropriately named sections of this chapter. With these functions in place, you can easily set the speed and direction of any sprite without directly dealing with dx and dy.

Setting up direction constants

The best way to move objects in a computer game is to manipulate the object's dx and dy properties. Although this is a very powerful technique, it's a little bit messy. I recommend thinking in terms of an object's direction and speed and then let the computer do all the math required to translate these ideas into dx and dy.

Think about actual directions (like NORTH and SOUTHEAST) instead of worrying about dx and dy properties.

If you create a limited number of directions, your program can translate all these directions into the appropriate dx and dy values whenever needed.

Chapter 11 shows a technique that works with any direction (not just the eight basic directions described in this chapter). The technique in Chapter 11 works with any speed and direction but requires more math than the technique that I describe here.

The carMove code I use to demonstrate movement begins with the standard comments and continues with an init() function that's called immediately:

```
//carMove
//move the car random direction and speed

init();

function init(){
  //initialization

  //direction constants
  NORTH = 0;
  NORTHEAST = 1;
  EAST = 2;
  SOUTHEAST = 3;
  SOUTH = 4;
  SOUTHWEST = 5;
  WEST = 6;
  NORTHWEST = 7;
```

The first order of business is to determine a series of constants. These are variables that are used to describe the various directions. In this game, all sprites go in the eight cardinal directions only. To keep track of the directions, I use numeric codes. Numeric values are convenient because it's easy to change directions by addition or subtraction. However, it can be cumbersome to remember that SOUTHEAST is direction 3, so I declare special variables to keep track of the variables. When you use variables in this way, capitalizing them is traditional.

Later in the turn() function, I show how to convert these somewhat arbitrary numeric values to the actual directions they represent.

Programmers often use variables with numeric values to represent certain kinds of information like I do with the direction variables.

- ✔ Many languages have constructs called *constants* and *enumerations,* which are handy in this kind of situation. ActionScript doesn't have these features yet, so I simulate them with these direction variables.

- ✔ Chapter 8 shows that Flash's own keyboard handling uses a similar scheme to assign names to the keyboard values.

Determining sprite properties

All the sprites in this game have the same general properties:

- ✔ **Custom properties,** such as speed, dx, dy, and dir (direction). I add these properties to most of my sprites so I can control them better.
- ✔ **Built-in properties,** such as _x and _y.

In my demo, the car goes in a randomly chosen speed and direction. Listing 9-1 shows the code inside the init() method that gives the random initial values.

Listing 9-1:   carMove init() Function

```
//carMove
//move the car random direction and speed

init();

function init(){
  //initialization
  //randomly position car
  car._x = Math.random() * Stage.width;
  car._y = Math.random() * Stage.height;
  car.dir = Math.random() * 8;
```

```
car.dir = Math.floor(car.dir);
car.speed = Math.random() * 10;
turn(car);

/ * debugging code
trace ("dir: " + car.dir);
trace ("rot: " + car._rotation);
trace ("dx: " + car.dx);
trace ("dy: " + car.dy);
*/
} // end init
```

To create a sprite with random initial values, follow these steps:

1. **Build the sprite object, including any animations or layers.**

   Be sure that the object's default position points north.

2. **Give a random starting position by setting the object's _x and _y properties.**

   I derive both properties with `Math.random()`:

   - *The x position should be somewhere between 0 (zero) and the width of the Stage.*

     This is determined with a call to `Math.random()`. `Math.random()` * `Stage.width` gives a result between 0 (zero) and the width of the Stage.

   - *car._y is positioned by multiplying a* `Math.random()` *value by the height of the Stage.*

     `Math.random()` * `Stage.height` gives a result between 0 (zero) and the height of the Stage.

   Multiplying the floating point value of `Math.random()` by the integer values of `Stage.height` and `Stage.width` produces floating point values within the range of the screen's dimensions. If you feed these floating point values to the _x and _y properties of a sprite, the object is moved to the nearest pixel automatically. Thus, that floating point value doesn't need to be converted to an integer.

3. **Establish the car's direction.**

   I designated in this program that directions are integers between 0 and 7, inclusive. For example, 3 is a valid direction (SOUTHEAST), but 3.5 is not. Here's how I produce a random integer between 0 and 7:

   a. *Begin with* `Math.random()` * 8.

     This returns values between 0 and 7.9999999.

   b. *The* `Math.floor()` *function lops off any trailing decimal points.*

This leaves a random integer between 0 and 7, inclusive.

4. **Give the object a random speed.**

The car's speed is simply a random number between 0 and 10.

Floating point values are fine here, so I didn't convert to an integer.

5. **Call the `turn()` function to generate dx and dy values.**

ActionScript needs `dx` and `dy` properties to move an object, but it's more natural to think in terms of direction and speed. The `turn()` function's job is to translate a direction and speed into `dx` and `dy` properties.

6. **Give yourself some debugging hints.**

The final piece of code in the `init()` method is a set of `trace()` statements. I use these statements for debugging purposes. I write code for `turn()` and `move()` in the next sections, but there's really no point in moving on to those functions if these variables haven't been created correctly. After the variables all appear to be working well, I comment out the code. I don't remove the comments entirely, though, because there is some chance that things will go wrong again, and it's useful to have the diagnostic tool already in place in case I need it.

7. **Move the sprite in the `enterFrame()` event.**

After all the initialization is done, write a `move` function that moves the object according to its direction and speed. That function is called in the sprite's `enterFrame()` event.

Turning a sprite

The `turn()` function is designed to translate a speed and direction into `dx` and `dy` properties. It is specially written so it can work on any movie clip object. You can use it to turn any object in any program.

The function gets its flexibility by accepting an object as a parameter. Within the function, the object is called `thing`. If you call the function `turn(car)`, `thing` refers to the `car` movie clip. You can also turn the monster or anything else in your program by calling `turn(monster)` or whatever.

Write your functions to be as flexible as possible. If you can make a function work so it can turn anything, you can reuse the function and easily add functionality to your program. The final version of the Monster Traffic game has up to five objects moving around the screen at a time (and later projects have many more). All of them can use the same `turn()` and `move()` functions. If you design those functions upfront so they can manipulate any object, it's trivial to upgrade the program.

This function converts the numeric direction and speed of any object to appropriate values for its `dx` and `dy` properties. Listing 9-2 shows the `turn` function of the `carMove` program. As you look at the code, note the use of negative and decimal values for `dx` and `dy`. I explain these values after this listing.

Listing 9-2:   carMove turn() Function

```
function turn(thing){
  thing._rotation = thing.dir * 45;

  switch (thing.dir){
    case NORTH:
      thing.dx = 0;
      thing.dy = -1;
      break;
    case NORTHEAST:
      thing.dx = .7;
      thing.dy = -.7;
      break;
    case EAST:
      thing.dx = 1;
      thing.dy = 0;
      break;
    case SOUTHEAST:
      thing.dx = .7;
      thing.dy = .7;
      break;
    case SOUTH:
      thing.dx = 0;
      thing.dy = 1;
      break;
    case SOUTHWEST:
      thing.dx = -.7;
      thing.dy = .7;
      break;
    case WEST:
      thing.dx = -1;
      thing.dy = 0;
      break;
    case NORTHWEST:
      thing.dx = -.7;
      thing.dy = -.7;
      break;
    default:
      trace("there's a problem here...");
  } // end switch
  thing.dx *= thing.speed;
  thing.dy *= thing.speed;
} // end turn
```

To make the car point in the direction in which it will move, I modify the built-in `rotation` property. It's important to understand that `rotation` changes the orientation of the physical sprite onscreen but doesn't directly affect how the object moves onscreen. The `rotation` property takes degree measurements with 0 as north. I was very sneaky about the numbers I used for the constants. Table 9-1 shows the relationship among the direction constants, their values, and the corresponding rotation value.

Table 9-1		Rotation Values
Direction	*Value*	*Rotation (Degrees)*
NORTH	0	0
NORTHEAST	1	45
EAST	2	90
SOUTHEAST	3	135
SOUTH	4	180
SOUTHWEST	5	225
WEST	6	270
NORTHWEST	7	315

Each rotation is exactly 45 degrees more than the previous direction, making it easy to calculate the appropriate rotation for each direction. Simply multiply the direction by 45, and you have the appropriate rotation value.

This is why I design the sprites so that they face north as a default. If the sprite is heading in any other direction, you'd have to compensate for that beginning angle. If the sprite begins by heading in direction 0, it's pretty easy to find the appropriate rotation value for the sprite.

The function then generates a large `switch` structure that examines the direction. I set up direction as an integer between 0 and 7. I already converted that direction to a rotation, which changes the visual appearance of the object. To make the object move in the desired direction, I have to change the `dx` and `dy` properties. The following chunk of code handles the behavior when the player is moving to the north:

```
switch (thing.dir){
    case NORTH:
        thing.dx = 0;
        thing.dy = -1;
        break;
```

If `thing` is moving to the north, its `dx` property should be set to `0`, and its `dy` property should be set to `-1`. This makes the pixel move one pixel to the north. After the `switch` statement is over, both the `dx` and `dy` properties are multiplied by the object's speed, so if the speed is `8`, the object now moves eight units to the north.

Moving in the other cardinal directions (east, south, and west) is pretty much the same as moving to the north. You might be surprised at the code for the diagonal directions. As an example, here's the code for moving to the southeast:

```
case SOUTHEAST:
    thing.dx = .7;
    thing.dy = .7;
    break;
```

You might expect in this case that the `dx` and `dy` properties should both be set to `1`, but they are `.7` instead. The explanation for this requires a little math review. (I promise it won't be too painful.) If you set `dx` and `dy` to `1`, the object actually moves about 1.41 pixels to the southeast. When you multiply these values by the speed, you'll find that the car appears to move much faster on the diagonals than it does in the cardinal directions. Don't take my word for it. Write your own program or modify mine so that the `dx` and `dy` properties are both `1` when you move southeast. When the program is running, objects moving to the southeast seem to move much faster than objects moving to the south or the east. If you want to move in diagonal directions at a speed of `1`, use `dx` and `dy` values of `.7`. If you want to understand how I came up with the value `.7`, Figure 9-10 explains the math. (Your geometry teacher would be so proud of your use of the Pythagorean theorem.)

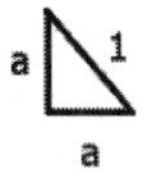

Figure 9-10:
Pythagoras did all his work just to help you animate monsters and cars.

$$a^2 + a^2 = 1^2$$
$$2a^2 = 1$$
$$a^2 = 1/2$$
$$a = \sqrt{1/2}$$
$$a \approx 0.7$$

Table 9-2 shows the dx and dy values for the various directions.

Table 9-2		dx and dy Values for Various Directions		
Direction	*Value*	*Rotation (Degrees)*	*dx*	*dy*
NORTH	0	0	0	−1
NORTHEAST	1	45	−0.7	−0.7
EAST	2	90	−1	0
SOUTHEAST	3	135	−0.7	0.7
SOUTH	4	180	0	1
SOUTHWEST	5	225	0.7	0.7
WEST	6	270	1	0
NORTHWEST	7	315	0.7	−0.7

In Table 9-2, all these directions add up to a distance of (roughly) one pixel. (That is, if you square dx and dy for a given direction and then add them, you get something close to 1.) If you calculate how to move one pixel in any direction, it's easy to move at any other speed (even backward) by multiplying the dx and dy values for moving one pixel by that speed. The last few lines of the turn() function handles this process:

```
switch(thing.dir){
   /// I'm leaving out most of the code for this example ...
   default:
     trace("there's a problem here...");
} // end switch
thing.dx *= thing.speed;
thing.dy *= thing.speed;
} // end turn
```

The turn code closes with some housekeeping:

- ✔ A default clause acts as a safety net if the unexpected happens and the program is sent a direction I didn't expect.

- ✔ The multiplication lines multiply the dx and dy properties of thing by its speed.

By the time this function is done, the object's dir property is converted to a number of other properties that are more useful to finally update the object's position onscreen. That's the next project.

Moving the sprite

After you set up an object's dx and dy properties with the turn function, it's time to move the object. (In this case, the car, but you're setting up your functions to move anything.) The move function is called immediately after the turn function. Listing 9-3 shows the move function for the carMove program.

Listing 9-3:   carMove move() Function

```
function move(thing){
  //moves any thing, wrapping around boundaries

  //move
  thing._x += thing.dx;
  thing._y += thing.dy;

  //check boundaries - wrap all directions
  if (thing._x > Stage.width){
    thing._x = 0;
  } // end if

  if (thing._x < 0){
    thing._x = Stage.width;
  } // end if

  if (thing._y > Stage.height){
    thing._y = 0;
  } // end if

  if (thing._y < 0){
    thing._y = Stage.height;
  } // end if
} // end move
```

This move function is unsurprising: It simply moves thing by its own dx and dy properties. As usual, when you move something, you should check for screen boundaries. In this program, I assume that all objects wrap around all walls because it makes the code easier. If I want, I can write different behavior later.

Animating the car

The car's animation code is pretty simple because the car's direction is set one time, when the car is created. The following code sets up the car's behavior in the program's init() function:

```
//randomly position car
car._x = Math.random() * Stage.width;
car._y = Math.random() * Stage.height;
car.dir = Math.random() * 8;
car.dir = Math.floor(car.dir);
car.speed = Math.random() * 10;
turn(car);
```

The preceding code has two main jobs:

1. Set up a random position and direction for the car.

2. Call the `turn()` function to convert `speed` and `dir` to `dx` and `dy`.

The remainder of the car's (very simple) behavior is contained in its `enterFrame()` event:

```
car.onEnterFrame = function(){
  move(car);
} // end car enterFrame
```

Put code in an object's `enterFrame()` event when you want that code to repeat every frame. Any code that doesn't need to be checked every frame should go someplace else.

Creating a User-Controlled Sprite

The car's direction is set one time at the beginning of the program. The monster requires a bit more effort because his direction and speed change dynamically according to keyboard input.

The next few examples refer to the `monsterMove` program on the book's companion Web site. The `monsterMove` program is very much like the `carMove` program shown in this chapter. I'm reproducing only the parts of `monsterMove` that differ from `carMove`. Please check the companion Web site to see the `monsterMove` code in its complete state.

Fortunately, the monster can use the same `turn` and `move` functions as the car. The monster's `enterFrame()` event code shows how to build a sprite under keyboard control:

```
monster.onEnterFrame = function(){
  checkKeys();
  turn(monster);
  move(monster);
} // end monster enterFrame
```

As you can see in the monster's `enterFrame` function, the program must perform three actions in each frame:

- ✔ Check for any key presses.
- ✔ Turn the monster.
- ✔ Move the monster.

Gosh, I *love* encapsulation!

The only thing that's really new in `monster.enterFrame` is the `checkKeys()` function. This function (not surprisingly) responds to keyboard input:

1. Scans the keyboard to see whether the user wants to change the monster's speed or direction.

   If the user presses a relevant key, the `checkKeys()` function changes appropriate properties in the `monster` sprite.

2. The `turn()` function sets `dx` and `dy` properties to the appropriate values.

3. The `move()` function (I bet you're ahead of me here) moves the monster.

Planning keyboard input

Keyboard input isn't very difficult to write, but it can be overwhelming if you don't plan what should happen. Before you write any code, consider building a chart something like Table 9-3.

Table 9-3	Keyboard Plan for Monster Move			
Key	**Action**	**Code**	**Boundary**	**Overflow**
Up	Speed up	`.speed ++`	`speed > 8`	`speed = 8`
Down	Slow down	`.speed --`	`speed < -3`	`speed = -3`
Left	Turn left	`.dir --`	`dir < NORTH`	`dir = NORTHWEST`
Right	Turn right	`.dir++`	`dir > NORTHWEST`	`dir = NORTH`

It makes a lot of sense to think carefully about all these things before you start writing code. Make a chart with this information:

1. **Write down the action associated with each key press.**

2. **Determine what code will occur.**

   Usually, you can summarize the action by changing a property or variable. You don't have to think about all the code here. You need to isolate only

   • The critical variable or property that changes when the user presses the key

   • How that property changes (increase by 1?, decrease by 50?)

3. **Think about boundary conditions.**

   Any time a variable changes, it could be given an illegal value. Decide what condition summarizes the boundary for this particular situation:

   • *If you're increasing a variable,* you need to think about the upper boundary only.

   • *If you're decreasing a variable,* you need to think about a lower boundary only.

4. **Provide an overflow statement.**

   Think about what you should do when the boundary is passed.

   Usually, the overflow statement should set the variable to a value within the variable's legitimate range.

Checking for motion keys

The checkKeys() function scans the keyboard for user input. You can check for any keys you want, but it's usually a good idea to stick with the standard arrow keys and spacebar unless you have a good reason to do something else. Chapter 8 describes why you might want to use other keys, such as W, A, S, and D.

To check for keyboard input, follow these steps:

1. **Determine your control scheme.**

   Think about what each keyboard input should do. Create a keyboard chart (like the chart in the preceding section).

   Plan boundary conditions and overflow statements.

2. **Create some kind of checkKeys() function.**

   This function contains all the keyboard code.

3. **Call `checkKeys()` from an `enterFrame` event.**

   Keyboard checking should occur frequently to give the user plenty of control. The `enterFrame` event is the easiest way to make this happen.

4. **Write a condition for each key press.**

   Each line in your control scheme table is easily translated into a few lines of code.

   For example, here is the code for handling the up arrow:

   ```
   if (Key.isDown(Key.UP)){
     monster.speed++;
     if (monster.speed > 8){
       monster.speed = 8;
     } // end if

   } // end if
   ```

The items in the keyboard planning chart directly correspond to code. Every key press contains similar code.

The `keyboard demo` program in Chapter 7 shows general keyboard input.

Controlling the monster

In this program, the user can

- ✔ Speed the monster with the up-arrow key.
- ✔ Slow the monster with the down-arrow key.
- ✔ Turn left and right with the left- and right-arrow keys, respectively.

I show you how to add a `fire` command for the flame in Chapter 10.

The complete keyboard-checking routine looks like Listing 9-4.

Listing 9-4:   Monster Move checkKeys() Function

```
function checkKeys(){
  //check keyboard to move monster
  if (Key.isDown(Key.UP)){
    monster.speed++;
    if (monster.speed > 8){
      monster.speed = 8;
    } // end if

  } // end if
```

(continued)

Listing 9-4 *(continued)*

```
if (Key.isDown(Key.DOWN)){
  monster.speed--;
  if (monster.speed < -3){
    monster.speed = -3;
  } // end if
} // end if

if (Key.isDown(Key.RIGHT)){
  monster.dir++;
  if (monster.dir > NORTHWEST){
    monster.dir = NORTH;
  } // end if
} // end if

if (Key.isDown(Key.LEFT)){
  monster.dir--;
  if (monster.dir < NORTH){
    monster.dir = NORTHWEST;
  } // end if
} // end if

} // end checkKeys
```

The `checkKeys` function responds to key presses:

1. Checks each key to determine whether it is being pressed.

2. If a key is selected, changes the appropriate variable.

Whenever you change a variable, you should check for boundary conditions. The monster has the following boundaries:

✔ **In the up-arrow code, the speed increases.**

If the monster's speed increases indefinitely, the monster will be impossible to control. I set the maximum speed to 8 ppf. If the user tries to accelerate past that rate, nothing happens.

✔ **In the down-arrow code, I set the minimum speed to –3.**

Because of how I calculate the speed, negative speeds make the sprite move backward. If you play around with the `moveMonster` Flash file (on the book's companion Web site), you see that backward movement works great. The monster can move and turn backward without any special programming.

Turning the monster involves changing the direction. I set up directions using constants, so turning to the right involves simply adding 1 to the direction. If the user tries to turn right from EAST (direction number 6), the program simply adds 1, making the new direction NORTHWEST (direction number 7). Turn to the left by subtracting 1 from the dir property.

The directions have boundaries, too:

✔ If the user tries to turn right from NORTHWEST (direction number 7), adding 1 makes the new direction number 8 (which doesn't exist in this scheme).

✔ If the direction gets past 7 (NORTHWEST), it should move to 0 (NORTH).

The code for checking the right-arrow key handles this situation with a standard if structure:

```
if (Key.isDown(Key.RIGHT)){
   monster.dir++;
   if (monster.dir > NORTHWEST){
     monster.dir = NORTH;
   } // end if
} // end if
```

Before you can run the monsterMove program, add some initialization code to give the monster some initial values. Specify the monster's initial speed and position as I did in the init() function:

```
//set monster initial values
monster.dx = 0;
monster.dy = 0;
monster.speed = 0;
monster.dir = NORTH;
```

All the other code in the monsterMove program is identical to the carMove program because both the monster and the car use the same functions for movement and turning.

Chapter 10

Building the Monster Traffic Game

In This Chapter

▶ Working with more sprites

▶ Handling many collisions

▶ Sprucing up your program with basic animations

▶ Solving problems and creating functions

Many skills are involved in game programming, but the ultimate skill is simply building games. Rather than introducing a lot of new ideas in this chapter, I take you step by step through the design and creation of a complete arcade game.

Reviewing the Basic Design

The examples in the last few chapters center around a game called Monster Traffic. This chapter shows how to put that game together. No new programming ideas are presented here, just a description of how to build the game after you understand all the component skills.

The Monster Traffic game looks like Figure 10-1 when it's running.

The main characters of the Monster Traffic game are the same as in Chapters 8 and 9. The complete monsterTraffic game builds on the moveMonster game developed in Chapter 9. See that chapter for more information on how to build that version of the game. The final game has other features that are worth noting:

✔ Three cars to avoid.

✔ A fire-breathing monster. (Try some mouthwash, buddy.)

✔ Sound effects when the monster breathes fire, fire hits a car, or a car hits the monster.

✔ A scorekeeping mechanism, win and lose screens, and a help screen.

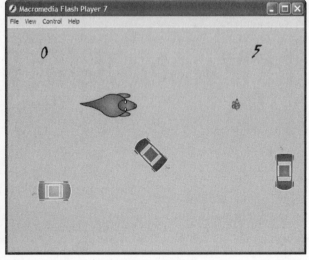

Figure 10-1:
The user controls a flame-breathing monster being pursued by cars.

Adding More Opponents

One opponent is too easy. It's much more fun if the monster has to dodge more cars. The easiest way to generate new opponents is to simply create new MovieClip objects. Figure 10-2 shows the threeCars program with three different cars.

Figure 10-1 is the play screen of the complete game, with flames and score-keeping (and much more that is not visible in a screen shot). Figure 10-2 is the first step toward that goal.

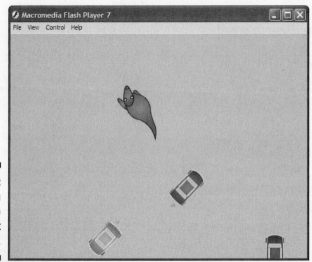

Figure 10-2:
Now you have three different yet similar cars.

Cloning the movie clips

The basic task is to build more than one car. You could, of course, make three instances of the same car from the Library. If you give each instance a different name, they all function independently. However, they're also all the same color. I chose to make several new movie clip objects and give them different colors. Here's the easiest way to do that:

1. **If the Library isn't open, press F11 to open it.**

2. **Select the movie clip you want to modify from the Library.**

   Make sure all the animations and elements that you want duplicated are finished in the first clip. After you duplicate the clip, you make individual changes in the clips.

3. **Duplicate the movie clip by right-clicking it (in the Library) and choosing Duplicate from the contextual menu.**

4. **Rename the new movie clip in the resulting dialog box and click the Export for ActionScript button.**

5. **Edit the new movie clip from within the Library.**

6. **If necessary, change all layers and frames.**

   If the duplicated object has multiple layers and frames, make your changes on all these parts, not just the visible elements.

7. **Make instances of your new objects on the Stage.**

   Don't forget to name the instances.

If you want to build a number of identical objects automatically, see Chapter 13.

Coding for multiple enemies

Games are more interesting with more enemies onscreen, but simply placing more objects onscreen doesn't mean they act how you want. Anything you put onscreen must be animated. Fortunately, the code you've been using is designed to be reused. It's no big deal to add code to the extra cars, but it requires a slight change in the program's code design. Instead of placing all the code for initializing a car in the `init()` function as previous examples do, I built a new function to reset any car. The `init()` function now contains this code:

```
//from threeCars.fla init function
reset(car1);
reset(car2);
reset(car3);
```

The `reset` function simply moves all the car initialization code to a separate function that expects a car as a parameter:

```
//from threeCars.fla
function reset(sprite){
  //given a car sprite, resets its parameters
  sprite._x = Math.random() * Stage.width;
  sprite._y = Math.random() * Stage.height;
  sprite.dir = Math.random() * 8;
  sprite.dir = Math.floor(sprite.dir);
  sprite._rotation = sprite.dir * 45;
  sprite.speed = Math.random() * 10;
  turn(sprite);
} // end reset
```

This is another example of the joy of encapsulation. Any time you're tempted to repeat code, consider putting it in a function.

If you're an advanced programmer, you might know another solution: When you repeat code on very similar objects, consider creating an array and a loop. However, arrays of movie clips aren't so simple in Flash. I show a workaround approach in Chapter 13.

Somehow you also need to add code to move the object every frame. For the `threeCars` game, I move all the cars in the monster's `enterFrame` event because I don't need to create three new event handlers that are all the same. The following code shows the `monster.onEnterFrame` event from `threeCars.fla`:

```
//from threeCars.fla
monster.onEnterFrame = function(){
  ...

  //move the cars, too
  move(car1);
  move(car2);
  move(car3);
  ...
} // end enterFrame
```

In this version of the program, the car's direction and speed still don't change, so there's no need to call the `turn()` function for any of the cars each turn.

Firing Missiles

What arcade game is complete without some firepower? The flames in the Monter Traffic game work very much like missiles in many 2-D arcade games:

- ✔ The missile is attached to some object onscreen.
- ✔ When the missile is fired, it travels in the same direction as the object that fired it, but faster.

Missiles usually have a very short lifespan. They die when they either

- ✔ Hit something (often damaging or destroying what they hit).
- ✔ Leave the screen.
- ✔ You fire another missile. (There's actually only one missile.)

Missiles usually travel in straight lines. You generally don't expect missiles to bounce off the walls. Of course, it's your game, so you can do what you want. Still, it's nice to start with the most standard behavior. After you understand the basic technique, you can add your own flourishes.

The `flame.fla` program begins with the monster and three cars, and then adds the flame behavior to the monster. I show you only the new code here for firing flames. You can view the whole program on the book's companion Web site:

www.dummies.com/go/flashgameprogrammingfd1e

To add a missile, follow these steps:

1. **Create the movie clip visual representation.**

   Use the ordinary Flash tools to create the visual design of your object.

   In this version of the program, I just made a bunch of circles filled with a custom gradient that looks (to me) like flames. I made several keyframes, each with its own set of circles. When these are played in succession, it looks like a little fireball. Figure 10-3 is a composite image showing my fireball.

   Make your graphics large; then shrink them for a good effect.

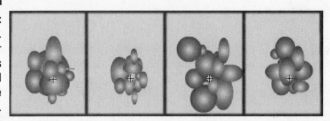

Figure 10-3:
The fireball.
Believe it or
not, it looks
pretty good
in the
program.

One nice thing about the fireball is it doesn't have a particular direction. If you design a rocket or torpedo, you must be willing to rotate the object in the game. (Otherwise, your torpedo appears to slide sideways through the water.) If you use the generic turn and move functions I suggest in Chapter 9, your objects already are rotated in the proper direction.

If the visual orientation of your object matters, build it so it's facing north, in the default position.

2. Place an instance of the missile off the Stage.

Usually, you place movie clip objects on the Stage so the user can see them. However, you don't want the flame showing unless the monster is shooting. You can drag items to the space that surrounds the Stage. As far as Flash is concerned, the object is onscreen, but it isn't visible to the user.

If you want an object to be invisible to the user but still on the Stage area, place the object to the top or left of the Stage. Otherwise, if the object is on the bottom or right, the user might resize the screen and see the object.

3. Set initial properties of the missile object.

This is usually done in the `init()` function. It looks much like the initialization of any object:

```
//set flame initial values
//from flame.fla
flame.dx = 0;
flame.dy = 0;
flame.speed = 0;
flame.dir = NORTH;
```

The flame initialization code shows that

- The flame's `dx` and `dy` properties are set to `0` (zero).

- The speed is set to `0` (zero).

- The direction is set to `NORTH`.

    This guy isn't going anywhere until you tell it to move.

4. **Set up a situation for firing the missile.**

This is usually a keyboard event, often pressing the spacebar.

To fire the flame ball, I add the following code to the `checkKeys()` function, which is called once per frame:

```
//from flame.fla checkKeys()
if (Key.isDown(Key.SPACE)){
    //shoot flame
    flame._x = monster._x;
    flame._y = monster._y;
    flame.dir = monster.dir;
    flame.speed = monster.speed + 20;
    turn(flame):
} // end if
```

When the user presses the spacebar, `moveFlame` moves from its off-Stage position to a place directly under the monster and also moves in the same direction as the monster but at a faster speed.

5. **Move the missile underneath the firing object.**

To fire a missile, you first move the missile sprite that has been hiding patiently off-Stage. Missiles are fired from some other clip, so it should look like the missile is emerging from the parent (in this case, the monster). Copy the _x and _y properties of the monster to make the fireball appear at the same position onscreen as the monster.

```
//from flame.fla checkKeys()
flame. x = monster. x:
flame._y = monster._y;
```

If you overlap two movie clip objects, one appears on top of the other. Typically, you want the missile to appear underneath the monster. To make sure this happens

a. *Drag the two movie clips together in your editor and see which clip appears on top.*

b. *Select either object.*

c. *Press Ctrl+↑ or Ctrl+↓ to change which object appears on top.*

6. **Give the missile appropriate speed and direction.**

Both these properties are inherited from the object launching the missile.

Typically, you want to launch the missile in the same direction that the launcher (in this case, the monster) is pointing. Simply copy the direction from the monster to the flame to get that effect.

```
//from flame.fla checkKeys()
flame.dir = monster.dir;
flame.speed = monster.speed + 20;
```

Of course, you can change how missiles are fired. If you want the bullets to go off at an angle to the object's nose — say, always at 90 degrees (or even somewhat randomly) — you can arrange it, but start with the most simple situation and embellish it after you have the basic form working.

If you want a turret that operates independently of the main vehicle (like for a tank game), make two different movie clips:

- The turret always travels with the tank, but the turret can be rotated independently from the tank chassis.

- When the user fires, the bullet goes where the turret is pointed.

The speed of the bullet or missile should be faster than the speed of the firing object, or your firing platform will outpace its projectiles. (This was a problem for some of the first supersonic fighter planes.) I simply added 20 to the monster's speed to get a firing rate that's quick enough to look like flames but slow enough to see.

7. Turn the missile.

Even if your missile doesn't have a visible direction, you should still set its dx and dy properties according to the direction you want it to travel. Use the turn() function in Chapter 7 to automatically set the dx and dy properties of your missile:

```
turn(flame);
```

8. Move the missile.

You could move missiles with the move() function that's been handling all your other sprites so well, but there's a difference. All the other sprites have wrapped around the screen when they hit a Stage boundary. Missiles need a different behavior from the other objects. When missiles hit the edge of the screen, I want them to disappear and stop moving. For that reason, I made a special variant of the move() function specialized for moving the flame (as shown in Listing 10-1).

Listing 10-1: Flame Program moveFlame() Function

```
//from flame.fla
function moveFlame(){
  //the flame has different behavior on borders, so give it
  // its own movement function

  //move
  flame._x += flame.dx;
  flame._y += flame.dy;

  //rotate not needed
  //flame._rotation = flame.dir * 45;
```

```
    //hide on all boundaries
    if ((flame._x > Stage.width) ||
        (flame._x < 0) ||
        (flame._y > Stage.height) ||
        (flame._y < 0)){

      //move off screen and stop
      flame._x = - 200;
      flame._y = - 200;

      flame.speed = 0;
    } // end if

} // end moveFlame
```

The movement hasn't changed. I disabled the feature that turned the flame because I didn't need it.

9. **Remove your missiles.**

Sounds like a peace protest, doesn't it?

Missile objects must have short lifespans, or they clutter the screen and bog down the processor. I chose to "kill off" my missiles when they hit any boundary. I use a special condition to check for borders:

```
    //from flame.fla moveFlame()
    if ((flame._x > Stage.width) ||
        (flame._x < 0) ||
        (flame._y > Stage.height) ||
        (flame._y < 0)){
```

This behemoth is actually one `if` statement, with one condition. The `||` symbol stands for *logical or*. It works just like the word *or* in English: If the flame's X is greater than the stage width *or* the flame's X is less than 0 (zero); *or* the flame's Y is greater than the stage height *or* the flame's Y is less than (0) zero; then do something.

Faster than a speeding bullet?

The rate at which your bullets fly is an important consideration in the game:

- ✔ If projectiles move very quickly, hitting your target is relatively easy.

- ✔ Slower projectiles require the player to anticipate or lead the target, making a more interesting game situation.

Many games actually use slow, weak bullets to make the game more exciting. Counterintuitive, but true.

The || symbol lets you combine two or more conditions to make a compound condition.

This particular condition evaluates to true as soon as the flame leaves any frame boundary. Because I'm doing the same thing no matter what edge of the screen the flame leaves on, I need to simply write a more complex condition — and write the code for it but once.

To remove the missiles, simply move them off the Stage and set the speed to 0 so they don't sneak back where it isn't wanted:

```
//from flame.fla moveFlame()
//move off screen and stop
flame._x = - 200;
flame._y = - 200;

flame.speed = 0;
```

You can dynamically create and destroy movie clip objects, but this approach works fine for now.

To see how to make sprites truly live and die, check Chapter 13.

Testing for Collisions

When you have all kinds of sprites moving around onscreen, they're bound to crash into one another. Collisions are the key events of most video games. Figure 10-4 illustrates collisions.swf running from within the editor. (The output window shows a list of collisions that have occurred.)

Figure 10-4:
When a collision occurs, a note appears in the output window.

```
▼ Output
hit by car 2!
hit by car 3!
hit by car 1!
burned car 3
```

This is the easiest way to test that all the collision routines are working correctly. After you know all the various types of collisions that you want to register are working, you can add other behavior, including sound effects, scoring, and whatever else you want.

Planning your collisions

You'll have a lot of things crashing into each other, and the game often depends on what bonks into what.

Summarize what happens in various collisions with a chart like Table 10-1, which summarizes all the possible collisions between all of the sprite objects in my game.

Table 10-1	Collision Summary			
	monster	*car1*	*car2*	*car3*	*flame*
monster	x	Monster hit	Monster hit	Monster hit	x
car1	Monster hit	x	x	x	Car reset
car2	Monster hit	x	x	x	Car reset
car3	Monster hit	x	x	x	Car reset
flame	x	Car reset	Car reset	Car reset	x

Certain collisions aren't important at all. No sprite can collide with itself (or maybe it's *always* colliding with itself . . . ooh, that's deep . . . I think I need some chocolate), so I won't even check those collisions. When a monster collides with any car, the monster takes a hit, so I need to check for that collision. When the flame hits a car, that car's position, direction, and speed are reset.

To get a good handle on collision detection, build a collision chart for your game. Based on your game's logic, determine what will happen on each collision. You'll be very glad to have this information while you're writing code and debugging.

Adding collision code to your game

After you know the collisions you're checking for, write the actual code. To add collision detection to your game, follow these steps:

1. **Determine which collisions you are concerned with**.

   Anything that moves can potentially crash into anything else. Organize your plan so you know what will happen in various situations.

2. **Build a routine to check for collisions**.

   If you need to check a lot of collisions (as I need for this program), put them all in one function that can handle all the collisions. My function is cleverly named `checkCollisions()`. I call it from one of the `enterFrame` events.

3. **Create a `hitTest` `if` structure for each potential collision**.

   Look over your chart for the collisions that require some sort of behavior. Build an `if` structure for each potential collision using the `hitTest()` function to determine whether the two movie clips collide. Your code for one collision might look like this:

   ```
   if (monster.hitTest(car1)){
     //code will go here
   } // end if
   ```

4. **Write a `trace` statement to describe the hit**.

   Don't write any actual code now. Simply write a `trace` statement in each `if` structure that tells you what kind of collision occurred:

   ```
   if (monster.hitTest(car1)){
     trace("hit by car 1!");
     reset(car1);
   } // end if
   ```

   After you write code that starts moving and hiding your sprites, testing for the various collisions is much harder.

5. **Add some basic functionality**.

   After you know that all the collisions are being checked correctly, start adding code. Use the chart (refer to Table 10-1) to determine what should happen. For example, when a car and monster collide, the car should get a new position, speed, and direction.

   This fragment from the `monster.hitTest` function in `collisions.fla` illustrates one collision check.

   ```
   //from collisions.fla
   if (monster.hitTest(car1)){
     trace("hit by car 1!");
     reset(car1);
   } // end if
   ```

Test constantly. When trouble happens, you'll be more likely to know when things went bad as well as what probably caused the problem.

Building the checkCollisions () function

The details of your collision-checking routine will be unique, but the general structure will look something like mine (as shown in Listing 10-2).

Listing 10-2:   Collisions Program checkCollisions() Function

```
//from collisions.fla
function checkCollisions(){
  //check for various collisions

  if (monster.hitTest(car1)){
    trace("hit by car 1!");
    reset(car1);
  } // end if

  if (monster.hitTest(car2)){
    trace("hit by car 2!");
    reset(car2);
  } // end if

  if (monster.hitTest(car3)){
    trace("hit by car 3!");
    reset(car3);
  } // end if

  //look for flame collisions
  if (flame.hitTest(car1)){
    trace("burned car 1");
    resetFlame();
    reset(car1);
  } // end if

  if (flame.hitTest(car2)){
    trace("burned car 2");
    resetFlame();
    reset(car2);
  } // end if

  if (flame.hitTest(car3)){
    trace("burned car 3");
    resetFlame();
    reset(car3);
  } // end if
} // end checkCollisions
```

Listing 10-2 shows some good strategies for collision routines:

✔ **I left the `trace` statements in place.**

When you finish the collision code, you will use more code in each of these code segments to handle playing audio, scorekeeping, and game-ending situations. `trace` statements are useful when code goes wrong so you can see where the program processes in the code.

✔ **The `trace` statements are descriptive.**

When I run this program, I can look at the output window and see exactly what's happening. I didn't simply report that a collision occurred but rather exactly which object hit what as well as what should happen next.

✔ **Each segment calls some other functions.**

I avoid putting too much code in these segments. Whenever possible, I want to call other functions to do the heavy lifting so I can clearly see the logic flow here. (Gotta love that encapsulation!)

✔ **It looks like I need a new function to reset the flame.**

Any time a flame hits a car, I need to take it off the screen. That code needs to happen in many places, so it's a candidate for a function.

Building the ResetFlame() function

When you find yourself copying and pasting code, you have a good candidate for a function. I need to reset the flame sprite from several places in my program, so that looks like it would be a good function.

Code for the `resetFlame` function is actually quite simple. I could just give it to you as I've been doing throughout this book, but I want to take a moment to talk about how functions are built.

At this point in your travels, you're probably pretty good at following code, and you probably understand most of what's going on in my programs. However, when you try to write your own code from scratch, knowing where to start can be really hard.

Building any function begins the same way:

1. Describe in English what you want the function to accomplish.

2. Look for tools to help you do the job.

   They might be

   • Built-in Flash functions

   • Functions you've previously written

- Programming concepts (such as a loop, `hitTest`, or `if` structure)
- Other intangibles (an idea, a strategy, or an inspiration)

3. Rewrite your problem with the tools you've identified.

4. Test your code to see whether it does what you expected.

5. Refine the code to get it working better.

The `resetFlame()` function was pretty easy to build using this technique. As I was writing the `checkCollision()` function, it became apparent that I'd need to deal with the flame collisions. The code didn't simply flow out of my brain. I had to go through this process:

1. Describe the plan in English.

I want the flame to move off the screen and stop.

2. Look for tools.

In this case, all the key tools are properties of the `flame` object. If I set the right values to the right properties, I can accomplish all the goals of the function.

3. Rewrite the problem.

I can move the flame off the screen by setting both its `_x` and `_y` properties to a negative number. (I use `-200`.) I can stop the flame by setting its speed to `0`.

`_x` and `_y` are built-in properties of the `MovieClip` object, so they always work. The `speed` property is something I invented, so it works only in the context of the move techniques I show you throughout this book. If you choose to implement movement in some other way, your code must reflect your technique.

4. Test.

At some point, you must write actual code and see whether it works. Here's my code:

```
//from collisions.fla
function resetFlame(){
  //move off screen and stop
  flame._x = - 200;
  flame._y = - 200;
  flame.speed = 0;
} // end resetFlame
```

It's pretty easy to write the code if you went through all the planning steps outlined here, but it's much harder if you simply blurt out the code with no planning.

I ran the code and tested many ways to make sure the flame was reset each time the flame hit a car.

STAIR and programming

I once attended a conference of computer programming teachers. (Sounds dull, huh?) Everyone agreed it was very difficult to teach students how to get from an idea to code. We spent a lot of effort analyzing good programmers. We finally worked out a variation of the problem-solving technique I described. Of course, you aren't allowed to do anything in the academic world without a good acronym. I was assigned to come up with an acronym for the problem-solving process. I thought about it for a long time but couldn't come up with anything. One night I had a dream about walking up some stairs. I shot out of bed and knew I had it!

- **S:** State the problem
- **T:** Tools

- **A:** Algorithm
- **I:** Implement
- **R:** Refinement

As things go in the university world, this thing got way out of control. Overzealous teaching assistants began making people memorize STAIR, like some sort of mantra. People had to submit STAIR analysis of all their programming assignments. I got a little sad. Still, I think the idea has merit. When you find yourself staring (get it? STAIRing!) at a blank screen, think about applying the STAIR technique (or any other organized problem-solving methodology) to get over the hump.

5. **Refine the code to get it working better.**

Sometimes code works the first time. That rarely happens. Even experienced programmers don't expect code to work on the first try. If it isn't working right

    a. Try to isolate the problem.

    b. Make sure the condition is being triggered. (That's why you include those trace *statements.)*

    c. If the code is being called from several places, check whether it's wrong in all of them.

    d. Try to separate code that works from code that doesn't.

Eventually, you will find the problem. After you locate a problem, solving it is usually pretty easy.

Adding the Sound Effects

Sound is an important part of games. Because many game sounds happen in response to collisions, I often code sound right after getting the basic collision behavior.

The basics of sound programming are covered in Chapter 8.

To add sounds to your game, follow these steps:

1. **Gather your sound files**.

   You might need to create some sounds, modify them, or adjust their compression settings. Make sure all your sounds are working correctly before you begin adding the sound code to your programs. Check Chapter 8 for information on incorporating sounds.

    Store all the audio files for your project in the same place so you can find them easily.

2. **Import the audio files into your Library.**

   Follow these steps for each audio file:

    a. *Load the sound file into the Library.*

      You can load all the sound files at once, but you must repeat the following steps for each individual sound file.

   b. *Right-click the sound's name in the Library and choose Linkages.*

   c. *Set the linkage to Import for ActionScript.*

    If you don't get the linkage right, the sound doesn't play no matter how you write the code.

3. **Create all the sound objects.**

   The program's `init()` function is the best place to create the sound objects.

   Here's the code I added to `init()` in my program:

   ```
   //set up sounds
   //from sounds.fla init() function

   sndCrash = new Sound();
   sndCrash.attachSound("crash.wav");

   sndFlame = new Sound();
   sndFlame.attachSound("flame.wav");

   sndAlarm = new Sound();
   sndAlarm.attachSound("alarm.wav");
   ```

4. **Play the sounds where appropriate.**

   After the sound objects are created, use the sound's `start()` method to play the sound when it's needed in the program.

In my game, all the sounds are played as a response to collisions, so I add code to the collision routines, like this:

```
//from sounds.fla checkCollisions() function
if (monster.hitTest(car1)){
  trace("hit by car 1!");
  sndCrash.start();
  reset(car1);
```

5. Test your program.

Make sure sounds are happening when they are supposed to and aren't happening anywhere else.

When you're working on code for hours, the sound can really get on your nerves. If you're sick of the sounds (or one sound), comment out the line that starts that sound, like this:

```
//from sounds.fla collisions()
if (monster.hitTest(car1)){
  trace("hit by car 1!");

  //sound temporarily turned off
  //sndCrash.start();
  reset(car1);
```

If you turned the sounds off to preserve your sanity, turn them back on before you publish your final version of the program!

Completing the Program

Although much of the basic functionality is done, you can't call a game complete if it doesn't have winning and losing situations. Winning and losing a game are usually attached to scorekeeping.

Adding an intro frame

For the Monster Traffic game, I created various games states. Chapter 3 illustrates how to implement the concept of state in a program:

1. Think of your game as a series of nodes.

In my game, I have four distinct states: Introduction, Play, GameOver, and Instructions. Figure 10-5 shows the states. Although these states share certain elements, they are distinct and thus require separate attention.

Figure 10-5:
Each state
of the
game is
represented
by a
different
frame.

2. **Rebuild your main Timeline to incorporate the states.**

Each node translates to a keyframe on the main Timeline. Separate
each keyframe by a few frames and add clear labels to your frames.
My Timeline looks like Figure 10-6.

Figure 10-6:
Final
Timeline for
Monster
Traffic
game.

 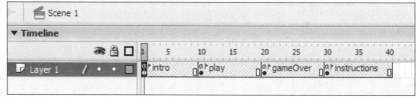

When you're building a game, you often begin with all the action in
Frame 1, Layer 1. Your final game will probably incorporate one or more
screens before the main play screen, so you need to add a keyframe or
two before the keyframe containing most of your code. To move your
code to a new keyframe, do the following:

a. *Create a new keyframe at Frame 10.*

By default, all the movie clip objects in the previous frame are
duplicated in the new frame.

b. Add new keyframes to Timeline Frames 20, 30, and 40 as well.

These new keyframes represent other states in your final game.

c. Place a blank frame in Frame 50.

The last frame doesn't really do anything: It's just there to make sure the label for the last keyframe is readable.

After this procedure, you have four keyframes, all containing the same movie clip objects. Give each keyframe a meaningful label.

3. Copy the code from Frame 1 to the play frame.

So far you've written all the code in Frame 1, Layer 1 because it's easy to work with there. For your final game, you have an intro screen in Frame 1, so all the code belongs in the play frame. Follow these steps to migrate code to the play frame:

a. Select all the code from Frame 1.

b. Copy the selected code.

c. Paste the copied code into the play frame.

d. Delete the original code from the first frame.

Be absolutely sure you have the code available in the new frame before you delete it from the original. Do not delete anything from Frame 1 until you're sure that you have the code duplicated in the play frame.

4. Clean up the intro frame.

If the first frame is no longer the play frame, remove everything that you don't need from that frame. On the intro frame, you need the monster, one car, a text box for the game's title, and two buttons. Begin by clearing all the stuff you don't need from the intro frame. Add a text box for the game title.

5. Create a button to start the game.

Eventually, you need two buttons on the intro frame, but you can begin with one. You reuse this button in several other parts of the game, so take some time to make it something you like. (You can review button creation in Chapter 2 if you need a refresher.) Don't forget to name the button instance something clever, like btnBegin. Add static text on top of the button to tell the user what the button does.

6. Code the button.

Check again to ensure that all the code that was in Frame 1 is now duplicated in the play frame. Remove all the other code from the intro frame. Add some button code something like this:

```
//from monsterTraffic.fla init frame
stop();

//button events
```

```
btnBegin.onRelease = function(){
  _root.gotoAndStop("play");
} // end button event
```

Because this is now a multi-frame program, the `stop()` function turns off the automatic Timeline progression.

When the user clicks the button, program control moves to the play frame.

7. **Test the program.**

Be sure that the program begins with the intro screen. Also ensure that the program moves to the play screen when the user clicks the button.

Don't worry about animating the car and the monster in the intro screen now. I show you how to do that in a following section.

Create the other states

My program has four other states, so I need to create them. They're all pretty similar to the intro screen, so if you want, you can simply copy the elements from the intro Stage onto the game over the instruction frames. After you have all the basic components in place, follow these steps to get the functionality working:

1. **Add an Instructions button to the intro screen.**

   You can use another instance of the same button that you use for beginning the game. Drag another instance of the button from the Library; add a static text field on top of the button; and give the button the new name, like `btnInstructions`.

2. **Code the new button.**

   Add code to control the button so that when it is clicked, program control moves to the instructions frame. The following code shows the button's event handler:

   ```
   //from monsterTraffic.fla init frame
   btnInstructions.onRelease = function(){
       root.gotoAndStop("instructions");
   } // end button event
   ```

3. **Modify the instructions frame.**

   Add a second text field to the instructions frame and modify the new text field so that you can put instructions for the game on this page. You might also need to modify the font on both text fields so that you have room for all the text to fit at once. Both of these fields should contain static text because their values don't change during the program's run. Add enough instructions so that the user can get started in the game.

Don't get carried away with your instructions. People playing online games have notoriously short attention spans.

4. **Add a button to the instructions frame.**

   Drag another instance of the button onto the instructions frame. Give this new button a sensible name and label, and then add code, such as the following:

   ```
   //from monsterTraffic.fla instructions frame
   //button event
   btnBegin.onRelease = function(){
     _root.gotoAndStop("play");
   } // end button event
   ```

5. **Test your program to ensure that program control moves correctly from the intro screen to the instructions page as well as from the instructions to the main game screen.**

6. **Create the GameOver screen.**

   Because this node is very much like the intro screen, you can use many of the same elements. Modify the text field so that it reads Game Over and create or copy a button that returns the user to the play screen. The code for that button is identical to similar code in the intro and instructions screens, so I won't repeat it here.

7. **Test once again.**

   As always, make sure your new changes work before you move on to something else.

Adding the scorekeeping functionality

When you have all the states in place, you can add the code that

- ✔ Increments the player's score
- ✔ Keeps track of the number of times the player has been hit

This code goes into the checkCollisions() function described earlier in this chapter. To add scorekeeping capability, follow these steps:

1. **Find conditions that should change the score.**

   The Monster Traffic game has two kinds of conditions:

   - *When the flame hits a car (a good thing), the player's score increases.*

     There's no maximum score (except for that imposed by the player's ability level), so don't worry about the score getting too high.

- *When a car hits the monster (a bad thing), the number of lives decreases.*

  The player has a limited number of lives, so when the monster has been hit too many times, the game ends.

2. **Add text fields to track the current score and lives.**

   For scorekeeping, you need two dynamic text fields on the play screen:

   a. *Attach one dynamic text field to the* `monster.points` *variable.*

   b. *Attach the other dynamic text field to the* `monster.lives` *variable.*

3. **Add code to modify the player's score when the flame hits a car.**

   When the flame hits the car, the player's score increments. In typical arcade-game grade-inflation fashion, every hit is worth 100 points.

   This is the code for changing the player's score lives in the `checkCollisions()` function on that play screen. The following code is repeated for each car:

```
//from monsterTraffic play frame checkCollisions function
//look for flame collisions
if (flame.hitTest(car1)){
  trace("burned car 1");
  sndAlarm.start();
  resetFlame();
  reset(car1);
  monster.points += 100;
} // end if
```

Because the `monster.points` variable is already connected to a dynamic text field, simply modifying the variable automatically places the score onscreen.

4. **Add code to decrease the number of lives when the monster is hit by a car.**

   Each time the monster is struck by a car, the number of lives is reduced by one. Code for this situation also goes in the `checkCollisions()` function. The following code is repeated for each car:

```
 //from monsterTraffic play frame checkCollisions()
if (monster.hitTest(car1)){
    trace("hit by car 1!");
    sndCrash.start();
    reset(car1);
    monster.lives--;
    if (monster.lives <= 0){
      _root.gotoAndStop("gameOver");
    } // end if
  } // end if
```

The number of lives decreases, and it has a limit. If the monster has fewer than 0 (zero) lives, the player has lost, and the game is over. This is signified by sending program control to the gameOver keyframe.

5. **Test your program.**

After you add scorekeeping code, check your program to make sure that

a. The score increments correctly.

b. When the number of lives becomes less than 0, program control reverts to the gameOver state.

Adding the animations

The complete version of the monsterTraffic game features a simple animation of the monster chasing the car on all the screens. These animations aren't necessary, but they add charm to the game and are very easy to create. They simply reuse the objects already created for the main game and animate them in a much simpler way.

To add these animations to your intro, instructions, and game over screens, repeat the following steps for each frame:

1. **Make sure the frame has instances of the objects you want to animate.**

The animations in the monster game each need the monster and one car:

- *For my game, the intro frame needs instances of the monster and one of the cars.*

Name the monster instance monster and the car instance car.

- *For each screen, make sure that you name the instances of the monster and car objects correctly.*

2. **Initialize the objects.**

In the *auxiliary* frames (everything but the play state), the objects in this animation are much simpler than in the main game:

- Because the objects move straight up, only the dy property is important.

- All the other properties are determined by the initial placement of the objects on the Stage.

Follow these steps to build a simple animation:

a. Create an initialization function (called init()).

b. Call the newly created init() function from the Timeline code.

c. Add the following code to `init()`:

```
//from monster traffic init frame
init();

function init(){
  monster.dy = -5;
  car.dy = -5;
} //end init
```

In `monsterTraffic`, the `monster.dy` property and the `car.dy` property are both set to –5, indicating that both of these objects move up the screen five pixels per frame (ppf).

3. **Add simple animation code to the frame.**

The following code is a simplification of the animation loop:

```
monster.onEnterFrame = function(){
  monster._y += monster.dy;
  car._y += car.dy;

  //very limited boundary checking
  if (monster._y < 0){
    monster._y = Stage.height;
  } // end if

  if (car._y < 0){
    car._y = Stage.height;
  } // end if
```

Because the monster and car animation is so limited, you need to change only the `y` properties of the two objects. The only necessary boundary checking determines whether the monster or the car has moved off the top of the Stage and then wraps the offending object to the bottom.

Retest your program after you build the animation. Run your program through its paces and make sure that

- The monster and car animations are working in all the right places.

- Your new code hasn't broken anything that was working.

Part V
Phun with Phuzzy Physics

The 5th Wave   By Rich Tennant

"So, someone's using your credit card info to buy stylish clothes, opera tickets and exercise equipment. In what way would this qualify as 'identity theft'?"

In this part . . .

At some point, you probably want to make your games a little more realistic. Maybe you want a catapult to shoot things in an arc, a car that slows when you release the accelerator, or a spacecraft that orbits properly around a planet. The bad news is all these things are explained by the basic rules of math and physics. The worse news is we all hate math and physics. However, there *is* some good news: It's not nearly as bad as you probably think. Dig in, and you'll wonder why your math professor didn't explain all that icky stuff by having you write a few games. You never know: You might finally understand why vectors, radians, and cosines really matter. Of course, if this stuff truly freaks you out, you don't have to pay any attention at all, but play with the examples from these chapters, anyway. You'll find them pretty intriguing, and you might eventually decide that they're worth a try.

Chapter 11 describes the concept of vectors and how you can use them to give objects a much more realistic motion than the techniques shown earlier in the book. You also discover the important principle of *vector projection* as well as how to simulate the effect of gravity on an object like a cannonball.

Chapter 12 applies the vector ideas to vehicles and illustrates how you can simulate various forces acting on a moving sprite. Read here how to build objects that skid, spin, and orbit. You can also read about the basic physics models for various kinds of vehicle motion.

Chapter 13 is about creating and destroying sprites. You see how to build a sprite from an object in the Library and then how to destroy it with code. Read how to build and manage an entire fleet of sprites and how to use Flash's new object-oriented paradigm to build extremely powerful custom sprites easily.

Chapter 11

Vectors and Gravity

. . . .

In This Chapter

▶ Introducing vectors

▶ Converting from angle and length to dx and dy

▶ Converting from dx and dy to angle and length

▶ Managing gravity

▶ Following the mouse

▶ Responding to mouse input

. . . .

Games usually have some relationship to reality. If you want your game to model the real world — or even exaggerate aspects of the real world — you need to know how things work in the real world. You don't need a degree in math or physics to make more realistic games. Some basic ideas can provide you a lot of capability. In this chapter, you see how to use vectors and gravity to improve your games.

Tower, Give Me a Vector

Sprite objects moving around onscreen are the core of 2-D video games. On each frame of a game, every object moves a given direction and speed. In Chapter 10, I show you how to convert the direction and speed into the dx and dy values that are used to move the object. The technique in that chapter is fine if you're willing to limit your sprites to a limited number of directions. However, many games call for a lot more flexibility. Fortunately, a really neat concept — a *vector* — is perfect for this kind of situation. Vectors can make your sprites do all kinds of cool things.

Objects don't normally just move without outside influence. Gravity, which plays a big part in many games, is essential for realistic behavior in your games. Fortunately, the math technique for working with any angle is closely related to an easy way to work with gravity.

Throughout this chapter, I show you how to work with angles, speed, and gravity by using variations of the `gravityTrace` program featured in Figure 11-1. The user can control a cannon's angle and charge, and the cannon fires cannonballs in realistic arcs.

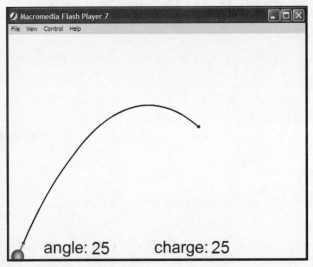

Figure 11-1:
In this game, users control a cannon's angle and charge.

Working with vectors

The `gravityTrace` program in Figure 11-1 is remarkably similar to many other programs throughout this book. Compared with the Monster Traffic game developed in Chapters 8 through 10, the new elements are

- ✔ **Gravity**

- ✔ **Moving objects in any direction at any speed**

  You can move an object in any angle at any speed with a math trick called *vector projection,* which is a lot easier than it sounds. The basic problem is this: When objects move, think of the motion in terms of direction and speed. Mathematicians refer to this type of information as a *vector*.

It's natural to think about vectors when you're describing motion, even if you aren't familiar with the term *vector*. In everyday language, if you say, "Drive east for five miles" or " I walked 100 yards at a bearing of 35 degrees," you're using vectors to describe motion.

Flash (and most computer animation systems) doesn't work directly with vectors. To move an object on the screen, you need dx and dy properties. You can convert any speed and angle into the appropriate x and y values.

Okay, you caught me. There's some math in this chapter. However, any math in this book is used because it makes your job easier, not harder. Basic math can do incredibly powerful things. If you've ever asked when you'll really use math, *today's the day!*

Math is much less painful when you use it to launch a cow over a castle wall!

Examining the vector

Figure 11-2 shows the most basic type of vector: a line superimposed onto a coordinate system. One end of the line is on the origin (center) of that coordinate system.

If you want to look at this diagram or any of the other diagrams in this section more closely, you can find them all in the vectorAngle.fla file on the Web site that accompanies this book:

www.dummies.com/go/flashgameprogrammingfd1e

As I was trying to figure out how to draw the math and figures for this section, I realized I had one of the world's best vector-drawing packages in front of me.

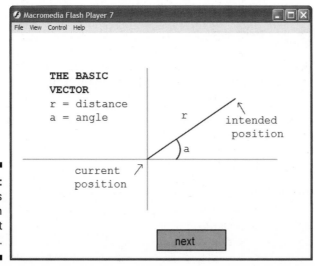

Figure 11-2:
A vector is a line with one end at the origin.

A *vector* is usually described as a length and an angle measured against some other standard. Math usually uses these terms:

- **Length of the line:** r
- **Angle of the line (against the x axis):** a or Θ (theta)

  I use a in this chapter to avoid Greek symbols.

Mathematicians normally measure angles counterclockwise from the x axis. This makes the math a little easier later on, but it might be confusing to you because you're probably used to measuring angles clockwise from the y axis. Don't worry about it. I show you the basic ideas of working with angles now. I show you how to convert from common measurement to mathematical techniques when you need them later in this chapter.

In your games, you'll encounter the following terms:

- The *angle* represents the direction you want the sprite to travel.
- The *length* of the line represents how far in that direction you want to go.
- The *origin* of the coordinate system is the current position of the object.
- The other end of the line represents where you want to position the object in the next frame.

Technically, mathematicians refer to a vector's *magnitude,* not its *length.* However, length and magnitude can be considered interchangeable for programming purposes.

Making a triangle

The angle and length are what you start with, but what you really need to know is what you should set dx and dy to get the object to the other end of the line. Draw two lines to make your vector into a triangle, like in Figure 11-3.

You now have a right triangle that shows the difference between the current and desired location:

- The vertical line represents the difference in y values.
- The horizontal line represents the difference in x values.

Seeing things the trig way

Right triangles are wonderful because of the many tricks for getting information from them. The ancient Greeks discovered ways to determine all the lengths and angles of a triangle based on very small bits of information. With trigonometry, you give different names to the parts of the triangle. You're usually thinking about one angle still called a, but the sides have different names.

- ✔ **hyp:** The longest side of the triangle is the *hypotenuse*.
- ✔ **adj:** The side touching the angle is the *adjacent side*.
- ✔ **opp:** The remaining side is the *opposite side*.

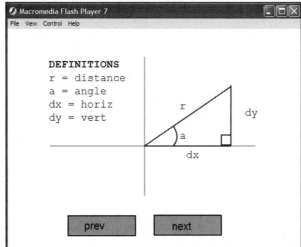

Figure 11-3:
The sides of
the triangle
represent
dx and dy.

Figure 11-4 shows the triangle using trigonometry notation.

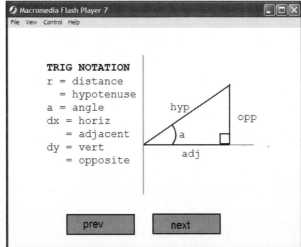

Figure 11-4:
The trig
names of
the triangle
parts.

Trigonometry notation is useful because it describes how the sides of a triangle relate to a specific angle of the triangle.

Getting help from Chief SOHCATOA

The ancient Greeks recognized that certain ratios persist in right triangles, and that if you understand these ratios, you can calculate any side of a triangle based on an angle and one of the other sides.

Math teachers often use the mnemonic SOHCAHTOA to help people remember the relationship. SOHCAHTOA is a summary of the three basic trigonometry ratios, as shown in Figure 11-5:

- ✔ **SOH:** The **s**in of angle a is the **o**pposite side divided by the **h**ypotenuse.

- ✔ **CAH:** The **c**osine of a is the **a**djacent angle divided by the **h**ypotenuse.

- ✔ **TOA:** The **t**angent of a is the **o**pposite side divided by the **a**djacent side.

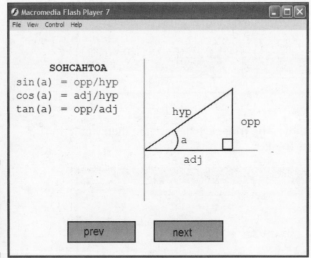

Figure 11-5:
The trig functions are nothing but ratios.

How do I get dx and dy?

In every frame of your game, you'll know the current position of each object, what direction it should move in, and how many pixels you want it to move in that direction. You need to resolve these values into something more practical: How much should you add to the object's x value (dx), and how much should you add to the object's y (dy)?

I want to write games. Why the math lesson?

You might wonder whether all this theory is absolutely necessary in a book as eminently practical as a *For Dummies* book. I can (and will, later in the chapter) just give you exactly the formulas that you need to handle most of the vector issues you encounter. But you shouldn't write games just like mine — think of new variations. The only way you can truly create new ideas is from a fundamental understanding of the underlying principles. If you truly know how vector projection works, for example, you have a much better chance of changing how it's done to simulate a black hole onscreen or to make some other variation I've never thought of. Sometimes the most practical thing of all is a little bit of well-applied theory. I show you several ways to enhance these ideas in Chapters 12 and 15.

Getting the dy value

Finally, the trig and math stuff pays off. You know an angle and a distance, and you want to generate dx and dy values. Figure 11-6 shows how you can use math to do exactly that.

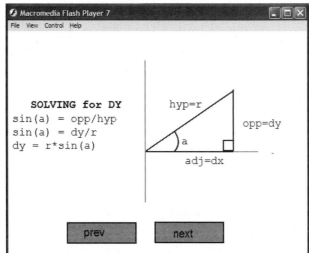

Figure 11-6: Derive a formula to get dy from any angle and distance.

Trig notation says that

sin(a) = opposite/hypotenuse

This formula can be translated into the original terminology:

sin(a) = dy/r

From there, you can use some basic algebra to create a formula that solves for dy given any angle (a) and length (r). The formula requires that you know the sin of angle a, but the computer can do that for you. The resulting formula is

dy = r * sin(a)

In traditional mathematics, most variables are one letter long, so dy means d * y. In the context of this book, dy is a property used to determine how an object moves in y. Programmers avoid one-character variable names. I always explicitly multiply variables together with the asterisk or parentheses conventions. Two characters placed together are a variable name, not a multiplication.

Getting the dx value

Of course, the formula for deriving dx is nearly the same. Figure 11-7 shows how I derived that formula.

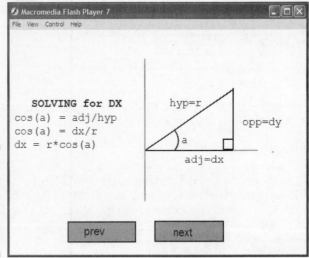

Figure 11-7: The dx formula uses the cosine function.

To solve for dx, just recognize that dx is also the adjacent side, so the cosine function that relates the hypotenuse to the adjacent side is also used to compare the vector distance with its angle. Here's the final formula:

dx = r * cos(a)

Going the other direction

Sometimes you need to work the angle and length of the vector from dx and dy. These problems have well-recognized formulas.

Solving for the angle

Solving for the angle uses the tangent function, as illustrated in Figure 11-8.

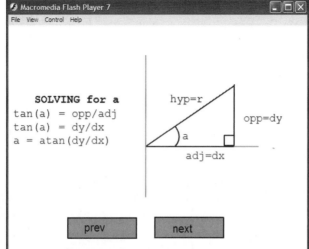

Figure 11-8: Use the tangent function to determine the angle if you know dx and dy.

The tangent of angle a is the opposite side divided by the adjacent side. In dx/dy terminology, you can say it this way:

tan(a) = dy/dx

To solve for a, you need to use the inverse tangent function (arctan). Of course, ActionScript has this function built in; you just have to know when you need it. The final formula for determining the angle when you know dx and dy is this:

a = atan(dy/dx)

Solving for the distance

If you know dx and dy, you can determine the vector angle with the atan function, but how do you determine the vector's length? That is best done with our old friend Pythagoras. Figure 11-9 illustrates how to figure out the vector length r given dx and dy values.

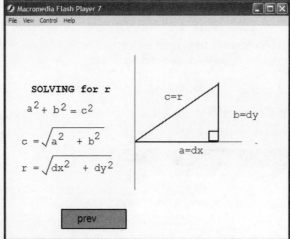

Figure 11-9:
The
Pythagorean
theorem
comes to
the rescue
once again.

Unfortunately, the Pythagorean theorem uses yet another terminology to describe the same triangle. The theorem is traditionally worded

$$a^2 + b^2 = c^2$$

where c is the hypotenuse and a and b are the two other sides. If you solve this function for c, c equals the square root of a squared plus b squared.

Translating to dx and dy notation, you can find the length of the vector (r) by

1. Squaring dx.

2. Squaring dy.

3. Adding these two values.

4. Finding the square root of the sum.

Doing Vector Conversion in Flash

When you can translate between angle and speed to dx and dy with vector projection, you can modify the turn function to translate speed and direction to dx and dy. However, there are other tricky details when you want to do the math in Flash or another computing environment:

✔ **Inconsistent angle measurement units:** ActionScript uses different angle units in different parts of the language:

  • *radians:* The math functions built into ActionScript use *radians* (the radius of a circle wrapped around a part of its circumference).

- *degrees:* The _rotation property that is used to change the visual orientation of a sprite uses degrees.

Degrees and radians are easy to convert:

- Degrees to radians

```
degrees = (180 * radians)/pi
```

- Radians to degrees

```
radians = (pi * degrees)/180
```

In the vecProj code described in the next section, I show you how to convert units when necessary:

- *Opposite rotation:* Mathematicians begin angle measurements at the x axis, working counterclockwise. In ActionScript, built-in math functions work the same way.

- *Offset by 90 degrees:* In mathematics, most angle measurement is done from the x axis. In navigation, angles are usually measured in relationship to north. In ActionScript, when you work with degrees, zero is north. When you work in radians, zero is the positive x axis. The vecProj code in the next section illustrates how to compensate for this inconsistency as well.

Introducing the vector projection demo

Figure 11-10 shows vecProj.fla, a simple program that illustrates these concepts.

Figure 11-10:
Given a length and angle (in degrees), generate dx and dy.

![Macromedia Flash Player 7 window showing a form with "angle" field set to 90, "length" field set to 2, a "calculate" button, and output "dx 2" and "dy 0".]

The vecProj program has dynamic text boxes linked to the variables angle, length, dx, and dy. Note the button named btnCalc that has the following code attached:

```
btnCalc.onRelease = function(){
    //calculate DX and DY from angle and length
    //use vector projection to get DX and DY

    //offset the angle
    degrees = angle -90;

    //convert to radians
    radians = degrees / 180 * Math.PI;

    //get DX and DY (normalized: length is one)
    dx = Math.cos(radians);
    dy = Math.sin(radians);

    //compensate for length
    dx *= length;
    dy *= length;
} // end btnCalc
```

When you're running the vecProj program, you see very strange numbers every now and then. For example, if you enter an angle of 180 and a length of 1, you might expect dx to be 0 and dy to be 1 (because you're moving down one pixel). In this case, dy is 1, but dx is 6.12303176911189e-17! Before you send me an angry e-mail about the defective program, look at the result. The e stands for *exponential notation,* so the actual value being suggested for dx is approximately

0.00000000000000006123

Computers are famous for not being capable of exact calculations on real numbers. This number is close enough to 0 for game development.

Calculating the values

The code uses the angle and length variables to calculate new dx and dy values.

The general procedure for generating dx and dy from angle and length is this:

1. **Determine the angle and length of your vector.**

   In most cases, you extract these values from various sprites in your game. In this first example, they are input directly from the text fields shown in Figure 11-10.

Generally, the input values follow these conventions:

- The angle is measured in degrees using normal navigation mode.

- The distance is measured in pixels.

2. Offset the angle.

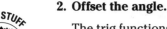

The trig functions measure angles from the x axis. You can compensate for this by subtracting 90 from the original angle. I call this new variable `degrees` because it's measured in degrees.

```
//offset the angle
degrees = angle -90;
```

3. Convert to radians.

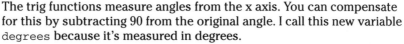

The trig functions require angle measurements in radians. Fortunately, it's a pretty easy conversion:

```
//convert to radians
radians = degrees / 180 * Math.PI;
```

The `Math` object has a built-in constant called `Math.PI`, so you don't have to remember the value of pi. Of course, a computer can't get pi completely right, but this approximation is more than good enough for game development purposes.

4. Derive the normalized dx and dy values.

Use the trig functions to get the `dx` and `dy` values that would generate a vector of length `1` in the desired direction. (A vector of length one is a *normalized* or *unit* vector.)

```
//get DX and DY (normalized: length is one)
dx = Math.cos(radians);
dy = Math.sin(radians);
```

The trigonometry functions in ActionScript (such as `Math.cos` and `Math.sin` syntax) are built into ActionScript's incredibly useful `Math` object. The `Math` object in the ActionScript dictionary shows other useful tricks.

5. Multiply dx and dy by the distance.

After you know how to build a vector of length one in any direction, multiply both `dx` and `dy` by the length value to generate `dx` and `dy` values corresponding to the desired length.

Using Vector Projection in Motion

You generally use vector projection in terms of motion. Chapter 10 describes how to use a basic `turn()` function to convert direction and speed into dx and dy by using a very crude algorithm. You can use vector projection to vastly improve the turn() function. The cannon.fla program illustrated in Figure 11-11 shows a cannon that fires bullets in any direction at any speed.

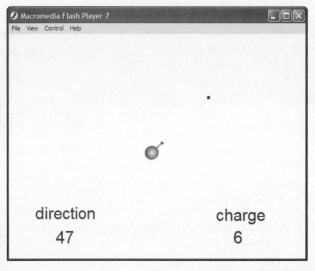

Figure 11-11:
The user aims the cannon by adjusting the angle and speed of the projectile.

The cannon program demonstrated in Figure 11-11 uses these keys for adjustments:

- **Direction:** Left- and right-arrow keys

  The cannon's direction is indicated in degrees.

- **Initial velocity of the cannonball:** Up- and down-arrow keys

In this example, the cannonball continues to travel in the same speed and direction until it reaches the edge of the Stage.

Building a cannon

Much of the Cannon program is similar to some of the other programs presented in this book. Begin your cannon game by building the visual elements on the screen:

1. **Create a cannon movie clip.**

   My cannon looks like a sphere with a barrel sticking out of it. I built the sphere as a circle with a radial gradient and the barrel as a rectangle with a linear gradient. I was careful to ensure that the registration point of the cannon was near the center of the circular part so that the cannon appears to rotate around the center of that circle.

2. **Create a bullet.**

   The bullet also is a movie clip.

   My projectile is a simple dot, so I don't have to turn it in the direction of travel. You might want to use the `ctl-up` and `ctl-down` commands to ensure that the ball appears underneath the cannon sprite so that it appears to shoot out of the barrel instead of appearing on top of the turret.

   For now, move the bullet sprite off the Stage. It's summoned when it's needed.

3. **Add text fields to display the angle and speed.**

   Even if you don't show this information to the player (or if you use some kind of graphical representation), it's good to see the actual input values while you're testing.

   To display the angle and charge, build two dynamic text boxes:

   - A dynamic text box linked to the `gun.dir` property
   - A dynamic text box linked to the `gun.charge` property

   The variables associated with the text fields are the two properties that are controlled from the keyboard.

4. **Initialize your program.**

   As usual for moving sprites, you need to set up a number of properties in some sort of `init()` function:

   ```
   //from cannon.fla
   init();

   function init(){
     gun.dir = 0;
     gun.charge = 0;
     bullet.dir = 0;
     bullet.speed = 0;
   } // end init
   ```

   In `init()`, the gun object has the following properties:

   - *The `gun.dir` property: This indicates the direction the gun is pointing.*

     In this program, the gun is stationary. When it's fired, this is the direction in which the shells fly.

   - *The gun also has a `gun.charge` property that indicates how fast the bullet flies when the gun is fired.*

   The bullet has two important properties of its own:

   - *The `bullet.dir` property indicates the direction that the bullet travels in each frame.*

   - *The `bullet.speed` property indicates the distance the bullet travels in each frame. (Unlike the cannon, the bullet actually moves.)*

5. Set up the bullet's motion with the normal `enterFrame` code, like this:

```
//from cannon.fla
_root.onEnterFrame = function(){
  checkKeys();
  move(bullet);
} // end enterFrame
```

The next two sections show you how to make these two functions:

- The `checkKeys()` function checks the keyboard for user input.

- The `move()` function moves the bullet when it has a speed greater than zero.

Reading the keyboard

In this case, you want to check for five different keys:

✔ Left and right arrows control the angle of the gun.

✔ Up and down arrows control the gun's charge.

✔ The spacebar launches the bullet.

The keyboard routine is, well, routine! (Chapter 8 describes the details about reading from the keyboard.) Listing 11-1 shows the `checkKeys` function from the `cannon.fla` program.

Listing 11-1:   Cannon Program checkKeys() Function

```
//from cannon.fla
function checkKeys(){
  if (Key.isDown(Key.LEFT)){
    gun.dir--;
    gun._rotation = gun.dir;
  } // end if

  if (Key.isDown(Key.RIGHT)){
    gun.dir++;
    gun._rotation = gun.dir;
  } // end if

  if (Key.isDown(Key.UP)){
    gun.charge++;
  } // end if

  if (Key.isDown(Key.DOWN)){
    gun.charge--;
  } // end if
```

```
if (Key.isDown(Key.SPACE)){
  bullet._x = gun._x;
  bullet._y = gun._y;
  bullet.speed = gun.charge;
  bullet.dir = gun.dir;
  turn(bullet);
} // end if

} // end checkKeys
```

Listing 11-1 shows these controls:

✔ **Direction control**

- The left-arrow key decrements gun.dir by one degree.

- The right-arrow key increments gun.dir by one degree.

I don't check for a lower boundary because negative angles are completely acceptable. I then rotate the gun sprite by the new dir.

✔ **Charge**

- The up and down arrows simply modify the gun's charge.

- This doesn't change anything visible on the screen, so it's good to have the text field displaying the gun's charge.

✔ **Firing**

The spacebar fires the gun. In general, this simply involves transferring information from the gun to the bullet. Follow these steps to fire the cannon:

 a. *Place the bullet under the gun by copying the _x and _y properties from the gun to the bullet.*

 b. *Copy the* gun.charge *value to the* bullet.speed *property.*

 c. *Copy the* gun.dir *property to* bullet.dir.

The last line of Listing 11-1 calls a turn function, which translates the bullet's speed and direction into dx and dy properties.

Moving the bullet

The bullet is moved on the screen by using a typical move() function, as shown in Listing 11-2:

✔ Move the bullet by its dx and dy properties.

✔ Stop the bullet at the screen boundary.

Listing 11-2:   Cannon Program move() Function

```
//from cannon.fla
function move(sprite){
  //moves an object. Kills it if it moves off stage

  sprite._x += sprite.dx;
  sprite._y += sprite.dy;

  if ((sprite._x > Stage.width) ||
      (sprite._x < 0) ||
      (sprite._y > Stage.height) ||
      (sprite._7 < 0)){
    //stop sprite and move it off stage
    sprite._x = -100;
    sprite._y = -100;
    sprite._speed = 0;
  } //end if
} // end move
```

When the bullet hits a Stage border, it is quietly moved off the Stage and stopped until it's needed again.

Turning the bullet

As you learn more sophisticated techniques, you can modify your programs to use these techniques. The `turn()` function described in Chapter 10 is useful for moving any object in eight standard directions. You can make an even better `turn()` function using the vector projection principles described in this chapter.

The Cannon game uses a `turn()` function like many of the other programs in this book, but this version of `turn()` uses the more sophisticated vector projection scheme to produce the same results. It still uses a direction and speed to generate `dx` and `dy` values.

It's pretty common to look at a particular function and figure out a way to keep the same input and output but change the internal coding. This is useful because you could presumably retrofit a more sophisticated algorithm without having an adverse effect on the other parts of the program. This capability is one of the biggest advantages of encapsulation. Used correctly, upgradeable functions can make it very easy to improve your programs incrementally.

Listing 11-3 shows an improved `turn()` function implementing vector projection.

Listing 11-3:   Cannon Program turn() Function

```
function turn(sprite){
  //use vector projection to get DX and DY

  //offset the angle
  degrees = sprite.dir -90;

  //convert to radians
  radians = degrees / 180 * Math.PI;

  //get DX and DY (normalized: length is one)
  sprite.dx = Math.cos(radians);
  sprite.dy = Math.sin(radians);

  //compensate for speed
  sprite.dx *= sprite.speed;
  sprite.dy *= sprite.speed;
} // end turn;
```

When you use vector projection for motion instead of the pure math version described in vecProj.fla, you're still worried about angles and distance, but there are two special considerations:

- ✔ The r variable refers to the distance covered in one frame, so you generally think of the variable as speed rather than distance.

- ✔ Because you're moving a sprite, the variables generally are properties of that sprite, not global variables.

To turn a sprite object using vector projection, follow these steps:

1. **Initialize your sprites.**

   Any sprite that's moved using this scheme must have properties for dx, dy, dir, and speed. Prepare initial values of these variables in an init() function.

2. **Create a generic turn function that works with any sprite.**

   For the cannon game, this turn function is different from the turn functions in preceding chapters: You calculate the new dx and dy from the angle and speed properties (instead of moving in one of a preset number of directions).

3. **Extract the angle from the sprite's dir property.**

   Derive the degrees variable from the direction of the sprite.

4. **Use the sprite's speed property as the vector length.**

   The speed property should indicate how many pixels the object should move in a given frame, so the sprite speed equals the length of the vector.

Fun with Ballistics

Cannon games are very popular. The `cannon.fla` demonstration featured earlier in this chapter makes sense if you're looking at a cannon from the top down. However, if you look at a cannon from a side view, as in the `gravityTrace.fla` program, the shell's trajectory is never a straight line. Figure 11-12 illustrates the track of the shell for various starting criteria.

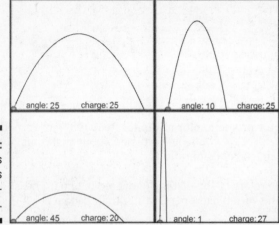

Figure 11-12:
Trajectories
of various
firing combi-
nations.

If you look at the trajectories in Figure 11-12, you can tell that things look right, but it's better to actually run the program to see how it works under your own control.

Table 11-1 illustrates what happens to the vertical speed of an object pointed straight up at an initial velocity of 10 with a gravitational pull of 1 ppf.

Table 11-1		Example of a Shell's Vertical Speed			
Frame	*Velocity*	*Frame*	*Velocity*	*Frame*	*Velocity*
Frame 0	10 ppf	Frame 7	3 ppf	Frame 14	−4 ppf
Frame 1	9 ppf	Frame 8	2 ppf	Frame 15	−5 ppf
Frame 2	8 ppf	Frame 9	1 ppf	Frame 16	−6 ppf
Frame 3	7 ppf	Frame 10	0 ppf	Frame 17	−7 ppf
Frame 4	6 ppf	Frame 11	−1 ppf	Frame 18	−8 ppf
Frame 5	5 ppf	Frame 12	−2 ppf	Frame 19	−9 ppf
Frame 6	4 ppf	Frame 13	−3 ppf	Frame 20	−10 ppf

Gravity is serious

Projectiles should behave in certain ways:

- **What goes up must come down.** The Earth's gravitational field has an effect on things. If you fire a bullet upward, it eventually comes down (unless, of course, you shoot it into orbit, but let's forget about that for now because it's a little more complicated). For side-view games that occur inside a gravity field (which is most of them), you need to somehow compensate for that gravity. (In games with a top-down perspective, all objects are perceived at the same height, so gravity isn't an issue.)

- **Projectiles move in parabolas.** Any `trace` you can create with the `gravityTrace` program is a parabola. This is good because objects like bullets (that don't have some sort of onboard propulsion system) travel in parabolic paths when in the presence of some major gravitational feature like Earth. (Of course, you can easily modify your games to simulate the gravity of other planets.)

- **Movement is smooth and continuous.** Objects move in smooth curves. They don't suddenly change direction, jump, or drastically change speed.

- **`dx` remains constant.** Unless acted upon by some other force, the horizontal speed of an object shouldn't change. In this case, I'm not modeling drag, which would in fact slow a cannonball because the effect is much less important than the effect of gravity on `dy`.

- **`dy` changes throughout the trajectory.** When the `gravityTrace` program is running, you see that the cannonball's vertical speed changes. If you fire straight in the air (angle 0) at 20 units, the ball leaves the gun's barrel at 20 pixels per frame (ppf), but it slows every frame until it appears to hang for a moment. It gradually accelerates until it hits the ground at 20 ppf. In the absence of any other force, the ending `dy` is exactly opposite of the starting `dy`.

From Table 11-1, you can see some important characteristics of an object moving in gravity:

- At the beginning of the exercise, the bullet is moving very quickly at its initial speed. The bullet begins moving at 10 ppf.

- On each frame, the upward speed of the projectile slows until its vertical motion stops altogether.

- On each successive frame, the bullet picks up speed downward until it hits the ground at a velocity the same speed at which it left the cannon! The bullet hits the ground at –10 ppf, which is the same speed as its initial charge.

Understanding the gravity of the situation

A ballistic trajectory works in a very specific way, so adding a gravity model might seem intimidating. In fact, it's incredibly simple. It's amazing how easy the gravity model in the `gravityTrace` program is despite the fact that it tends to follow all the rules of a good ballistics model.

The secret to simulating gravity on a planet is very simple:

1. **Generate a gravitational constant.**

   My `gravityTrace` demonstration uses a gravitational constant of 1 ppf. In the following example, I add a line to the Cannon program's `init()` function to set up the gravity:

   ```
   //from gravityTrace init() function
   gravity = 1;
   ```

   The preceding function uses an arbitrary gravity value instead of attempting to simulate actual Earth gravity. The sidebar, "My physics teacher says you're wrong about gravity" describes the process of simulating gravity.

2. **Add the gravitational value to each object's `dy` in the `move()` function.**

   ```
   //from gravityTrace move() function at end of function
   //incorporate gravity
   sprite.dy += gravity;
   ```

   During each frame, add a small amount to the `dy` property of each object that is affected by gravity.

   This form of gravity relies on changing the value of an object's `dy` property.

   - Negative `dy` values make the object move up.

   - Adding a positive value to `dy` makes it tend to go up more slowly if it's going up or to go more quickly if it's going down.

3. **Leave `dx` alone.**

   Doing nothing doesn't sound like a step, but it's part of making the gravity work correctly.

   The traces from the `gravityTrace` program show that when you aren't firing straight into the air, the arc of the bullet looks like a parabola. This is because the `dy` changes, but `dx` remains constant. If you're firing high (like 10 degrees), the initial change in `y` is much more than the change in `x`, making a nearly vertical line. As your bullet nears the top of its trajectory, the change in y becomes smaller and smaller, but the change in x remains constant, causing a more nearly horizontal path. Eventually, the dy gets larger again, and the angle approximates the starting angle as the bullet hits the ground.

4. **Don't forget to hit the ground.**

   It seems silly, but it's even more important to do certain kinds of boundary checking when you're incorporating gravity. When the bullet hits the ground, it should either bounce or stop.

   The simpler code is to stop the bullet, so that's what I do here. Make sure to set the bullet's $speed$, dx, and dy properties all to 0.

5. **Adjust gravity as necessary.**

   I chose 1 as an arbitrary gravitational constant. The mass of your objects in relationship to the planet is the most important characteristic. The key is to play your game but also fiddle with the gravitational constant until it works for your game.

   • *If things plummet to the ground too fast,* make your gravitational constant a little smaller.

   • *If they're floating too much,* make gravity more powerful.

   This simple gravity technique works only when you simulate a small object interacting with a very large object (like a bullet and a planet). When you work with orbits and objects with similar masses, the calculations for gravity are different. Chapter 12 describes how to simulate orbits, and Chapter 14 includes more formal descriptions of the gravity formulas.

My physics teacher says you're wrong about gravity

The gravitational constant of Earth (third planet from the Sun) is approximately 9.8 meters/second^2. I don't usually use that value in game programming because I rarely use either *meters* as my unit measurement or *seconds* as my time segment. Game programmers usually do their calculations in pixels per frame. This is an arbitrary measurement. The actual constant you should use varies based on the scale of your game. You generally need to experiment the actual value until it feels right. For this example, start with a gravity value of 1; that value is easy to understand as you work on the rest of the gravity code. The last step of the process involves tweaking the gravitational constant so it works well for your game.

Gravity is out of this world!

If you want to simulate gravity on a planet other than Earth, begin with a gravitational constant that works well for Earth and then adjust that by the appropriate scaling factor, as in these examples:

✔ If you have gravity working well for Earth at a gravity constant of 1 and you want to simulate the moon, simply divide by six because the moon has one-sixth of the gravitational effect of Earth. A gravity of .1667 is close enough to simulate the moon's gravity.

✔ The gravitational pull on the surface of Jupiter is about 2.6 times that of Earth, so changing the gravitational constant to 2.6 effectively simulates Jupiter's gravity.

Drawing on a movie clip

The code that traces the path of the bullet onscreen isn't critical to understanding how to work with gravity, but it has two advantages:

✔ Tracing the bullet's trajectory makes the program easier to understand.

✔ The tricks I use in `gravityTrace` are useful in other programs when you want to draw directly on the screen.

The `MovieClip` object as defined by Flash has methods built in that let you draw on a movie clip. You can look them up in the ActionScript dictionary for more details.

In `gravityTrace`, I use the following methods:

✔ `lineStyle(thickness, rgb, alpha)`

This method specifies the color and thickness of the line:

- *thickness is measured in pixels.*

- *rgb is the color.*

  The color code uses `0x` plus six hexadecimal characters. For example, `0xFF0000` is red, `0xFFFFFF` is white, and `0x000000` is black.

For a complete guide to hexadecimal colors, check the excellent reference at Wikipedia:

```
http://en.wikipedia.org/wiki/Web_colors
```

- *alpha is the line's transparency.*

`100` is completely opaque (solid), and `0` is completely transparent.

✔ `moveTo(x,y)`: Given an `x`, `y` coordinate pair, this moves a pen to that spot on the movie clip without drawing a line.

✔ `lineTo(x,y)`: This draws a line between the last `lineTo()` or `moveTo()` command and the given `x` and `y` coordinates.

✔ `clear()`: This clears anything drawn with the drawing methods.

Drawing the path

The drawing methods make it very easy to trace the path of the cannonball:

1. Initialize the line.

The line is redrawn every time the user fires the cannon, so I initialize the line when the user fires the cannon with the spacebar:

```
//from gravityTrace.fla checkKeys function
if (Key.isDown(Key.SPACE)){
    ...

    //initialize line
    _root.clear();
    _root.lineStyle(2,0x000000,100);
    _root.moveTo(gun._x, gun._y);


} // end if
```

The preceding code shows how to initialize the line:

- Clear any line that was on the Stage (with the `clear()` method).

- Make the line 2 pixels wide, black, and completely opaque with the `lineStyle()` method.

- Move the pen to the gun's position with the `moveTo()` command.

2. Draw the line as the bullet moves.

Each time the bullet moves, a small line segment should be drawn between the bullet's previous position and its current position. This is quite easy to accomplish:

```
//from gravityTrace.fla move function
//use drawing tools to trace the path
_root.lineTo(sprite._x, sprite._y);
```

The `lineTo()` method draws a line from the previous point to the sprite's current position. A series of small straight lines creates an illusion of a curved line.

3. **Turn off the line drawing when the bullet stops.**

When the bullet leaves the Stage, I move it off-Stage. You don't want the user to see that motion, so whenever the bullet hits a screen boundary, I turn off the line drawing capability by setting the line style to invisible. The following code shows how to turn off the line-drawing mechanism:

```
//from gravityTrace.fla move function boundary checking
//turn off line drawing
_root.lineStyle(0,0x000000,0);
```

The lineStyle property is changed to make the line invisible.

- The line style is set to a width of 0 points and a transparency of 0, so the line is indeed drawn, but it's invisible.

- The next time the player fires the cannon, the line style is reset to be visible again.

Calculating the Vector from dx and dy

It's common to have a vector that you need to convert to dx and dy values, but sometimes you must go in the opposite direction. You might have a situation where you

✔ Know the location of two objects

✔ Need the angle and distance between the objects

The followMouse.fla program featured in Figure 11-13 is such a situation. The program calculates the cannon's angle and velocity by calculating the relative position between the mouse and the cannon.

In this program, the difference between the mouse's position and the cannon's position is used to determine the values for dx and dy. By using some other calculations, the dx and dy values are turned into angle and speed. As usual, I start with a simpler example that boils down the key ideas. The dxdyToVec.fla program, as shown in Figure 11-14, is just such a utility.

I copied much of the design from the vecProj program, simply moving around the variables. Once again, all the code is in the button press event handler.

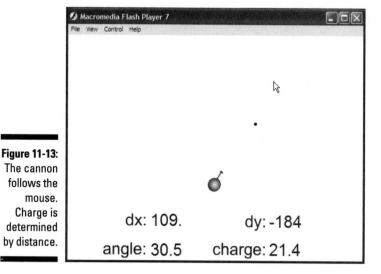

Figure 11-13:
The cannon
follows the
mouse.
Charge is
determined
by distance.

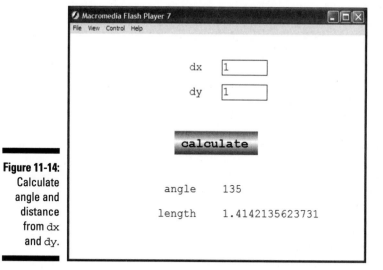

Figure 11-14:
Calculate
angle and
distance
from dx
and dy.

Listing 11-4 shows the button code for dxdyToVec.

Listing 11-4: dxdyToVec Program btnCalc() Function

```
//from dxdyToVec
btnCalc.onRelease = function(){
  //calculate angle and length from dx and dy
  //use atan to get angle, pythagoras to get length

  radians = Math.atan(dy/dx);

  //convert to degrees
  degrees = radians * 180 / Math.PI;

  //offset the angle
  degrees += 90;

  //handle negative dx angles
  if (dx <0) {
    degrees -=180;
  } // end if

  angle = degrees;

  //use pythagorean theorem to calculate length
  length = Math.sqrt(dx*dx + dy*dy);

} // end btnCalc
```

Determining the angle

Converting values from dx and dy to the angle is done by using the arctangent function. If you know dx and dy, you can derive the angle a by the formula

$$a = atan(dy/dx)$$

To process the angle, follow these steps:

1. **Calculate the angle by using the arctangent function.**

   The arctan result is in radians, so you should use a variable name to help you remember that fact:

   ```
   radians = Math.atan(dy/dx);
   ```

2. **Convert the measurement to degrees.**

   If you rotate an object using the _rotation property, you need the angle measured in degrees.

   ```
   //convert to degrees
   degrees = radians * 180 / Math.PI;
   ```

3. **Offset the measurement by 90 degrees.**

   The math world and navigation worlds have different 0 marks. When you measure in degrees, north is usually 0, so add 90 to your new variable to compensate.

   ```
   //offset the angle
   degrees += 90;
   ```

4. **Manage negative dx values.**

   The arctangent function is based on triangles, so it gets a little mixed up when angle measurements are larger than 180 degrees. (A triangle can't have an angle larger than or equal to 180 degrees.)

   To deal with this problem, check whether dx is negative. If dx is negative, subtract 180 degrees from the measurement, like this:

   ```
   //handle negative dx angles
   if (dx <0) {
     degrees -=180;
   } // end if
   ```

   The result is the vector's angle:

   ```
   angle = degrees;
   ```

Determining the vector length

The vector length is actually a lot easier to calculate than the angle. A simple application of the Pythagorean theorem does the trick:

```
//use pythagorean theorem to calculate length
length = Math.sqrt(dx*dx + dy*dy);
```

Generate the square root by using the `sqrt` method of the `Math` object.

You could also use a `Math.pow()` method to generate the squares, but in this case, I find it easier to simply multiply the values by themselves.

Following the Mouse

You can modify the `dxDyToVec` technique to make the cannon follow the mouse.

Most of this program is just like the other cannon programs, so I highlight only those areas that make it unique.

Programming the EnterFrame event

In the previous versions of the program, you check the keyboard and move the bullet in the `enterFrame` event. Now all the tasks formerly assigned to the keyboard are delegated to the mouse. The `enterFrame` method is still simple:

```
_root.onEnterFrame = function(){
  followMouse();
  move(bullet);
} // end enterFrame
```

Building the followMouse routine

Following the mouse is very much like the vector projection routine described earlier in this chapter. Listing 11-5 shows the `followMouse()` function.

Listing 11-5:   Follow Mouse Program followMouse() Function

```
//from followMouse.fla
function followMouse(){
  //calculate gun's direction based on its relationship to
  //the mouse

  dx = _root._xmouse - gun._x;
  dy = _root._ymouse - gun._y;
  radians = Math.atan(dy/dx);
  degrees = radians * 180 / Math.PI;
  degrees += 90;
  if (dx <0) {
    degrees -=180;
  } // end if
  gun.dir = degrees;
  gun._rotation = degrees;


  //charge is distance from gun to mouse divided by 10
  distance = Math.sqrt(dx*dx + dy*dy);
  gun.charge = distance / 10;

} // end followMouse
```

The process for making an object point toward the mouse is straightforward:

1. **Determine the difference in location between the object and the mouse.**

   - Use the _root._xmouse and _root._ymouse properties to determine the location of the mouse.

   - Use the _x and _y properties of the object to determine where it is.

2. **Calculate dx by subtracting the object's x position from the mouse's x position.**

   ```
   dx = _root._xmouse - gun._x;
   ```

3. **Calculate dy by subtracting the y position of the object from the y position of the mouse.**

   ```
   dy = _root._ymouse - gun._y;
   ```

4. **Calculate the angle in radians with the arctangent function.**

   ```
   radians = Math.atan(dy/dx);
   ```

5. **Convert the angle to degrees.**

   ```
   degrees = radians * 180 / Math.PI;
   ```

6. **Offset the degree measurement by 90 degrees.**

   ```
   degrees += 90;
   ```

7. **Compensate for negative dx values.**

   ```
   if (dx <0) {
      degrees -=180;
   } // end if
   ```

8. **Set the direction property of the object.**

   ```
   gun.dir = degrees;
   ```

9. **Set the rotation property of the object to change the visual orientation of the object.**

   ```
   gun._rotation = degrees;
   ```

10. **Calculate the power of the charge based on the distance.**

    Often when you have objects follow the mouse, the relative angle between the mouse and the object is the only thing you're worried about. In this case, you also use the distance to get an initial charge for the gun.

    In the followMouse() routine, I modify the speed of the bullet. I divide the length of the vector by 10 because when I use the actual distance as the initial velocity of the ball, it often shoots across the screen too quickly to be seen.

    ```
    //charge is distance from gun to mouse divided by 10
    distance = Math.sqrt(dx*dx + dy*dy);
    gun.charge = distance / 10;
    ```

When you see an animation of a person or creature with eyes that seem to follow the mouse, it works basically like this program. In most of those animations, only the angle matters.

Responding to the mouse click

Movie clip objects (including the _root object) can respond to mouse clicks. In fact, they have an event designed specifically to look for this type of situation.

In the followMouse version of the game, the cannon is fired by clicking the mouse — not by keyboard action. The following code shows how to respond to the mouse click:

```
_root.onMouseUp = function(){
    //move the bullet
    bullet._x = gun._x;
    bullet._y = gun._y;

    bullet.dir = gun.dir;
    bullet.speed = gun.charge;
    turn(bullet);
} // end mouseUp
```

Responding to a mouse click is pretty easy:

- The onMouseUp event automatically occurs when the mouse is released anywhere over the application.

- All the code that had been attached to the keyboard spacebar event is moved to the mouse's release event.

    Mouse input is often preferred if the user is already using the mouse for navigation.

Chapter 12

Vehicle Motion

· ·

In This Chapter

▶ Understanding basic physics principles

▶ Generating motion vectors

▶ Building a realistic car

▶ Modeling spacecraft

▶ Making sprites with multiple states

▶ Adding drift to vehicles

· ·

Many arcade games involve various kinds of vehicles. If you've looked at some of the other chapters in this book, you've seen several good ways to handle vehicles. More interesting and realistic vehicles require a closer approximation to the actual behavior of these objects. The study of how objects move is a part of physics, but you don't need a lot of fancy physics to use it in your games. Frankly, the most realistic physics models require so much mathematics that are very difficult to write and run very slowly on interpreted platforms like Flash. Most games use approximations of physics rules, not actual physics. This chapter shows several ways to move an object onscreen so it behaves more naturally.

Newton without the Figs

Isaac Newton would be a great game programmer. He was interested in understanding how objects move. He proposed three laws of motion that guide all game programmers.

Newton's First Law

Newton's First Law seems really simple at first:

An object in motion stays in motion. An object at rest stays at rest.

I have my own summary of this law:

If it ain't movin', it ain't movin'. If it is, it is.

There's one strange thing about this simple rule: It doesn't seem to be true. Sure, if you have a rock in the middle of the field and nothing touches it, the rock doesn't move. But so far, every time I've ever thrown a rock, it stopped moving eventually.

Newton was aware of this. The reason why balls stop rolling and things stop moving is that lots of forces act on things:

- **An object moving in a perfect vacuum indeed keeps moving at the same trajectory indefinitely.** When you code a spaceship flying in space, you need it to have that behavior. An object on the surface of a planet is different because it eventually stops. When you roll a ball on a flat plane, the ball faces wind resistance and friction from the ground. These forces slow the ball.

- **When you drive a car, you constant apply gas to keep a constant speed.** You're actually applying the force necessary to compensate for air resistance and friction.

Whenever you model the motion of some object, you need to compensate for Newton's First Law regarding these forces. You can simulate different kinds of motion by understanding and manipulating the forces. For example, a spaceship has no rolling resistance nor wind resistance but also no *traction* (the tendency to go in the direction it's pointed). You model its motion differently than how you model a racecar, which has wind resistance, rolling resistance, and traction. If you can change these values, you can easily model the behavior of a racing car or cargo truck. With a little more modification, you can model the behavior of a boat or spacecraft.

In game programming, think of each force acting on an object as a vector. Each vector can be broken into dx and dy components:

- Add all the dx components to get the object's total change in x.

- Add all the dy components to get the object's total change in y.

Newton's Second Law

Newton's Second Law helps you figure out exactly how much force you need to overcome Newton's First Law.

Some basic definitions

Force is the amount of work necessary to move an object. Force is a vector with a magnitude and a direction.

Mass is the amount of matter in an object. Things with more mass are more difficult to move and stop.

In normal conversation, you might use the terms *mass* and *weight* interchangeably, but that isn't precisely correct:

✔ **An object's *mass* never changes (unless the object changes).**

An object with a mass of 10 *kilograms* always has that mass, whether sitting on Earth, orbiting Earth, or sitting on the Moon.

✔ **An object's *weight* depends on its mass and the local gravity.**

A 10-kilogram object (on Earth) weighs about 1.6 kilograms on the Moon, or nearly 0 pounds in orbit.

Acceleration is a measurement of how the object's motion is changing. It is a vector quantity.

My own eloquent summary of this law is this:

The faster you want something to move, the harder and longer you kick it.

Newton's Second Law is more officially summarized by this formula:

```
Force = Mass * Acceleration
```

This is sometimes shortened to `F = ma` or `a = F/m` (but I think my version is much less stuffy).

The `F = ma` equation neatly summarizes the relationship among force, mass, and acceleration:

✔ Force is required to move something.

✔ You need more force to move something faster.

✔ You need more force if the object has more mass.

If you know two of these variables, you can solve for the third. In game programming, you often know the amount of acceleration you want to apply, and you might need to calculate the force necessary. You use a variation of the formula `a = F/m` to derive this value.

Just make a bigger engine!

You'd think that Newton's Second Law would give you a simple formula for making really fast vehicles, but it isn't always that simple. The classic example of this is the famous Gee Bee racing planes of the 1930s. The designers took a huge bomber engine and wrapped the tiniest possible airplane around it. The plane was fast because the amount of force available through the engine was enormous, and the mass was quite small. Unfortunately, the small lifting and control surfaces made the aircraft difficult to fly. Several pilots were killed trying to fly the beast.

Newton's Second Law is useful because you can use it to account easily for the mass of a vehicle or object. Game programmers often take shortcuts in the actual calculations (as I do in most of the programs presented in this book). Still, you need to understand this principle because you can use it to make different kinds of objects act differently. For example, a big boat with a small motor doesn't accelerate nearly as well as a small boat with a big motor.

Newton's Third Law

Newton's Third Law describes how rocket engines can move spacecraft:

Every action is coupled with an equal and opposite reaction.

If you stand on a skateboard and throw a bowling ball off the front of the board (preferably not in a china shop), the skateboard moves backward. Once again, I will illustrate why these are called Newton's laws and not Harris' laws:

When you throw a rock, the rock throws you.

Newton's versions sound a lot more official, but I think my interpretations have their own cachet.

Every action has an equal and opposite reaction.

Newton's Third Law explains how to add force to make something move. If you want something to move in some direction, you must apply force in the opposite direction.

A car moves forward by pushing back on the Earth with its tires. When an apple moves toward the Earth, the Earth moves, too! Of course, because of the relative masses of the two objects, the motion of the Earth is miniscule.

Newton's Third Law isn't used as much as the other two in game programming. Game programmers don't usually worry about *how* to move an object. Your code moves it. Still, it's a handy tool to know.

Physics terminology 101

I use a lot of physics words in this chapter. You can also use these terms in everyday conversation, but they have important specific meanings for programmers. Position, velocity, and acceleration are related but are different things. In the context of game programming, these terms mean the following:

✔ **Position** is the object's location on the Stage.

In this book, I use an object's built-in _x and _y properties to determine the object's position. Position is often seen as an ordered pair (x and y); however, it can also be viewed as a vector.

✔ **Velocity** is the movement of the object.

Velocity is a vector. Velocity can be viewed as either an angle and a direction or as a coordinate pair. An object's velocity is denoted by its dx and dy properties. Some objects have direction and speed properties, but in most of my games, speed and direction are used to generate dx and dy.

✔ **Speed** is the magnitude of the velocity vector.

Speed isn't the same as velocity. Speed is an ordinary number (scalar); velocity is a vector.

✔ **Acceleration** is the rate of change in an object's speed.

If velocity (dx) is the change in x, acceleration is the change in dx (ddx). In practice, when you add some value to dx or dy, you accelerate the object. Acceleration is a vector although I don't always have specific acceleration properties. I simply add values to dx and dy to effect acceleration.

✔ **Deceleration** isn't really important! Deceleration is simply acceleration in the opposite direction.

To decelerate, add a motion vector in the opposite of the direction of travel.

Newton and Vectors

The reason all this talk about Newton, forces, and vectors is important is that the vectors that act on an object can be combined to create one motion vector. A balloon floating in the air looks very simple, but it's a very complex balance of forces.

Empty balloons fall to Earth

Figure 12-1 shows an empty balloon in the `balloon.fla` program.

No other forces are at work, so the balloon moves downward.

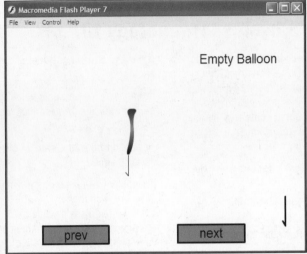

Figure 12-1:
Gravity pulls down an empty balloon.

The `balloon.fla` program illustrated in Figure 12-1 (and on the book's companion Web site) shows that the balloon is moving downward. It's much better to see the actual motion than just to look at these still pictures in the book.

The little diagram at the lower right of Figure 12-1 illustrates the total force acting on the balloon. You could call gravity a vector, with its own dx and dy values. Gravity is the only force acting on the balloon, so you could use the following formula:

```
balloon.dx = 0;
balloon.dy = 0;
balloon.dx += gravityDX;
balloon.dy += gravityDY;
```

Adding helium to the balloon

Figure 12-2 shows the balloon after it's filled with helium. Gravity still exerts a downward force, but that force is counteracted by the buoyancy of the helium.

The vectors drawn onto the balloon illustrate the two opposing forces. The small diagram at the bottom right duplicates these vectors. If gravity pulls the balloon downward some amount (for argument, say 3 pixels per frame [ppf]), but buoyancy pulls up the balloon (how about 5 ppf?), the resulting vector is a compromise. The balloon rises 2 ppf.

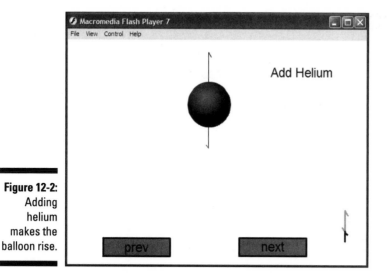

Figure 12-2:
Adding
helium
makes the
balloon rise.

The code looks something like this:

```
balloon.dx = 0;
balloon.dy = 0;
balloon.dx += gravityDX;
balloon.dy += gravityDY;
balloon.dx += bouyancyDX;
balloon.dy += bouyancyDY;
```

Bringing wind into the mix

You can keep adding vectors all day long if you need to represent other forces. Figure 12-3 shows what happens if a breeze is blowing.

In Figure 12-3, the balloon appears to move diagonally upward. This simple diagonal vector is actually the combination of three forces at work:

The vector diagram in Figure 12-3 shows how the forces interact. Here's the code to compensate for the wind:

```
balloon.dx = 0;
balloon.dy = 0;
balloon.dx += gravityDX;
balloon.dy += gravityDY;
balloon.dx += bouyancyDX;
balloon.dy += bouyancyDY;
balloon.dx += windDX;
balloon.dy += windDY;
```

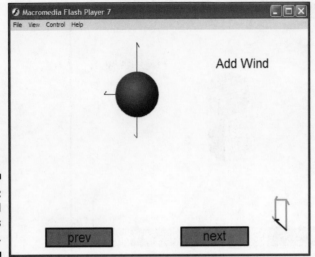

Figure 12-3:
The wind
adds its
own vector.

This code shows that you can model as complicated of a system as you want. For every force that you want to add to your system, simply

1. Break the force into `dx` and `dy` variables.

2. Add the force's `dx` to the object's `dx`.

3. Add the force's `dy` to the object's `dy`.

Don't tie me down

Sometimes what seems to be the simplest situation is actually quite complex. Imagine a balloon filled with helium, drifting in the wind but tied down with a string. Even if the balloon seems to be motionless, many forces are acting on the balloon.

Figure 12-4 illustrates the forces acting on a tied-down balloon.

If the balloon is tied to a string, it seems motionless, but the forces acting on it haven't gone away. This apparent contradiction is solved by noting that the string itself exerts force on the balloon. If the string is strong enough, it can counteract the buoyancy and wind forces and keep the balloon in place. Notice that the vector has turned into a simple dot.

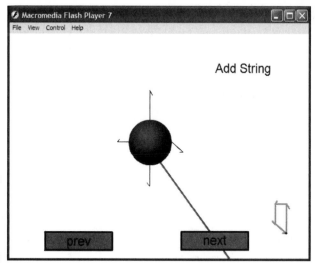

Figure 12-4:
Now the
balloon is
tied down.

If an object is still, all the forces acting on it are balanced, and the net motion vector is 0 (zero).

I used Flash's built-in motion tweening to make this example program. It worked, but it wasn't easier than writing the code by hand. After you know how to use code, it's often easier to code your programs than to use the "easy" way.

Baby, You Can Drive My Car

Some of the preceding chapters in this book show an example of basic vehicle motion. Chapter 11 describes how to work with basic vectors. You can create all kinds of vehicles with interesting motion when you

- ✔ Use Newton's laws of motion.
- ✔ Translate standard (speed and direction) vectors to the dx and dy values needed by ActionScript.

The first variation is a simple car shown in Figure 12-5. It doesn't look very different from the car featured in earlier chapters, but the car steers much more smoothly. It combines two major ideas:

- ✔ The basic car (and monster) motion routines in Chapter 9
- ✔ The vector techniques described in Chapter 11

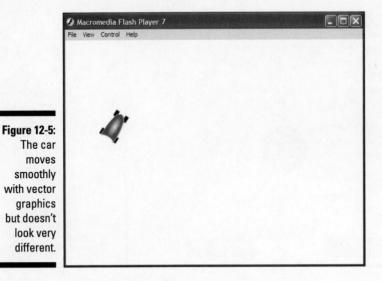

Figure 12-5:
The car
moves
smoothly
with vector
graphics
but doesn't
look very
different.

I use vector projection so that the car can turn at any angle. Listing 12-1 is the code for the car vector program.

Listing 12-1: carVector Program

```
//carVector
//use vector projection to go any speed, any direction

init();
function init(){
  car.speed = 0;
  //direction is now in degrees
  car.dir = 33;
}

car.onEnterFrame = function(){
  checkKeys();
  turn(car);
  move(car);
} // end enterFrame

function turn(sprite){
  //use vector projection to get DX and DY

  //offset the angle
  degrees = sprite.dir -90;

  //convert to radians
  radians = degrees / 180 * Math.PI;
```

```
    //get DX and DY (normalized: length is one)
    sprite.dx = Math.cos(radians);
    sprite.dy = Math.sin(radians);

    //compensate for speed
    sprite.dx *= sprite.speed;
    sprite.dy *= sprite.speed;
} // end turn;

function move(sprite){
    //moves any sprite, wrapping around boundaries

    //move
    sprite._x += sprite.dx;
    sprite._y += sprite.dy;

    //rotate changed slightly.
    sprite._rotation = sprite.dir;

    //check boundaries - wrap all directions
    if (sprite._x > Stage.width){
        sprite._x = 0;
    } // end if

    if (sprite._x < 0){
        sprite._x = Stage.width;
    } // end if

    if (sprite._y > Stage.height){
        sprite._y = 0;
    } // end if

    if (sprite._y < 0){
        sprite._y = Stage.height;
    } // end if
} // end move

function checkKeys(){
    //check keyboard to move car
    if (Key.isDown(Key.UP)){
        car.speed++;
        if (car.speed > 8){
            car.speed = 8;
        } // end if
    } // end if

    if (Key.isDown(Key.DOWN)){
        car.speed--;
        if (car.speed < -3){
            car.speed = -3;
        } // end if
    } // end if
```

(continued)

Listing 12-1 *(continued)*

```
if (Key.isDown(Key.RIGHT)){
  car.dir += 5;
  if (car.dir > 360){
    car.dir = 5;
  } // end if
} // end if

if (Key.isDown(Key.LEFT)){
  car.dir -= 5;
  if (car.dir < 0){
    car.dir = 355;
  } // end if
} // end if

} // end checkKeys
```

Checking keys for vector input

The basic setup of the carVector program is nothing new. I create a car sprite facing north. The carVector code contains

✔ The same init(), move(), and enterFrame() functions used in the Monster Traffic game in Chapters 9 and 10

✔ A different turn() function than the turn function in the Monster Traffic game

The following code fragment shows a minor change in the checkKeys() function:

```
//from carVector.fla checkKeys function
if (Key.isDown(Key.RIGHT)){
  car.dir += 5;
  if (car.dir > 360){
    car.dir = 5;
  } // end if
} // end if

if (Key.isDown(Key.LEFT)){
  car.dir -= 5;
  if (car.dir < 0){
    car.dir = 355;
  } // end if
} // end if
```

The code for the arrow keys shows a couple of new ideas:

- ✔ The car's direction is stored in degrees instead of the arbitrary directions used in Chapter 9. When the user presses the right- or left-arrow key, the car's direction changes by 5 degrees.

- ✔ The boundary-checking code reflects 360 degrees in a circle.

Turning the car

In carVector, the turn() function calculates dx and dy (like other the turn() functions in Chapter 9).

The following version of turn() incorporates the vector projection principles so the user can turn in arbitrary angles:

```
function turn(sprite){
  //use vector projection to get DX and DY

  //offset the angle
  degrees = sprite.dir -90;

  //convert to radians
  radians = degrees / 180 * Math.PI;

  //get DX and DY (normalized: length is one)
  sprite.dx = Math.cos(radians);
  sprite.dy = Math.sin(radians);

  //compensate for speed
  sprite.dx *= sprite.speed;
  sprite.dy *= sprite.speed;
} // end turn;
```

Making an object-oriented car

Object-oriented programming (OOP) makes code elements easier to reuse. You can add properties to your objects with reckless abandon, or convert functions to methods.

Methods are a lot like functions, but methods are attached to a specific object.

The following `carVectorOOP` program is functionally identical to the `carVector` program from the preceding section (Listing 12-1). Listing 12-2 in the object-oriented programming (OOP) version shows how object-oriented features in Chapter 6 can be combined with vector projection.

Listing 12-2:   carVectorOOP Program

```
//carVectorOOP
//convert carVector to OOP notation
//by changing all functions to methods

init();
function init(){
  car.speed = 0;
  //direction is now in degrees
  car.dir = 33;
} // end init

car.onEnterFrame = function(){
  this.checkKeys();
  this.turn();
  this.move();
} // end enterFrame

car.turn = function(){
  //use vector projection to get DX and DY

  //offset the angle
  degrees = this.dir -90;

  //convert to radians
  radians = degrees / 180 * Math.PI;

  //get DX and DY (normalized: length is one)
  this.dx = Math.cos(radians);
  this.dy = Math.sin(radians);

  //compensate for speed
  this.dx *= this.speed;
  this.dy *= this.speed;
} // end turn;

car.move = function(){
  //moves any this, wrapping around boundaries

  //move
  this._x += this.dx;
  this._y += this.dy;

  //rotate changed slightly.
  this._rotation = this.dir;
```

```
    //check boundaries - wrap all directions
    if (this._x > Stage.width){
      this._x = 0;
    } // end if

    if (this._x < 0){
      this._x = Stage.width;
    } // end if

    if (this._y > Stage.height){
      this._y = 0;
    } // end if

    if (this._y < 0){
      this._y = Stage.height;
    } // end if
} // end move

car.checkKeys = function(){
    //check keyboard to move car
    if (Key.isDown(Key.UP)){
      car.speed++;
      if (car.speed > 8){
        car.speed = 8;
      } // end if
    } // end if

    if (Key.isDown(Key.DOWN)){
      car.speed--;
      if (car.speed < -3){
        car.speed = -3;
      } // end if
    } // end if

    if (Key.isDown(Key.RIGHT)){
      car.dir += 5;
      if (car.dir > 360){
        car.dir = 0;
      } // end if
    } // end if

    if (Key.isDown(Key.LEFT)){
      car.dir -= 5;
      if (car.dir < 0){
        car.dir = 360;
      } // end if
    } // end if

} // end checkKeys
```

In Listing 12-2, the actual code is the same as Listing 12-1, `carVector`. The only difference is how the functions are organized. For example, Table 12-1 is a line-by-line comparison of `carVector` and `carVectorOOP`. The OOP code in `carVectorOOP` changes the functions into methods.

Table 12-1	**Comparison of carVector and carVectorOOP**	
Line	*carVector*	*carVectorOOP*
1	`Car.onEnterFrame =` `function(){`	`car.onEnterFrame =` `function(){`
2	`checkKeys();`	`this.checkKeys();`
3	`turn(car);`	`this.turn();`
4	`move(car);`	`this.move();`
5	`} // end enterFrame`	`} // end enterFrame`

A *method* is a function attached to a particular object. Just like a property is a variable attached to some sort of object, a method is a function attached to an object.

A method is something an object knows how to do.

The keyword `this` refers to the current object. Inside the `car.onEnterFrame` event, the keyword `this` refers to the `car` object. Each of the standard functions changes as well:

```
function turn(sprite){
```

becomes

```
car.turn = function(){
```

There is no need to send a parameter to the function. Now that it's a method of the `car` object, you can use the `this` keyword to refer to the car. So, inside the `turn` method, you can refer to the sprite's properties through the `this` keyword, so

```
sprite.dx
```

becomes

```
this.dx
```

For many programs, it doesn't much matter whether you use objects. When code is more complicated, the object-oriented style makes it easier to build many copies of a complex object. Chapter 13 shows how to make swarms of objects.

Making an even better car

The `carParam` program shown in Figure 12-6 illustrates a car with so many nifty gadgets that even James Bond is jealous.

I haven't added a rocket launcher, but it's easy to do.

Figure 12-6:
This car has all kinds of parameters for you to test and change.

(Macromedia Flash Player 7 window)

drag % : 35
power : 3
turn : 5
brakes : 1

speed : 5.57142
dir : 35
dx : 3.19563
dy : -4.5638

The `carParam` program lets you experiment with various features of a car so you can make vehicles that act exactly as you want. You can type your own values into the top four text boxes and then drive the car onscreen to see how it works.

The car has four main parameters:

✔ `drag`: This is the sum of the forces that slow the car.

Think of this variable as a combination of friction and wind resistance.

You can separate variables for all the various types of friction, but for this simple model, I combine all elements that slow the car with drag.

In `carParam`, drag is expressed as a percentage:

- *100 percent* means the drag forces are so strong that the car will never move, no matter how powerful the engine is.

- *0 percent* means that the car is efficient, is never slowed, and has an infinite top speed.

The default setting for drag is 35 percent:

- Set a lower `drag` value for a zippier car.

- Set a higher `drag` value for a more sluggish response.

The `drag` and `power` variables work together to determine the top speed of the car. A force based on the `drag` value is multiplied by the car's speed each frame to slow the car. Even a fast-moving car eventually slows because of drag.

✔ `power`: This simulates the engine's power. Power is applied in the direction the car faces.

The `power` value affects the acceleration, which in turn affects speed. A car with high power accelerates well, but it might not have a high top speed if the drag is set high.

✔ `turnRate`: This is the turning rate of the car. It indicates how many degrees per frame the car turns when an arrow key is pressed. A high turn rate generates a car with a fast response.

This version of the program assumes a perfect suspension with no skidding. Later in this chapter, the boat example shows a program with a sliding effect.

✔ `brakes`: This is the stopping power of the car.

With the drag effect, you won't really need brakes unless the car's drag ratio is extremely low. What self-respecting arcade gamer wants to slow down anyway? Still, brakes can be used for some interesting effects, and they're easy to model.

Change the various parameters in the text boxes and use the arrow keys to drive the car. You can add a lot of variety to the car with these four variables. As you're driving, watch how the car's other characteristics (speed, direction, `dx`, and `dy`) change.

The most striking feature of this program is the smooth acceleration and deceleration (especially at low drag levels). The top speed of the car is no longer determined by a simple condition but rather by the interplay of the `power` and `drag` variables. When you stop accelerating, the car coasts for a while and eventually glides to a stop. You can adjust the turning rate so the car feels like anything from a roadster to an aircraft carrier.

Because the car drives quite quickly in this example, I changed the default frame rate from 12 frames per second (fps) to 24 fps to get smooth animation. You can change the frame rate easily by changing the frame rate property when the stage is selected. Change your frame rate before you start programming, so all your motion values will change with the frame rate. (For example, moving at 3 ppf at 24 fps is just like moving 6 ppf at 12 fps.)

Coding the parameter car

You can build many kinds of vehicles by adjusting a few well-designed parameters.

The physics model of the carParam program still isn't realistic, but it more nearly approximates the actual physical properties of a motorized vehicle. To build a car with these parameters, follow these steps:

1. **Build an object-oriented car like the car in carVecOOP.**

   Your car should have all the standard properties and methods as in the other car examples in this chapter. In Listing 12-3, the init code illustrates the standard parameters for my souped-up car.

Listing 12-3:   carParam Program init() Function

```
//from carParam
function init(){
  //direction is now in degrees
  car.dir = 0;

  //getting values from screen
  //would normally be initialized here
  //car properties
  //car.drag = 35;
  //car.power = 3;
  //car.turnRate = 5;
  //car.brakes = 1;

  car.speed = 0;
  car.dx = 0;
  car.dy = 0;

} // end init
```

The car needs speed, dir, dx, and dy properties, plus the four new properties: drag, power, turnRate, and brakes.

In the `carParam` init function, I get values for the car's `drag`, `power`, `turnRate`, and `brakes` properties from text boxes on the screen. Normally these values are written into the code. I include some property assignments but comment them out. In a normal situation, you don't pull initialization settings from the screen.

2. **Write the `enterFrame` code to indicate what things happen during each frame.**

For each frame, my code looks like this:

```
car.onEnterFrame = function(){
  car.getNumbers();
  car.checkKeys();
  car.turn();
  car.move();
} // end enterFrame
```

Most of this is familiar stuff. `checkKeys`, `turn`, and `move` are equivalent to the functions in `carVectorOOP` from earlier in this chapter. Only the `getNumbers()` method is new. This method takes the property values from the screen and converts them into a useable form.

3. **Incorporate the turning rate in the `checkKeys()` method.**

The following code shows how to use the turning rate to adjust how quickly the car turns:

```
//from carParam checkKeys function
if (Key.isDown(Key.RIGHT)){
  car.dir += car.turnRate;
    if (car.dir > 360){
    car.dir = car.turnRate;
  } // end if
} // end if

if (Key.isDown(Key.LEFT)){
  car.dir -= car.turnRate;
  if (car.dir < 0){
    car.dir = 360 - car.turnRate;
  } // end if
} // end if
```

The `checkKeys` code adjusts the car's direction by the `turnRate`. If the direction passes the 360-degree value, it is moved to the next appropriate value. (Similar code handles rotation to the left.)

4. **Get accelerator and brake input in the `checkKeys()` method.**

The up- and down-arrow keys control acceleration and braking. In this model, the input is actually much simpler, as the following code shows:

```
//from carParam checkKeys function
if (Key.isDown(Key.UP)){
  car.speed += car.power;
} // end if

if (Key.isDown(Key.DOWN)){
  if (car.speed > -3){
    car.speed -= car.brakes;
  } // end if
} // end if
```

Here's how the up- and down-arrow keys work in `carParam`:

- *When the user presses the up key, increment the car's speed by the car's power.*

  You don't need to look for an upper boundary for the speed because the `drag` value takes care of that.

- *The down arrow subtracts the car's braking force from the car speed.*

If the speed is less than –3, the braking force is not subtracted from the car's speed. This limits the car's backward velocity to 3 ppf regardless of the `drag` and `power` settings.

5. **Calculate `dx` and `dy` in the `turn()` method.**

   In Listing 12-4, the `turn` method uses the same vector-projection scheme as `carVectorOOP`, but `carParam` also incorporates the `drag` rating.

Listing 12-4:   carParam Program car.turn() Method

```
//from carParam.fla
car.turn = function(){
  //use vector projection to get DX and DY

  //offset the angle
  degrees = this.dir -90;

  //convert to radians
  radians = degrees / 180 * Math.PI;

  //get DX and DY (normalized: length is one)
  this.dx = Math.cos(radians);
  this.dy = Math.sin(radians);

  //incorporate drag
  tempDrag = 1 - (car.drag/100);
  this.speed *= tempDrag;

  //compensate for speed
  this.dx *= this.speed;
  this.dy *= this.speed;

} // end turn;
```

The only unfamiliar line in Listing 12-4 is the one that incorporates drag. The drag ratio is meant to be a value between 0 (zero) and 100. I use this value to calculate a percentage between 0 and 1. I then subtract this value from 1 and multiply the vehicle's speed by the result. When you multiply the speed by tempDrag, the speed decreases. This means that various forces are always causing the car to slow. The engine's power is strong enough to compensate, but when the car is no longer accelerating, the speed gets smaller and smaller until it becomes negligible.

6. Stop the car at slow speeds.

The sidebar, "Stop that car!" shows a special case to make a coasting car stop.

7. Grab variables from the screen if you need them.

Generally, you won't worry about pulling car data from onscreen text boxes, but I wanted an illustration that was easy to experiment with.

As I was working on the carParam program, I discovered a problem: ActionScript got really confused when I asked it to read numbers from text boxes. After some analysis, I discovered that ActionScript was trying to interpret the data from the text boxes as string data (instead of numbers), thus giving me bizarre results. This is a common problem in languages like ActionScript that allow loose variable typing.

The solution for reading numbers from text boxes is pretty easy: In the enterFrame event, I call a new method called getNumbers. The following method is an easy way to read all the text fields as numeric values:

```
//from carParam.fla
car.getNumbers = function(){
  //converts all text input to numbers
  //otherwise actionScript gets confused
  car.drag = parseFloat(car.drag);
  car.power = parseFloat(car.power);
  car.turnRate = parseFloat(car.turnRate);
  car.brakes = parseFloat(car.brakes);
} // end getNumbers
```

In the car.getNumbers method, all the relevant variables are linked to input text boxes, but they are interpreted as text. The parseFloat() function takes a String value and converts it into a floating-point real number. I simply converted every value into a float and had no further problems.

Don't bother with this conversion step if you don't need it. In most of your games, the property values for the vehicles are hard-wired into the game. This demonstration helps you pick out values that make sense in your game.

Stop that car!

Using a ratio to handle drag is a clever trick, but it has one annoying problem. If I multiply the speed (say, 10) by some fraction (say, .5), the new speed becomes half the original speed. Every frame, the speed gets smaller, but it never actually equals zero! As a result, the car continues to drift very slowly after common sense says it should stop. This is easy to rectify.

The following code at the end of the `move()` method makes the stop:

```
//stop at really slow speeds
if ((this.speed > -0.5) &&
    (this.speed < 0.5)){
  this.speed = 0;
} // end if
```

If the speed descends between -0.5 and 0.5, it is set to a value of 0. This "nails down the car," so it stops as it should.

Getting Lost in Space

The car I describe throughout this chapter has absolutely no skid. It sticks to the road perfectly, going in exactly the direction it's pointed. Of course, real cars usually do that, but arcade cars always skid around crashing into stuff.

To get a vehicle with skidding behavior, here's an example that's very different than a car. Figure 12-7 shows a spacecraft flying in open space. You can run the `space.fla` program from the companion Web site to see the real effect:

```
www.dummies.com/go/flashgameprogrammingfd1e
```

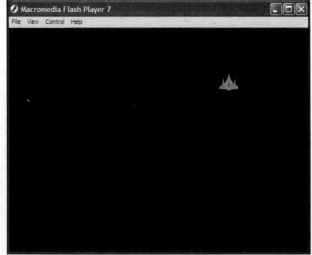

Figure 12-7: The spaceship is traveling to the right but is pointing up.

The biggest difference between the spaceship and the car is that the spaceship's direction of travel is completely decoupled from the direction it's pointing. The ship can easily travel sideways. When you press the up arrow for the spacecraft, you're actually adding a motion vector in the direction the spaceship is traveling.

Space doesn't have drag or traction, so an object in space conforms to Newton's First Law perfectly:

✔ **If it isn't moving, it stays put.**

✔ **If it's moving, it keeps moving unless a force stops it:**

　• Each time you apply thrust, you add to the ship's motion vector.

　• If you want to stop the ship, you must add the right thrust vector to cancel out *(oppose)* all the previous vectors.

The explanation given here is a simplification. Gravity is always acting on things in space. My method isn't perfect science, but it works great for space games.

Building a multi-state sprite

The spaceship has a special effect that shows little rocket thrusts when you press an arrow key:

✔ **Most of the time, the ship doesn't show any flames.**

✔ **When the user presses the arrow keys, the rocket changes to reflect its new status:**

　• The up arrow makes flames shoot out the back while accelerating.

　• The turn arrows fire little retro rockets while rotating the ship.

Figure 12-8 outlines the moods of the ship sprite.

Figure 12-8:
The ship has four states that can be activated by the program.

still　　　thrust　　　left　　　right

Each visual state is a named frame within the ship movie clip. To show any particular version, simply send the movie clip to the appropriate frame. For example, if a movie clip is named `ship`, you can call the `thrust` frame with this code:

```
ship.gotoAndStop(thrust);
```

Initializing the ship

The ship has all the typical properties and initialization.

The following code shows how to initialize the ship:

```
//from space.fla
function init(){
  //normal initialization
  myShip.dx = 0;
  myShip.dy = 0;
  myShip.speed = 0;
  myShip.dir = 0;
  myShip.gotoAndStop("still");
} // end init
```

In the `init()` code, the only new element is the code that sets the ship's visual representation to `still`. I don't want to see the flames unless I'm firing the rockets.

The `enterFrame` event is completely unsurprising:

```
myShip.onEnterFrame = function(){
  myShip.checkKeys();
  myShip.turn();
  myShip.move();
} // end if
```

As all the vehicle code has done, this program checks the keyboard, turns the ship, and moves it.

Checking for input

In Listing 12-5, the keyboard input has two differences from car games:

 ✔ The spacecraft has no brakes, so you don't need to trap for the down arrow.

 ✔ Each key press triggers a particular visual state on the ship.

Listing 12-5:   Space Program myShip.checkKeys() Method

```
//from space.fla
myShip.checkKeys = function(){
  //check for left and right arrows
  if (Key.isDown(Key.LEFT)){
    this.dir -= 10;
    this.gotoAndStop("left");
    if (this.dir < 0){
      this.dir = 350;
    } // end if

  } else if (Key.isDown(Key.RIGHT)){
    this.dir += 10;
    this.gotoAndStop("right");
    if (this.dir > 360){
      this.dir = 10;
    } // end if

  } else if (Key.isDown(Key.UP)){
  //thrust on up arrow
    this.thrustSpeed = 1;
    this.gotoAndStop("thrust");

  } else {
    this.thrustSpeed = 0;
    this.gotoAndStop("still");
  } // end if

} // end checkKeys
```

All the keyboard trapping has usually been in separate `if` statements, but in Listing 12-5, I use an `if...else if` structure. I did this so I could handle the case where none of the keys were pressed. The `else` clause handles that eventuality.

The up arrow doesn't directly control the ship's speed. Instead, it controls a special variable called `thrustSpeed`, which is either `0` or `1`. The directions are handled in the normal form. The `thrustSpeed` is used to calculate the speed in the `turn()` method.

Turning the ship

As in the car programs, the `turn()` method's job in Listing 12-6 is to convert the ship's speed and angle into `dx` and `dy` properties for the `move()` method.

Listing 12-6: Space Program myShip.turn() Method

```
//from space.fla
myShip.turn = function(){
  this._rotation = this.dir;

  //get new thrust vector
  degrees = this.dir
  degrees -= 90;
  radians = degrees * Math.PI / 180;
  thrustDX = this.thrustSpeed * Math.cos(radians);
  thrustDY = this.thrustSpeed * Math.sin(radians);

  //add thrust to dx and dy
  this.dx += thrustDX;
  this.dy += thrustDY;

} // end turn
```

In Listing 12-6, the `turn` method is different in this situation from the `turn()` function used in the car programs. The `space` program *adds* a vector to the current motion (instead of *creating* a new motion vector from the ship's current direction and speed). For example, if the ship is moving to the right but pointed up, pressing the up-arrow key adds an upward vector to the existing rightward vector, so the ship angles up and to the right.

To add to an existing motion vector, follow these steps:

1. **Calculate the dx and dy of the direction you're pointing.**

   The direction your craft is moving might or might not be the direction you're heading. Use the standard vector projection formulas from Chapter 11 to get `thrustDX` and `thrustDY` variables.

   You aren't changing the ship's dx and dy yet. Rather, you're simply figuring out how much you will change these values (if at all).

2. **Multiply your calculated dx and dy values by the thrust speed determined in the checkKeys() method.**

   In this program, there are two possible values for `thrustSpeed`:

   • *If the user is pressing the up arrow, thrustSpeed is 1.*

     If `thrustSpeed` is 1, the `thrustDX` and `thrustDY` variables have meaningful values.

   • *If the user isn't pressing the up arrow, thrustSpeed is 0.*

     If `thrustSpeed` is 0, thrustDX and thrustDY are 0.

In essence, if the thrust speed is 1, you add the calculated thrust to your spaceship's dx and dy values. If the thrust speed is 0, you add nothing to the sprite's motion vector, keeping the ship's motion the same.

3. **Add the thrust vector (thrustDX, thrustDY) to the object vector (dx, dy).**

   When vectors are broken into dx and dy components, you can add vectors by

   - *Adding the two dx components to get a new dx*
   - *Adding the two dy components to get a new dy*

With this technique, the ship's motion vector doesn't change every time the ship's direction changes. Instead, the ship's motion vector changes only when the user accelerates.

Moving the ship

The ship's move() method is just like the other move() methods throughout this chapter, so I don't show it here. If you want to see it in detail, you can view it on the Web site version of the program:

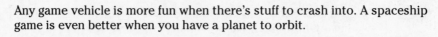

www.dummies.com/go/flashgameprogrammingfd1e

Captain, We're Caught in a Gravity Well

Any game vehicle is more fun when there's stuff to crash into. A spaceship game is even better when you have a planet to orbit.

The actual calculations for orbiting are complicated, but you can get a very realistic approximation of planetary orbits with a very simple technique.

Figure 12-9 shows the planet program, with a ship and a planet. The ship's path is traced onscreen so you can see that the pilot has skillfully (ahem) eased the craft into a parking orbit around the planet. Chapter 15 has a program called Orbit Matcher that extends the ideas of this program considerably.

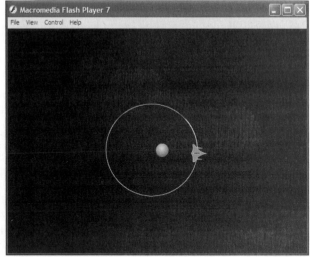

Figure 12-9:
Now the
ship has
a planet
to orbit.

Creating the universe

Adding gravitational pull to a ship is surprisingly simple:

1. **Begin with a spacecraft (as in the preceding example).**

2. **Add a movie clip called `planet` near the center of the screen.**

3. **Create a gravitational constant for the planet.**

   The following initialization code actually has two functions:

   • *Adds a gravity property to the planet*

   • *Turns on line drawing*

     I'm doing this so you see a trace of the ship's orbits in these pictures, but it's darn cool, anyway.

```
function init(){
  //create the ship

  myShip.dx = 0;
  myShip.dy = 0;
  myShip.speed = 0;
  myShip.dir = 0;
  myShip.gotoAndStop("still");

  planet.gravity = 1000;
```

```
    //set up drawing
    _root.lineStyle(.5,0xffffff,100);
    _root.moveTo(myShip._x, myShip._y);

} // end init
```

For `planet.fla`, most of the code is nearly the same as `space.fla`, but the ship's `enterFrame` event has this addition in `planet.fla`:

```
myShip.onEnterFrame = function(){
  myShip.checkKeys();
  myShip.turn();
  myShip.move();
  myShip.gravitate(planet)
} // end enter frame
```

In `planet.fla`, the `gravitate()` method tells the ship to calculate a gravitational pull from the planet based on that planet's `gravity` property.

I'm pulling for you . . .

In Listing 12-7, the `gravitate` method uses a very simple approximation of planetary gravitation.

Listing 12-7:   Planet Program gravitate() Method

```
myShip.gravitate = function(focus){
  //pull this element to the focus object
  //assumes focus object has a gravity property

  //figure angle difference between ship and planet
  tempDX = this._x - focus._x;
  tempDY = this._y - focus._y;

  //calculate distance between ship and planet
  tempDistance = Math.sqrt(tempDX * tempDX + tempDY * tempDY);

  //normalize vector (make it length of one)
  tempDX /= tempDistance;
  tempDY /= tempDistance;

  //compensate for the planet's gravitational pull
  tempDX *= focus.gravity / (tempDistance * tempDistance);
  tempDY *= focus.gravity / (tempDistance * tempDistance);

  //invert the vector so it pulls ship to planet
  tempDX *= -1;
  tempDY *= -1;
```

```
   //add vector to ship
   this.dx += tempDX;
   this.dy += tempDY;
} // end gravitate
```

You can create a simple planetary gravity well like this:

1. **Attach a `gravitate` method to the moving object.**

   This method should accept some other movie clip as its focus.

2. **Give the `focus` object a `gravity` property.**

   The `focus` sprite needs a `gravity` property. I've found that large values (in the range of 100–1000) seem to work best. The larger the value, the more gravitational pull the object has.

   The `gravity` property really refers to the focus object's mass. You probably should set the `gravity` property in the `init()` code of your program.

3. **Calculate the difference in `x` and `y` between the object and the focus.**

   I call the difference between objects `tempDX` and `tempDY` in the `gravitate()` code:

   ```
   //figure angle difference between ship and planet
   tempDX = this._x - focus._x;
   tempDY = this._y - focus._y;
   ```

4. **Determine the distance between the ship and the planet.**

   The good ol' Pythagorean theorem handles this task admirably (as shown in Chapter 11). The distance is used in a couple of ways.

   ```
   //calculate distance between ship and planet
   tempDistance = Math.sqrt(tempDX * tempDX + tempDY * tempDY);
   ```

5. **Normalize the distance vector.**

   To make any meaningful calculations on the direction between the ship and the `focus` object, you must convert the `dx` and `dy` values to a vector of length 1.

   Get the normal (length 1) vector by dividing both `tempDX` and `tempDY` by `tempDistance`:

   ```
   //normalize vector (make it length of one)
   tempDX /= tempDistance;
   tempDY /= tempDistance;
   ```

6. **Calculate the gravitational pull of the planet on the ship.**

The standard formula for this is $g = m/r2$: Check Chapter 14 for a variation used when both objects have similar mass.

- g *is the gravitational force.*
- m *is the mass of the dominant object.*

  In this program, m is the focus object's `gravity` property. I'm ignoring the mass of the ship, as it's much smaller than the mass of the planet.

- r *is the distance from the center of the object's mass.*

  In this program, r is the distance between the two objects.

To find a vector representing the gravitational pull of a planet, solve for `tempDX` and `tempDY`, like this:

```
//compensate for the planet's gravitational pull
tempDX *= focus.gravity / (tempDistance * tempDistance);
tempDY *= focus.gravity / (tempDistance * tempDistance);
```

7. Invert the gravitational pull.

If you run the program as shown here, the gravitational force pushes the ship away from the planet.

Gravity pulls objects together, so simply invert `tempDX` and `tempDY`. The following code accomplishes this:

```
//invert the vector so it pulls ship to planet
tempDX *= -1;
tempDY *= -1;
```

8. Add the gravity vector to the ship's normal motion vector.

After you calculate the gravitational pull and store its components into `tempDX` and `tempDY`, you can add these values to the `dx` and `dy` values of the actual object to get the required motion, like this:

```
//add vector to ship
this.dx += tempDX;
this.dy += tempDY;
```

If one planet is good . . .

You can use the basic gravity calculations in some interesting combinations For example, the `twoPlanets` program in Figure 12-10 shows how to calculate the seemingly complex problem of a spacecraft orbiting two large stationary planets. (I could also make the planets orbit each other as they would actually do, but I'll leave that as an exercise for the class.)

TECHNICAL STUFF

This isn't rocket science

Before I get e-mails from every scientist in NASA, let me give my standard disclaimer: This *really* isn't rocket science. You can improve your calculations after you have something good working. (I did have a friend who is a rocket scientist look it over, though.)

These simple calculations are good enough for arcade games:

✔ My model assumes that the focus object is so much heavier than the orbiting object that the force of gravity works in only one direction.

✔ My ships have ridiculous amounts of power. If you want a more accurate program, you must reduce the ship's thrust substantially.

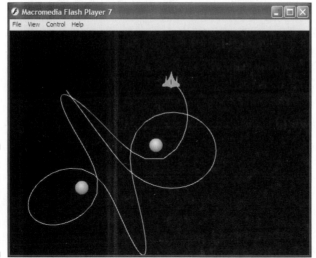

Figure 12-10:
Now the ship interacts with two planets.

In this program, I add another planet with a different gravitational pull. I check the gravitational pull of both planets in the `enterFrame` event:

```
myShip.onEnterFrame = function(){
  myShip.checkKeys();
  myShip.turn();
  myShip.move();
  myShip.gravitate(planet)
  myShip.gravitate(planet2)
} // end enter frame
```

Now the ship interacts with `planet` (the planet in the lower left with a gravity of 10000) and also interacts with `planet2` (near the center of the screen with a gravity of 15000) during each frame.

You can use the same scheme to manipulate complex systems and get some really fun results.

Building a Better Boat

A vehicle you are modeling might require slipping and sliding.

Most arcade vehicles fit somewhere between two extremes shown in this chapter.

- ✔ In the car examples, the direction in which the vehicle is pointing is the direction it moves. The vehicle doesn't skid at all.
- ✔ In the spacecraft examples, the vehicle can be traveling in any direction, not simply the direction in which it is pointed.

As an example of skidding behavior, look at the `boat` program displayed in Figure 12-11. This program features a boat that can

- ✔ Slip sideways
- ✔ Accelerate forward

The best way to see this effect is to run the `boat` program from the companion Web site:

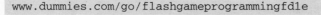
`www.dummies.com/go/flashgameprogrammingfd1e`

You can apply the same skidding concepts to any vehicle. I chose the boat for variety and because boats have pronounced skidding effects.

In `boat.fla`, I add lots of dynamic text boxes so you can see what's going on with all these variables. Although the final user doesn't usually want to see all this information, it can be very useful to you while you test your programs. The `carParam` program in this chapter shows you how to add this kind of dynamic output to your programs.

Figure 12-11:
The boat
can slip
sideways,
giving a nice
realistic
feel.

The Secret of Traction

To get a vehicle to skid well, you actually need to move it twice per frame. One time, you move it like the car, where it moves in the direction it's pointed. Then you move it in the direction of the thrust, like you do in the spaceship.

You can adjust which type of motion gets the highest priority with a property called `traction`:

- When you give a vehicle a high `traction` value, the vehicle tends to go in the direction it's pointed.

- When you give a vehicle a smaller `traction` value, the vehicle tends to skid.

To add traction to a vehicle, follow these steps:

1. **Begin with a vehicle object like the ones you create throughout this chapter.**

   The object should have the same methods as the car examples for movement, turning, and keyboard input.

2. **Add a `traction` property to the vehicle.**

   The best place to put any property definition is in the `init()` function, so that's where you should add the `traction` value, like this:

   ```
   //from boat.fla, init function
   boat.traction = .5;
   ```

3. **Determine the boat's current direction and speed.**

   The `turn()` method generates `dx` and `dy` values from the boat's other characteristics.

   To determine these values, I use the following code to calculate the object's

   • Direction in radians

   • Current speed

   ```
   //from boat.fla turn method
   this._rotation = this.dir;

   //get new thrust vector
   //thrust vector is direction boat is currently pointing
   degrees = this.dir;
   degrees -= 90;
   radians = degrees * Math.PI / 180;

   //calculate current speed
   speed = Math.sqrt(this.dx * this.dx + this.dy * this.dy);
   ```

4. **Calculate the boat's drift vector.**

   The following code calculates the drift amount from the boat's current speed and direction. Drift is stored in variables called `driftDX` and `driftDY`.

   ```
   //from boat.fla turn method
   //determine drift from boat's current direction
   driftDX = Math.cos(radians);
   driftDY = Math.sin(radians);

   //adjust drift for speed.
   driftDX *= speed;
   driftDY *= speed;
   ```

5. **Determine the boat's thrust vector.**

   This is the amount of change the user intends to apply.

The following code finds the user's intended change from the boat's current direction:

```
//from boat.fla turn method
thrustDX = this.thrustSpeed * Math.cos(radians);
thrustDY = this.thrustSpeed * Math.sin(radians);

//add thrust to dx and dy
this.dx += thrustDX;
this.dy += thrustDY;
```

6. Apply the boat's drift vector in the `move()` method:

```
//from boat.fla move method
//move according to current speed BEFORE applying thrust.
this._x += driftDX * this.traction;
this._y += driftDY * this.traction;
```

To move the boat with a skid factor

- Apply the drift vector to the boat's current position.

- Use the `traction` value to indicate how influential the drift is.

7. Apply the boat's thrust vector in the `move()` method, like this:

```
//from boat.fla move method
//move again AFTER applying thrust
this._x += this.dx * (1/this.traction);
boat._y += this.dy * (1/this.traction);
```

In the preceding code, the thrust vector is multiplied by the *reciprocal* (one divided by) of the `traction` variable:

- *If the traction amount is larger,* thrust has less influence.

- *If the traction amount is smaller,* thrust has more influence.

Chapter 13

The Life and Death of Sprites

In This Chapter

▶ Creating arrays

▶ Repeating code

▶ Building a sprite dynamically

▶ Creating a bunch of sprites

▶ Creating custom objects

▶ Making custom movie clip classes

*F*lash gives you the movie clip object, which is extremely useful because it does most of what a sprite should do. (For some background on sprites, skip back to Chapter 6.) Sometimes you want even more precise control over your objects, such as making objects pop up and disappear on command, or creating new kinds of movie clip objects that automatically do whatever you want them to do. Games should also have lots of sprites onscreen — to add to the fun and mayhem. You need to know how to create a number of sprites and control them at once. In fact, you often need to work with a list of things in programming, so start by reading about the incredibly useful `array` structure.

In this chapter, I cover how to build arrays, create sprites with your code, work with a lot of sprites at once, and investigate Flash MX 2004's new object-oriented features. With these skills, you'll be a master game programmer.

Here We Go Loop-de-Loop

This chapter is about repeated behavior. When you want a computer to do things several times, you can use a special programming device called a *loop*.

What are loops doing way back in this chapter?

Loops are a really big deal in traditional programming languages, so you might be surprised that I haven't mentioned them elsewhere in this book. Game development is based on the notion of a built-in animation loop. All your code is designed to happen several times per second in the `enterFrame` event. In essence, your program already has a huge loop built in, so there's usually no need to think about repeating behavior. However, when you work with several sprites at a time in this chapter, you will often use loops.

Loops are used to repeat code several times. Figure 13-1 shows the output screen for `loopDemo.fla`.

Figure 13-1: The `loopDemo` program does a lot of counting.

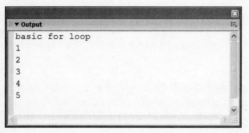

The `loopDemo` program, as shown in Listing 13-1, demonstrates several basic ways to perform repetitive behavior.

Listing 13-1:   Loop Demo Program

```
//loop demo

//basic for loop
trace ("basic for loop");
for (counter = 1; counter <= 5; counter ++){
  trace (counter);
} // end for loop
```

The `loopDemo` program uses counting to illustrate several kinds of looping mechanisms.

The most important kind of loop for game developers is the standard `for` loop. The `for` loop is used to repeat code a specified number of times. To build your own repeating loop

1. **Create a counting variable.**

   Mine is called `counter`, but you can call it whatever makes sense for your program. If you don't have a better name, programmers traditionally use `i` as a counting variable. The counting variable should be an integer.

2. **Begin the `for` statement.**

   The `for` statement indicates a loop will begin. The `for` statement contains three key elements (described in the following steps) that determine the loop's behavior:

   - A starting point for the counter

   - An ending condition for the counter

   - A mechanism for advancing the counter

3. **Initialize the counting variable.**

   Most of the time, you begin counting at 0 (zero) or 1. (See the next section for other variations.) The first clause of the `for` structure sets the starting value of the counting variable. In my basic example, I want to begin counting at 1, so I begin the `for` loop with the clause

   ```
   counter = 1;
   ```

4. **Determine the ending condition.**

   Create a condition that determines when the loop continues. As long as the condition is evaluated as `true`, the loop continues. When the condition is evaluated as `false`, the loop ends. My example counts to 5, so I specify the following condition:

   ```
   counter <= 5;
   ```

   If `counter` is less than or equal to 5, the code inside the loop continues. As soon as `counter` is evaluated as greater than 5, the loop exits, and the next line of code outside the loop executes.

5. **Update the counting variable.**

   Every time the loop executes, the counting variable needs to change. This can be easily accomplished through the `for` loop's last parameter: an update statement. Usually, this is a line of code that adds to or subtracts from the counter. My update statement looks like this:

   ```
   counter ++
   ```

   The `++` operator simply tells ActionScript to increment the `counter` variable by 1. Each time through the loop, `counter` is incremented by 1. Eventually, the condition triggers, and the loop ends.

6. **Create loop contents.**

   After defining the loop's parameters, write code inside a pair of braces. This code occurs as long as the loop's condition is `true`. As soon as the condition is evaluated as `false`, the next line of code outside the loop occurs.

There's more than for

Many other looping structures are available. Although the `for` loop will serve your needs for this book, you can adjust the basic loop so that it can count backward and even *skip count* (count by fives). You won't need those behaviors in this book, so I won't dwell on them here, but you can look up these procedures in the online Help. While you're at it, you might also investigate the powerful `while` loop, which is another popular looping structure.

Making Many Things with Arrays

Your game programming goal is to create a number of movie clip objects that are related yet unique. The good news is that programming languages have had the ability to create lists of elements for years. The bad news is that ActionScript doesn't use this capability in a clean way when it comes to `Movie Clip` objects. Still, the underlying technique for working with lists of variables can be extremely useful. Listing 13-2 is a demonstration.

Listing 13-2: Array Demo Program

```
//arrayDemo.fla
 //source: International Union for the Conservation of
         Nature

 ePop = new Array();
 ePop[1] = "Tanzania";
 ePop[2] = "Dem. Rep. Congo";
 ePop[3] = "Botswana";
 ePop[4] = "Gabon";
 ePop[5] = "Zimbabwe";
 ePop[6] = "Rep. Congo";
 ePop[7] = "Zambia";
 ePop[8] = "Kenya";
 ePop[9] = "South Africa";
 ePop[10] = "Cameroon";

for (i = 1; i <= 10; i++){
  trace(i + ": " + ePop[i]);
} // end for
```

This program records the ten countries with the largest population of African elephants. (Remember me when you win big on *Jeopardy!* with this factoid tidbit.) Any time you have a list of data, programmers usually like to use a special structure called an *array*. In ActionScript, an array is a built-in object type, created with the `new` keyword. Several values can be stored in the same array variable, where they are distinguished by a numeric index.

Arrays by any other name

If you're used to arrays in another language like Java or C, you might be shocked at how little information you need to create an array in ActionScript. ActionScript arrays are actually objects, so they're much more powerful than the arrays you might have seen in other languages. Pair that with the dynamic variable generation and loose typing of ActionScript, and it's really pretty easy to make an array in Flash.

To create an array, follow these steps:

1. **Build an array variable using the `new Array()` syntax.**

   You have a number of variations of this approach, but ActionScript arrays are unusually flexible, so you can simply use the `new Array()` syntax without any parameters at all, and it will usually work just fine.

2. **Add elements to the array.**

   The array can be seen as one variable with a lot of variables inside it. This might seem strange to you, but throughout earlier chapters, you can see this many times with Flash objects. Each object is a variable, but it also has many properties, which also are variables. In arrays, each subvariable has a numeric index rather than a name. Refer to a specific element in the array with its index in square brackets. For example

   ```
   ePop[1] = "Tanzania";
   ```

   can be read as *ePop sub 1 gets Tanzania*. You can assign values to array elements just like normal variables.

3. **Retrieve elements from the array.**

   After values are stored in an array, you can call them back by using the same square bracket syntax. Thus, `trace(ePop[1])` returns the first element of the `ePop` array, which is `Tanzania`.

4. **Consider using a `for` loop.**

   Because arrays have numeric indices, the `for` loop is a natural companion to the array. Frequently you'll find yourself wanting to do the same thing to every element in the array, and a `for` loop is a good way to accomplish this. For example (pun intended)

   ```
   for (i = 1; i < ePop.length; i++){
     trace(i + ": " + ePop[i]);
   } // end for
   ```

   Each time through the loop, the value of `i` increases by 1, so eventually each element of the array is displayed. Figure 13-2 shows the results in the output window.

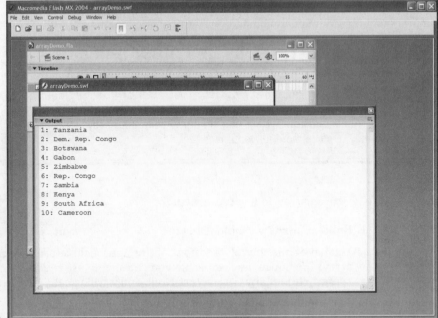

Figure 13-2:
One trace
statement in
a loop prints
the top ten
elephant
populations.

This program creates its output with the trace statement, so the SWF version doesn't produce any visible output. To see the results of this program, be sure to run the FLA version within the Flash editor. (Read about these file types in Chapter 2.)

5. **Use the length property to determine the number of elements in the array.**

   Usually, you build loops that step through all elements of an array. You could build a loop to work with the ePop array that looks like this:

   ```
   for (i = 1; i <= 10; i++){
     trace(i + ": " + ePop[i]);
   } // end for
   ```

   Such a loop runs ten times, with the value of i ranging from 1 to 10 just like it's supposed to do. Consider what would happen if you add one more value (making it a top 11 list). The loop still counts to 10 even though there are now 11 elements in the array. Arrays come with a built-in length property that tells how many elements are in the array.

Arrays begin counting elements with 0, so I wrote ePop originally (with elements numbering from 1 to 10) to include an element 0 and with a length of 11. Notice that I actually changed the condition to handle this fact.

Building Sprites Dynamically

In other parts of this book, I show you how to create a sprite on the Stage and then manipulate that existing sprite. If you want many copies of a sprite, you can drag them from the Library, but until this chapter, you didn't really have a good way to create a sprite if it weren't already on the Stage. Likewise, you didn't have a good way to make a sprite disappear when it's no longer needed. The makeaSprite program featured in Figures 13-3 and 13-4 shows a technique for creating a sprite from the Library. Master how to make one sprite, and then you can graduate to making a bunch of them.

The makeaSprite program doesn't look terribly different from anything you can see in earlier chapters of this book — from the user's point of view, that is. However, this program has an important design difference under the hood. In all previous examples, you create movie clip objects on the Stage or in the Library, and you can make more copies of a movie clip by dragging more instances of it from the Library to the Stage. You can also use code to create and destroy sprite instances. To create and destroy instances of the object after the program starts running, read the techniques in this chapter to see how to do exactly that and why it's such an important technique to master.

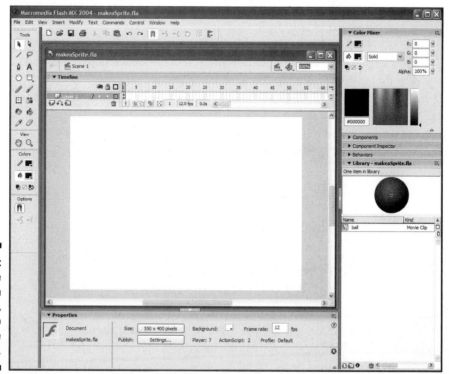

Figure 13-3:
In the design environment, there is no sprite on the screen.

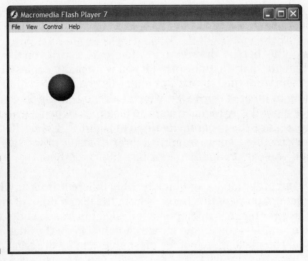

Figure 13-4:
When the program runs, there is a sprite!

Dynamically generating a sprite

You can create a sprite instance easily with the `attachMovie()` command. To build a movie clip instance, follow these steps:

1. **Create the movie clip class.**

   Build the visual representation of the movie clip object and place it in the Library. You don't need to have an instance of the movie clip on the Stage. When creating the movie clip, be sure to select the Export for ActionScript check box on the Properties tab, as shown in Figure 13-5.

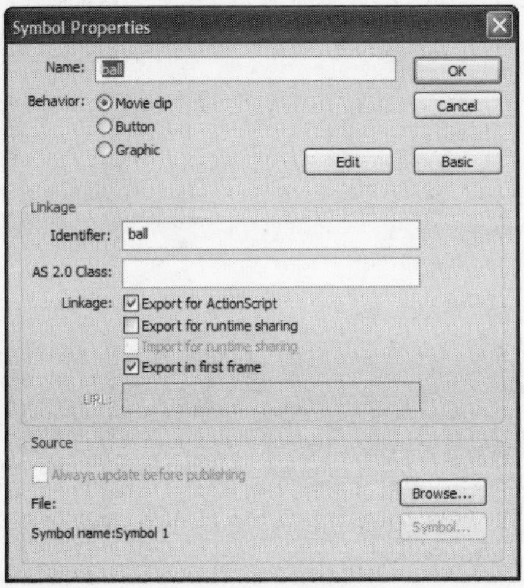

Figure 13-5:
Dynamically generated movie clips need exported for ActionScript.

By default, Flash ignores any items in the Library but not on the Stage. If you're building movie clips to be placed on the Stage by your code, be sure you link the movie clip, or Flash won't include the movie clip object in the final SWF file.

2. **Use the `attachMovie()` command to create an instance of the sprite.**

Add code to build the sprite wherever you want it to occur. The following code creates an instance of the ball called `theBall` and moves it to a particular spot (I chose 100, 100) on the Stage:

```
//makeaSprite.fla
//Demonstrates creating multiple sprites at run time

_root.attachMovie("ball", "theBall", 10);
theBall._x = 100:
theBall._y = 100;
```

`attachMovie()` is a method of `MovieClips`, so `_root.attachMovie()` creates a movie clip attached to the main program.

3. **Determine the class you want to create.**

The first parameter of `attachMovie` is the name of the object in the Library that you want to duplicate. This object must already exist in the Library.

4. **Name the instance.**

The second parameter is the instance name of the object that you're creating. When you build an instance in *design time* (that is, while you're working in the Flash editor), you name an instance by typing a name in the Properties box in the editor. When you generate an instance dynamically (as here), the sprite is generated while the user runs the program, so there is no Properties box. You must specify the instance name directly as part of the `attachMovie()` syntax. You can use this instance name to refer to the particular instance later in your code.

5. **Establish the z-order for the instance.**

The Flash documentation calls this third parameter — z — *depth*.

When you use the `attachMovie()` method to place instances on the screen, you must assign a number for the z-order. If you don't know what the z-order should be, you can use the `_root.getNextHighestDepth()` command to retrieve a valid z-order.

If you accidentally assign two or more elements to the same depth, only one appears. Be sure each instance is given a unique depth to avoid this problem. The `_root.getNextHighestDepth()` command generates a unique depth, but it does have some documented problems. It's often best to simply keep track of which depths you assign. I usually start adding elements at 10 or 100. In the upcoming "Making many copies of a sprite" section, I show you how to ensure unique z-order values even when working with a large number of elements.

6. Manipulate the instance.

After the instance is created, you can manipulate it through code just like an ordinary instance. In fact, you almost always need to change a few properties because the sprite appears in its default position. As a minimum, you want to change the _x and _y properties so the object appears somewhere other than the top-left corner of the screen. You can change properties, and you can also add methods, event handlers, and anything else you wish. In the preceding example, I move the sprite to 100, 100 by adjusting the _x and _y properties:

```
theBall._x = 100;
theBall._y = 100;
```

Building a suicidal sprite

This chapter's earlier makeaSprite example shows that you can change the properties of a sprite while it's being created. You can also attach methods to sprites while you create them. The killSprite program shown in Figure 13-6 automatically generates a sprite. However, this sprite has a new talent: When you click the sprite, it disappears. In earlier chapters, I show you how to make sprites leave the screen, but in those cases, the object stays in existence and simply moves off-Stage so the user can't see it. However, with the ability to create a sprite, you can also destroy it. When you can create and destroy sprites at will, your game can have as many sprites as you want without having to hide objects off-Stage.

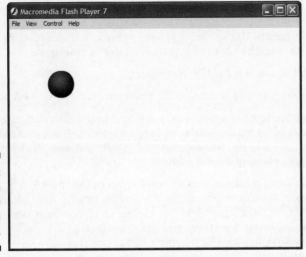

Figure 13-6:
Vaporize
this sprite
with a
mouse click.

Pick me! Pick me!

When Flash elements touch each other on the Stage, one element always overlaps another. Some objects appear to be closer to the user than others even though they're all on the same 2-D plane. This behavior is usually referred to as *z-order* because in a 3-D environment, the z axis usually refers to how close the object is to the viewer's nose:

✔ In normal Flash animation, you control the z-order by determining what layer an object is on.

✔ Objects in the same layer have their position determined by the order in which they were placed on the Stage.

✔ Elements placed later appear to be closer and have a higher z-order than those placed earlier.

The code for this new version looks like this:

```
//killSprite.fla
//Demonstrates adding methods to sprites,
//deleting them in real time

_root.attachMovie("ball", "theBall", 10);
theBall._x = 100;
theBall._y = 100;

theBall.onRelease = function(){
  this.removeMovieClip();
} // end onRelease
```

The new sprite has two important features:

✔ **Has a predefined method:** When I created the sprite, I added a method to it. This is done the same way in dynamically generated sprites as the ordinary (design-time) kind. Simply create a function associated with an event or method. This method is attached to the sprite as soon as it's created. The code does not run immediately, but the behavior is attached to the sprite, so it can act appropriately. In this case, I add code to the sprite's onRelease() event so this sprite acts like a button. When the mouse is released over the sprite, something ill happens.

✔ **Can be destroyed:** You can put any code you want in an event handler, but I want to demonstrate how sprites can be destroyed while the program is running. This behavior is handy for programs like *Asteroids* or *Breakout* in which the user can destroy a number of sprites. The sprite is killed by invoking its removeMovieClip() method.

It doesn't make sense to me to create a sprite using a method of the root object and then destroy it by using one of its own methods, but that's how you do it.

Inside the `onRelease` code, I refer to the sprite as `this` rather than its name (`theBall`). The distinction is unimportant when you have only one dynamically generated sprite, but when you use this technique to create lots of sprites (as you can see in the next section), each instance has its own name. The `this` keyword refers to the current object, so inside the `theBall` event handler, `this` means `theBall`, and you won't have to worry about exactly which instance you're trying to kill. Each sprite knows how to make itself "go gently into that good night."

Making many copies of a sprite

Creating a single instance of a sprite dynamically is kind of cool, but the technique really becomes crucial when you want to build a whole bunch of objects. As an example, take a look at the `lotsOfSprites` program that debuts in Figures 13-7 and 13-8:

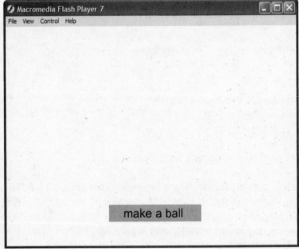

Figure 13-7:
Every time you click the button, a new sprite appears.

This program is noteworthy in a number of ways:

> ✔ **The user can make a lot of sprites.** Every time the user clicks the button, a new sprite appears. There is no limit to the number of sprites that can be generated (although they will eventually cover the button).

✔ **Each sprite is unique.** Each sprite has a unique position and a unique name. Each sprite also has a property called `index` that returns its ID.

✔ **Each sprite has an `onRelease` event.** When any ball is clicked, the program reports the ball's ID. This illustrates how a sprite can report on its identity.

Listing 13-3 shows the code for generating all the sprites.

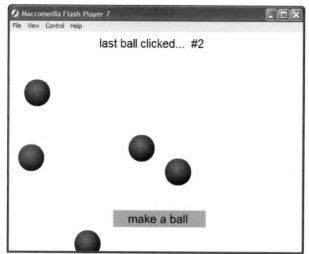

Figure 13-8:
When you click a ball, it reports its index.

Listing 13-3:   Lots of Sprites Program

```
//lotsOfSprites.fla
//Demonstrates creating multiple sprites at run time

i = 0;

theButton.onRelease = function(){
  i++;
  _root.attachMovie("ball", "ball_" + i, 10 + i);
  currentBall = eval("theBall_" + i);
  currentBall._x = Math.random() * Stage.width;
  currentBall._y = Math.random() * Stage.height;
  currentBall.index = i;

  currentBall.onRelease = function(){
    output = "last ball clicked... #" + this.index;
    this.removeMovieClip();
  } // end onRelease

} // end theButton
```

To build a number of sprites, follow these steps:

1. **Establish a counting variable.**

   Name the sprites `ball_1`, `ball_2`, and so on. The variable `i` keeps track of which particular version of the sprite you're talking about.

2. **Build a mechanism for creating sprites.**

   In this example, I use a button click to let the user create the sprites. You could also use a `for` loop to generate as many sprites as you wish. (Read about `for` loops earlier in this chapter.)

3. **Increment the counting variable.**

   Each time you build a new sprite, be sure you increment the counter so that the sprite gets a unique name.

4. **Create the sprite with `attachMovie()`.**

   Note the special way I define the instance name: `"ball_" + i`. I concatenate the literal value `ball_` with the value of the counter `i`. The first time the user clicks the button, the ball instance is called `ball_1`. The next time the user clicks the button, `ball_2` is created, and so on.

5. **Get a handle for the current ball.**

   Here's one tricky problem. Each sprite has its own name, so how do you assign the properties of the current ball? The easiest way to do this is to create a new variable that corresponds to the ball's name:

   ```
   currentBall = eval("theBall_" + i);
   ```

   The `eval` function takes a string and attempts to interpret it as ActionScript code. If `i` is 1, `eval("theBall_" + i);` tries to evaluate the string `"theBall_1"`. ActionScript recognizes that `"theBall_1"` is a sprite object, and `currentBall` becomes another temporary name for `theBall_1`. By using the `currentBall` technique, you can designate properties for whichever ball you're working on and not have to worry about its specific name.

6. **Generate a random position for the sprite.**

   After `currentBall` points to whatever sprite you just made, you can change properties of `currentBall` to modify the current sprite. Specifically, assign random values for the `x` and `y` properties to move the ball to a random position on the Stage.

   ```
   currentBall._x = Math.random() * Stage.width;
   currentBall._y = Math.random() * Stage.height;
   ```

7. **Create an index for the sprite.**

ActionScript doesn't provide an automatic way for the sprite to report which of many objects it is, so add an `index` property.

```
currentBall.index = i;
```

The index is copied from `i`. When the program runs, each instance has a different value for index to help you tell them apart.

8. Add an `onRelease` event handler.

Each ball should be capable of acting independently. Give each ball an event handler that reports its name before destroying the instance. (Of course, you can make your event handlers do whatever you want — change states, move the object, whatever.)

9. Report the ball's status.

Sometimes you need to know which particular instance you're dealing with. To illustrate, I have the movie clip report before self-destructing. The code looks like this:

```
output = "last ball clicked... #" + this.index;
```

This code presumes that a dynamic text box is linked to the variable `output`. The `this.index` reference indicates which particular instance is responding. When you click a ball, you don't want all the balls to disappear — just the one you click.

10. Self-destruct.

Just for fun, I make the ball disappear when you click it, using the `removeMovieClip()` syntax.

Using a similar technique, you could create armies of sprite objects by creating them inside a `for` loop. Each of the objects can have its own move methods, collision detection routines, or anything else you want.

How about creating an array of sprites? After all, arrays are great for this sort of situation. Unfortunately, Flash doesn't make it easy to build arrays of movie clips. The technique I show you here is a workaround, but as far as I'm concerned, I'm still building an array of sprites. I have to use the `eval()` technique to refer to a particular sprite, but otherwise, it works identically to an actual array.

Creating Custom Objects

Until the advent of Flash MX 2004, the best way to build customized objects was to build all the sprites as soon as the program starts, as I do in the preceding section. However, you can encounter problems with this approach. The technique involves lots of code that prebuilds the objects, and then you simply release these objects and let them interact. It doesn't take long before you start having to declare functions inside functions and to face other strange and mystical programming problems.

To skirt this potential pitfall, read through this section.

Making a really simple object

The latest version of Flash supports a stronger form of object-oriented programming than earlier versions did. Flash MX 2004 includes ActionScript 2.0, which can incorporate a new kind of class. As an example, take a look at the following code:

```
class Dude {
  //external definition
  var handle: String = "anonymous";

  function sayHi(){
    trace("Hi, my name is " + handle);
  } // end sayHi

} // end class def
```

Although the code looks similar to the ActionScript throughout this book, it's not exactly the same. This code is a *class definition*. It is a separate file, containing just code for describing one particular kind of thing. In this case, the class describes Dude. A class definition has the following characteristics:

- ✔ **It resides in its own file.** Classes are separate files; they aren't part of the FLA file. Use a text editor to build the class file. Classes must be stored in the same directory as the Flash programs that use them. Classes must also end in .as, and the capitalization of the filename does matter.

   If you're using Flash MX 2004 Professional, you can edit class files directly in the editor. If not, you can still use class files, but you need to edit them in Notepad or some other text editor.

- ✔ **It begins with the keyword class.** This indicates that the file describes a class.

- ✔ **It contains a name.** The name follows the class keyword directly. Class names are usually capitalized. All the code between the class name and the end of the file is contained in braces({ }) and is usually indented.

- ✔ **Classes can have properties.** Define a property with the var keyword. Then specify the type of property it is (usually String or Numeric) and provide a default value. The Dude class has a property called handle.

- ✔ **Classes can have methods.** If you define a function in the context of a class file, the function is interpreted as a method of the object class.

After you create an object, you can use it in your Flash projects. The
`Dude.fla` project uses the `Dude` object:

```
//Dude   Demonstrates ActionScript 2.0
// Simplest possible external object.
// expects a class file in same directory called "Dude.as"

theDude = new Dude();
theDude.handle = "Benjamin";
theDude.sayHi();
```

There is no other code or user interface elements in the `Dude.fla` program
because it's designed to be as simple as possible. When the program runs,
you see something like Figure 13-9 in the output window.

To incorporate a class file into your project, follow along:

1. **Create the class definition.**

   a. Begin with a very simple class like the one defined here.

   b. Store the class in its own text file.

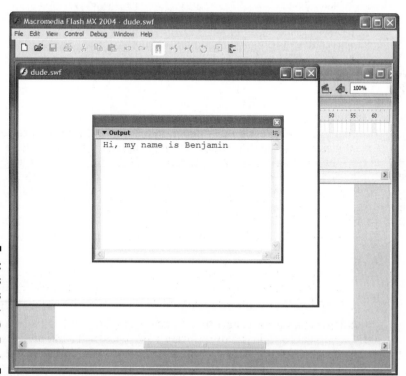

Figure 13-9:
The class
file code is
incorpor-
ated into
the Flash
project.

Be sure that the class name and the filename are the same (including punctuation) and that the class is stored in the same directory as the FLA file you use it in.

2. **Create an instance of the class.**

To use your class in the Flash environment, create an instance of that object with the `new` operator.

```
theDude = new Dude();
```

This generates a new `Dude` object and calls this instance of the object `theDude`. This behavior might seem strange to you, but it's much like a mechanism I use many times throughout this book. The object class (`Dude`) is much like a movie clip defined in the Library, and the particular instance (`theDude`) is like an instance of that class on the Stage.

3. **Use the object's properties and methods.**

After you create an instance of your class, you can use its objects and properties as if it were generated in the same program.

```
theDude.handle = "Benjamin";
theDude.sayHi();
```

You can assign new values to the `handle` property and call the `sayHi()` method. Because I wrote the `sayHi()` method to report the user's name, it works even though the code for this behavior isn't in the actual FLA file. Instead, it's in the AS file, which is loaded dynamically.

Building custom sprite objects

The real power of custom objects comes when you build custom variations of the movie clip class. When you create a graphical representation of an object in the Library, it's easy to drag that symbol onto the Stage to make multiple copies. It would be even better if you could define characteristics of that object (how it moves, the ability to check for keystrokes, or whatever) one time, and have those behaviors automatically duplicated whenever you make an instance of the object. That is exactly how custom `Sprite` objects work. Take a look at the `oopBall` program featured in Figure 13-10.

Each ball moves in a random speed and direction, bounces off the walls, and disappears when you click it. First imagine how much code it takes to get all these balls to do these things; then load `oopBall.fla` into the editor. You'll be amazed to find that it has no code at all! I simply drop some ball instances from the Library. I create an external class definition for the ball and associate it with the `ball` class in my Library. The class definition has all the code necessary for the ball encapsulated out of the way. In fact, after I create the external object definition, I can attach it easily to any movie clip in the Library.

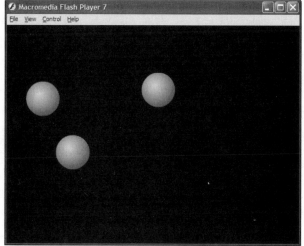

Figure 13-10:
These moving sprite instances were created without any code!

Using a custom movie clip class

Before writing your own custom movie clip classes, you can see how it works by using the `Ball.as` class file on this book's companion Web site. This definition causes the sprite to appear automatically at a random spot on the Stage, move in a random direction, bounce off all walls, and delete itself when clicked.

To build a sprite using a custom class definition

1. **Create the class in a separate file.**

   I show you in the following section how to create class files to modify movie clip objects.

2. **Create the visual representation of your movie clip in the Library as normal.**

3. **Modify the movie clip.**

   Use the Properties dialog box when you create the movie clip, or right-click the object in the Library and choose the Properties dialog box from that menu.

4. **Associate the class file to the movie clip.**

   Type the class file's name into the AS 2.0 Class text box, as shown in Figure 13-11.

   • Be sure the class file resides in the same directory as the FLA file you're working on (and that the FLA file has been saved).

• Be extremely careful of capitalization. The class file must have the same capitalization as the text in the Properties dialog box and the class name as defined in the file.

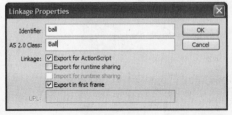

Figure 13-11:
Associate a
movie clip
with a class
file here.

5. Create instances of the movie clip.

• Drag the movie clip to the Stage.

or

• Use the `attachMovie()` function.

6. Test the program.

You don't have to write a single line of code for the movie clip object. If it's associated with the class file correctly, it automatically has all the right behaviors in place as soon as you put it on the Stage.

I added another class called `Rock.as` to the Chapter 13 examples on the companion Web site. This file has slightly different behavior: It rotates the movie clip and regenerates it in a new position when it hits a wall. Experiment by using different class files to change the behavior of your sprites.

Building a custom movie clip

As amazing as the `oopBall` program is, the code for animating the balls still has to go somewhere. It's stored in the separate `Ball.as` file, which is shown in Listing 13-4. Create this file with an external text editor (like Notepad).

Listing 13-4:   Ball.as Class Definition

```
class Ball extends MovieClip {

  var dx: Number;
  var dy: Number;

  function Ball(){
    _x = Math.random() * Stage.width;
```

```
  _y = Math.random() * Stage.height;
  dx = Math.random() * 20 - 10;
  dy = Math.random() * 20 - 10;
} // end constructor

function onEnterFrame(){
  move();
  checkBounds();
} // end function

function move(){
  _x += dx;
  _y += dy;
} // end move

function checkBounds(){
  if (_x > Stage.width){
    dx *= -1;
  } // end if

  if (_x < 0){
    dx *= -1;
  } // end if

  if (_y > Stage.height){
    dy *= -1;
  } // end if

  if (_y < 0){
    dy *= -1;
  } // end if

} // end checkBounds

function onRelease(){
  //delete when clicked
  removeMovieClip(this);
} // end if

} // end class def
```

A custom movie clip is a special type of class object. It has its own unique characteristics. If you want to make your own, follow these steps:

1. **Begin with a plain text file created in your text editor.**

   If you're using Flash MX 2004 Professional, you can create class files directly in the Flash environment. If you're not using the Professional edition, you can still create class files, but you must create them with your own text editor, like Notepad or SimpleText.

Inherit the wind and other stuff, too

The `extends` keyword is an example of the object-oriented principle of *inheritance*. That might be a handy piece of trivia if you find yourself magically transported to the middle of a computer science cocktail party. In this example, the new `Ball` object you're defining already has all the built-in characteristics of its mom: the movie clip class.

Name the file carefully because you need the filename when you associate the file with a movie clip class.

2. Extend the movie clip class.

The object you're making is actually an extension of an existing class. Because this object is attached to a movie clip, you want to be able to take advantage of all the great things movie clips already have, like the existing properties and methods. For example:

```
class Ball extends MovieClip {
```

establishes your class name as `Ball` and explains that the ball will be an enhanced movie clip.

3. Declare any properties.

Because the `Ball` object is an extended movie clip, it already has all the normal features of a move clip object. If you want to add other properties, you need to define them formally in the class file:

```
var dx: Number;
var dy: Number;
```

The naming convention is a little stricter than elsewhere in this book. To create a property, use the `var` keyword, the property's name, a colon, and the property type (`Number` or `String`, usually).

4. Build a constructor.

Look carefully to see that the `Ball` class also has a `Ball` function defined within it. This special function is a *constructor*, which is automatically called when the class is created. The constructor always has exactly the same name as the class. You can think of a constructor as an automatic `init()` function for a class. Usually, you put initialization code that should happen whenever the class is created in the constructor.

```
function Ball(){
    _x = Math.random() * Stage.width;
    _y = Math.random() * Stage.height;
    dx = Math.random() * 20 - 10;
    dy = Math.random() * 20 - 10;
} // end constructor
```

In my case, the constructor is used to initialize all the ball's key properties. If the ball hasn't been placed manually on the Stage, its position is randomly determined, and its dx and dy properties are likewise randomly generated.

5. **Add the object's methods.**

   Add methods to the object by defining functions. You can refer to any of the object's properties (whether built into the movie clip or custom properties that you add) by simply using the property as a name. Notice also that the method definition syntax is quite a bit simpler in the class context than in earlier projects. For example, rather than writing

   ```
   object.onEnterFrame = function(){
   ```

   as in other programs, you simply define onEnterFrame as a function because the object is already defined:

   ```
   function onEnterFrame(){
     move();
     checkBounds();
   } // end function

   function move(){
     _x += dx;
     v += dv:
   } // end move
   ```

   Likewise, the other methods can simply be defined as functions, and they are automatically attached to the movie clip associated with this class file.

6. **End the class definition.**

   The class definition is a code fragment and should end just like a loop or function definition.

7. **Test by saving your file and associating it with a movie clip in a Flash project.**

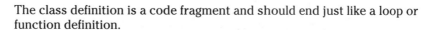

I'm doing properties the wrong way

If you've done some formal object-oriented programming, don't fire up your e-mail client to tell me how this method of creating properties is horribly flawed. Purists would agree that object properties should be controlled a little more strictly than I do here, through a technique called *access methods.* Although Flash does allow access methods, the Flash implementation doesn't provide the protection it should, so I choose not to use them. You'll be fine using the technique I present here in Flash, but when you move to a more formal object-oriented language, like Java or C#, you'll discover a better technique.

TIP

The removeMovieClip() method works only on movie clips that have been added through code. If you create an instance in design time by dragging from the Library, you can't delete it — yet another reason to create your sprites dynamically.

One loop to control them all: Making many custom movie clips

After you're happy with a custom movie clip's behavior, you can very easily build programs that seem much more complicated than they actually are. As an example, take a look at Figure 13-12 and the oopManyBalls program.

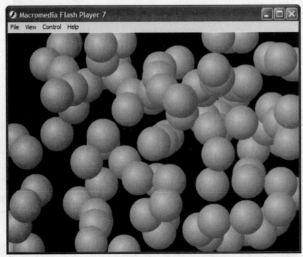

Figure 13-12:
All these balls are moving around, I built them with a simple loop.

The code for the oopManyBalls program is incredibly simple:

```
//oopBall
//uses an external definition for the Ball.

for (i = 0; i < 100; i++){
    _root.attachMovie("ball","ball_" + i, i + 10);
} // end for loop
```

I simply use the attachMovie() command to create all the balls I want in a big loop. All the behavior for the balls goes in the class definition file for the ball. When I change (or replace) that file, I can get different behaviors for every element in the set. With this tool on your belt, you have all the ammo you need to unleash swarms of aliens on an unsuspecting planet.

Part VI
The Part of Tens

The 5th Wave   By Rich Tennant

"We have no problem funding your Web site, Frank. Of all the chicken farmers operating Web sites, yours has the most impressive cluck-through rate."

In this part . . .

It's the law: You're reading a *For Dummies* book, so you know it will have a Part of Tens. These chapters have some of my favorite content in the entire book.

Chapter 14 summarizes ten key math and physics concepts for game programmers. It's a variation of a cheat sheet that I've kept by my computer for many years while writing games in any language. I took the most important nuggets of wisdom from the entire book and repeated them here in this easy-to-review section. If you did have to take a test on this book, this is the chapter you'd record and play all night to learn subliminally.

Chapter 15 is the most fun chapter in the book. I take the concepts described throughout the book and use them to build the genesis of ten different games. If you want to build an adventure game, a tile-based strategy game, a top-down scroller, or a game about matching planetary orbits, I provide you with a starting framework. Throughout the chapter, I show you where you can find the details you need to write each game.

Chapter 14

Ten Math Concepts
for Game Programmers

*Y*ou might not have loved math class in high school, but if you've looked through this book, you know that math can be really handy when you're making games. Here's a collection of my favorite math and physics concepts. Use this list as a review when you're trying to make interesting things happen in your own games. For each concept, I indicate where in the book you can turn to get more information about using the formulas in your own games.

Managing Velocity

If this book has one central pair of formulas, it's the pair that lets you move an object:

```
x += dx;

y += dy;
```

These two formulas are usually used in an `onEnterFrame` event to move an object, where

▶ x and y are the coordinates of the object.

▶ dx and dy indicate the desired change in x and y in the next frame.

These formulas specifically determine changes in position over a specific unit of time (one frame); standard physics formulas usually incorporate time as a variable. Look over Chapter 6 for an introduction to these concepts.

Accelerating an Object

Acceleration is accomplished by changing the values of dx and dy:

```
dx += x_accel
dy += y_accel
```

In this formula, dx represents the change in x, and x_accel indicates acceleration in the x axis.

If you want to speed your sprite, add some value to dx. (Read more about sprites in Chapters 6, 9, and 13.) If you want to slow a sprite, subtract a value from dx. The same ideas apply to dy, and you need to adjust both dx and dy to get the desired results. Usually, these values are changed in response to some kind of event. For example, you might want to accelerate when the user clicks the mouse button and then decelerate naturally over time. Use of acceleration is described most completely in Chapter 12.

Calculating a Distance

If you have two objects, with coordinates

```
(x1, y1)
```

and

```
(x2, y2)
```

you can determine the distance between these objects with a form of the Pythagorean theorem, as illustrated here in Figure 14-1.

Figure 14-1:
The
distance
formula.

$$d = \sqrt{\left(x2 - x1\right)^2 + \left(y2 - y1\right)^2}$$

Usually, the two objects are movie clips, and you use the _x and _y properties of the two objects for x and y.

You can use a variation of this technique as a special form of collision detection:

```
function collides (sprite1, sprite2, threshold){
  //returns true if the distance between sprite1 and
  //sprite2 is less than threshold. Otherwise returns false

  result = false;
  xDist = sprite1._x - sprite2._x;
  yDist = sprite1._y - sprite2._y;
  distance = Math.sqrt((xDist * xDist) + (yDist * yDist));
  if (distance <= threshold){
    result = true;
  } // end if
  return result;
} // end function def
```

The advantage of this function is that it tests based on the difference between the *registration points* (usually both in the center of the objects) and can be adjusted regardless of the actual size of the movie clip objects on the screen.

Chapters 11 and 12 use variations of this technique to determine the distance between either two sprites or a sprite and the mouse.

Projecting a Vector

In physics, the motion of objects is usually expressed in terms of *vectors,* which have an angle measurement and a length. In programming, breaking a vector into its dx and dy components is often more convenient, as shown in Figure 14-2. Trigonometry is used to perform this manipulation.

Figure 14-2:
Vector
projection
formulas.

$$dx = r \cos\theta$$
$$dy = r \sin\theta$$

Usually in game programming, you're not calculating x and y but rather dx and dy. Also, you rarely call the angle theta (Θ) because usually it's the direction property of a sprite.

The code for using these formulas for calculating a sprite's velocity is the primary topic of Chapter 11.

Generating a Vector

Sometimes you need the inverse of a vector projection:

- ✔ You know the dx and dy of an object (or the position of two objects, which amounts to the same thing).
- ✔ You want to know the angle and distance.

The angle is calculated through the arctangent function, as shown here in Figure 14-3:

Figure 14-3:
Angle calculation formula.

$$\theta = \arctan\left(\frac{dy}{dx}\right)$$

Use the Pythagorean theorem to determine the length of the vector, as shown in Figure 14-4.

Figure 14-4:
Distance formula for vectors.

$$r = \sqrt{dx^2 + dy^2}$$

These formulas are described fully in Chapter 11.

Compensating for Gravity

There are a number of ways to think about gravity. In simple games where the player is near a very large force (usually Earth), calculate gravity by adding some value to dy each frame:

```
dy += gravity;
```

This technique is illustrated in Chapter 11.

If you need to calculate the gravity between two objects in space, you can use the Law of Universal Gravitation, as shown in Figure 14-5.

Figure 14-5:
The Law of
Universal
Gravitation.

$$f = \frac{m_1 m_2}{d^2} G$$

This formal definition of gravity incorporates

✔ The mass of both objects

✔ A gravitational constant G

Chapter 12 describes a simpler variation for calculating the orbit of a spaceship around a planet. The variation in that chapter eliminates the need for the constant G.

Newton's Second Law

Newton's Second Law is usually expressed as a formula (see Figure 14-6).

Figure 14-6:
Newton's
Second
Law.

$$F = ma$$

In Newton's Second Law, *F* represents force, *m* represents mass, and *a* represents acceleration.

In game programming, you often know the mass and the force but need to determine proper acceleration. You can use the variation in Figure 14-7 to determine acceleration.

Figure 14-7:
A variant of
Newton's
Second
Law.

$$a = \frac{m}{F}$$

A discussion of this technique is found in Chapter 12.

Generating a Random Integer

If you want to generate a random integer between 0 and `highest`, use the following code:

```
randomVar = Math.ceil(Math.random() * highest);
```

Use variations of this formula to alter the range. For example, you can generate random values between –5 and 5 with this variation:

```
randomVar = Math.floor(Math.random() * 11) - 5;
```

Use random numbers to simulate random events, like the rolling of dice, or to add a level of uncertainty to a computer opponent's behavior.

Random number generation is described more fully in Chapter 4.

Combining Vectors

All forces acting on an object combine to generate the final motion vector for that object. If each vector (v) is expressed in its dx and dy components, you can easily add all the vectors by adding all the components, as shown in Figure 14-8.

Figure 14-8:
Add vectors
by adding
components.

$V_1 + V_2 + V_3:$

$dx = dx_1 + dx_2 + dx_3$

$dy = dy_1 + dy_2 + dy_3$

The components are the dx and dy components of the various forces acting on an object, and the results are placed in the object's dx and dy properties. This technique is described in Chapter 12.

Sophisticated Vehicle Motion

Sprite motion can be expressed more accurately in a form that incorporates speed, power, mass, and drag:

```
speed *= power/mass;
speed *= 1/drag;

dx *= speed;
dy *= speed;
```

Techniques using these formulas are the basis of Chapter 12.

Chapter 15

Ten Game Starters

In This Chapter

▶ Great ways to start ten games

▶ Building and enhancing these ten games

*T*he best part of game programming is, well, programming games. This chapter is almost like a cookbook of games. I give you the starting code for ten different styles of games. Each game is complete in the sense that it works and shows the basic functionality of its genre, but these games are meant as starting points for your own designs. If, for example, you want to build a version of *Space Invaders,* you can scan this chapter to see how such a game can be built by using the techniques described throughout the book. Get a version up and working by using mine as a template but then modify it however you want. As you look through the games, consider the following points:

✔ **Each game is a minimal demonstration.** I show the barest form that I could make work for each game. The code is simple and clean so that you can modify it yourself. Most are examples of classic gaming genres, but two (Egg Cannon and Orbit Matcher) are original ideas that show how you can combine ideas to make something new and interesting.

✔ **The graphics are merely placeholders.** I put very little effort into the graphics because you modify them and make your own. Let my graphics be a basic guide, but by all means, modify them for your own use.

✔ **I didn't end anything.** I didn't include ending conditions in any of these samples. I do suggest (in most cases) how you can end the game, but that's really up to you.

✔ **These games are silent.** Add your own sound effects and background music to spruce up the games. See Chapter 8 if you need more info on adding sound to games.

✔ **The code is on this book's companion Web site.** For length reasons, I didn't reproduce the code for any of these games here, but all code is available on the Web site:

www.dummies.com/go/flashgameprogrammingfd1e

✔ **Use the book as a reference.** Most of the ideas used in these games have been presented in other parts of the book. Rather than describing these concepts again, I point out where in the book you can find various techniques if you need a refresher.

✔ **I suggest many enhancements.** Each of the games presented here is shown in a basic form, but I suggest several ways how you can improve each. And you can probably think of a few enhancements on your own. I haven't tried all these enhancements myself. They're just meant to get you thinking how to improve on the basic framework I provide.

Asteroids

Asteroids is a classic game, as illustrated in Figure 15-1. The user controls a spacecraft drifting in an asteroid field, in which several large rocks float. When a player blasts an asteroid (so as to avoid getting smashed by it), it breaks into several smaller rocks. These can then be blasted again and broken up until all the rocks are toast and a new asteroid field appears.

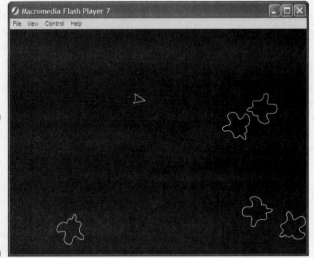

Figure 15-1:
Asteroids
is easy
to write
when you
generate
sprites
dynamically.

Building Asteroids

You can build your own version like this:

1. **Begin with the space game featured in Chapter 12.**

   You need a spacecraft that flies under user control with vector projection. The ship should wrap off the sides of the screen.

2. **Add the ability to fire a projectile from the ship.**

   See Chapter 10 for a refresher on creating missiles.

3. **Add the large rocks.**

   The easiest way to build a series of rocks is to use an external class file, as shown in Chapter 13.

4. **Manage collision detection.**

   When any rock hits the ship, the player loses a life. When a bullet hits a rock, the rock either splits or dies.

5. **Generate new rocks.**

   When a large rock dies (is shot), a number of medium rocks generate at that spot. When shot, a medium rock breaks into several small rocks. Small rocks simply disappear when shot.

Enhancements to Asteroids

Consider the following features:

- ✔ **Power-ups:** Various floating elements cause enhancements in the ship's behavior. A player can shoot or fly over a power-up to earn enhancement.
- ✔ **Shields:** These protect the ship from asteroids for a short time.
- ✔ **Warping:** This makes the ship reappear at a random destination.
- ✔ **A gravity well:** A star or planet, for example, acts on all the asteroids and your ship, changing the game completely. See Chapter 12 for details on including gravity in space games.

Lunar Lander

The *Lunar Lander* game is among the oldest computer games (and one of the first I played). The first computer I played this game on had no monitor: All output was through a teletype console. Your version can be quite a bit more colorful if you want. All versions of the *Lunar Lander* game work in pretty much the same way, as shown in Figure 15-2. The player controls a spacecraft landing on some sort of platform or surface. The planet pulls the ship downward, and the player uses arrow-key thrusters to control the descent. Retro-thrusters counteract the gravitational pull but consume fuel. Side thrusters provide side-to-side control and also consume fuel.

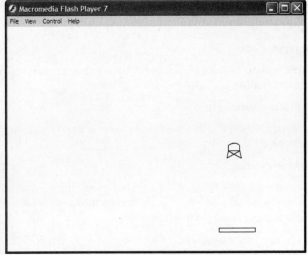

Figure 15-2:
Land your
ship safely
on the
platform.

Building Lunar Lander

You can build your own version like this:

1. Create the ship sprite.

The ship is just an ordinary sprite. Consider adding visual states for
no thrust, firing retro-rockets, thrusting to left, thrusting to right, and
crashing.

2. Add gravity and keyboard control.

Use the basic gravity technique from Chapter 11 to make the ship's downward speed accelerate. Add keyboard input as described in Chapter 8 to
let the user compensate for gravity and move in the x axis. Getting the
forces exactly right takes some careful tuning.

3. Add landing targets.

These targets can be platforms floating in space or smooth areas on a
planet's surface. Regardless, they should be represented by movie clips.

4. Determine safe landing parameters.

Just touching the landing site with the lander is not a landing. A safe
landing must include moving downward; that is, you can't hit a floating
platform from the bottom and call it a landing. Test for this by requiring
dy to be positive. The vertical speed should be small, so ensure that dy
is no larger than some threshold you determine. Also, the horizontal

speed needs to be within some reasonable limits. The easiest way to check for many conditions at once is to use a set of nested conditions. For example, the algorithm might go something like this:

```
if (lander touches platform){
  if (dy > 0){
    if (dy < 3){
      if (dx > -2){
        if (dx < 2){
          //safe landing
        } // end if
      } // end if
    } // end if
  } // end if
} // end if
```

5. **Limit the fuel supply.**

   Each time a key is pressed, reduce the value of the lander's fuel property. When the fuel is less than 0 (zero), don't respond to any more keyboard inputs.

Enhancements to Lunar Lander

Consider the following features:

- ✔ **Make smaller platforms.**
- ✔ **Change the gravitational pull.**
- ✔ **Add power-ups for fuel and performance enhancements.**
- ✔ **Move the landing platforms.**

Egg Cannon

Sometimes you can give an old game type new life by adding an interesting story and twist to the game. The Egg Cannon game of Figure 15-3 is a variant of the many cannon games. In this game, the player is a naturalist who discovers many eggs on the ground. He has a cannon that can fire the eggs into the air to return them to their nest — gently! — or they will break. Thus, the player must adjust fire to make the egg land as nearly motionless as possible.

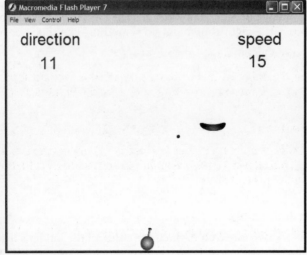

Figure 15-3:
Launch the eggs safely into the nests with your egg cannon.

Building Egg Cannon

You can build your own version like this:

1. **Begin with a standard cannon like the ones featured in Chapter 11.**

    The cannon should use vector projection and keyboard input to determine the charge and direction of the egg. Consider adding graphical feedback of the charge so that the user can tell exactly how much force is being applied to the egg. Maybe you convert the cannon into a slingshot or something if the idea of launching an egg out of a cannon bothers you, but the principle is the same.

2. **Allow the cannon to move from side to side along the bottom of the screen.**

    You might need to be inventive with the keys used for this because you'll probably already be using the arrow keys for changing the cannon's angle. You might consider using the Z and X or A and S keys for cannon motion.

3. **Randomly generate a bird's nest.**

    Use a movie clip object for the nest.

4. **Test for landings.**

    The landing should be soft, so give credit only for those landings when the egg is moving down, dx is small, and dy is small (much like the Lunar

Lander described in the preceding section). The eggs are much harder to control than the lander, so allow for a wider range of acceptable speeds.

5. **Penalize for broken eggs.**

   Of course, missing the nest or having an egg that hits the nest too hard should result in appropriate sound effects and animations as well as a loss of score or life.

6. **Set a time limit.**

   The best way to set a time limit in Flash is to employ the `setInterval` function. This allows you to designate a function to occur after a certain number of milliseconds.

Enhancements to Egg Cannon

Consider the following features:

- ✔ **Make smaller nests that are more difficult to land in.**
- ✔ **Add flying hazards such as birds or squirrels.**
- ✔ **Change the time limit so as the player progresses through the game, he has less time to land all the eggs.**
- ✔ **Require player to scoop up eggs before launching them.**

  Start each round with all the eggs on the ground. Make the player pick up an egg by moving the cannon over it and then let him fire the egg. Also add a state to the cannon so the player knows that he has scooped up an egg.

- ✔ **Add wind that adjusts the egg's horizontal velocity.** Wind works just like gravity except that it's constant. Add a small value to x (not dx) for each frame. Consider using a windsock or something to indicate the wind's speed and direction.

- ✔ **Add a parachute.** When the user presses a certain key, the egg deploys a parachute. This causes the egg to drop more slowly but also makes it much more susceptible to the wind.

Zelda

Nintendo introduced an entire new type of game in its ground-breaking *The Legend of Zelda*. In this type of game, the user controls some sort of character via the arrow keys. The character can move over certain kinds of terrain but is blocked from traveling over other types of terrain (such as buildings, rivers, and mountains). The player encounters various other characters and often receives clues or special tools from those characters. There are usually one or more ways to exit each screen, which takes the player to another screen with a new set of characters, monsters, problems, and treasure.

Figures 15-4 through 15-6 show a very short adventure typical of the genre.

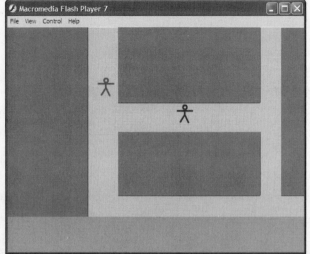

Figure 15-4: It's lonely in the big city, but I think I'll talk to that skinny guy on the left.

Figure 15-5: Hmmm. It seems to be some sort of clue. I wonder what it means?

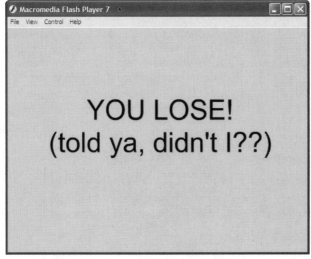

Building Zelda

You can build your own version like this:

1. **Diagram your plot and each screen on paper first.**

   First understand the plot and then figure out all the characters, the puzzles, monsters, and whatever else you want before you start coding. Draw a sketch of every room and an overall map that describes the relationships among the various rooms. This is invaluable as you design your game.

2. **Build a frame to represent each room.**

   In a sense, this game works a lot like the text-style adventure from Chapter 3. Each frame is a state, and the player moves from state to state by exiting rooms. Be sure to name the frames clearly as designated by your diagram. (You *did* make a diagram, didn't you?) A screen shot of one frame is shown in Figure 15-7.

3. **Create a movie clip object holding all the barriers in the current frame.**

   The barriers can look like anything you want (walls, lava pits, mountains). These are the things you won't let the player walk on. You can have several shapes in the same movie clip. Make sure to leave some empty space for the player to get around in.

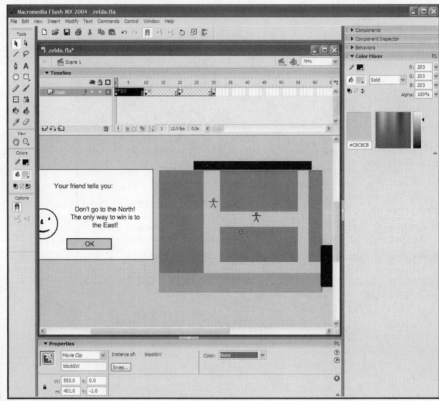

Figure 15-7:
A typical
room in
the editor
environ-
ment.

4. Make movie clips for all the exits.

Create a movie clip just outside each of the level's exits. This movie clip is used to determine which frame the game moves to when the user leaves a particular exit.

5. Build a movie clip for the player.

Start simple. However, you'll probably want to add animation to this character eventually because the player will stare at the main character animation for the entire game.

6. Build movie clips for any other elements in the scene.

If the scene features a non-player character (such as the skinny friend in my screen), a monster, a key, or some other important element, create a movie clip to represent that object and place it on the screen as desired.

7. Make a movie clip showing any dialog boxes that might occur in the scene.

The easiest way to make pop-ups like the one featured in Figure 15-5 is to simply create the entire dialog box as a movie clip and move it onto the Stage when desired.

8. **Add keyboard input to move the character.**

   Use keyboard commands to move the character around onscreen. Use a special version of the `hitTest()` method (shown on the included source code) to prevent walking through the barrier sprite.

9. **Use collision detection to handle various special events.**

   When the player collides with a special object or character, modify variables as needed to indicate the current situation. For example, add to the player's gold amount or indicate that the player now has the special blue key, or whatever. If you need to communicate something special to the user, display a custom dialog box sprite and then have the sprite remove itself when clicked.

10. **Check for collisions with the exit sprites to determine when the user is trying to exit the room.**

    When the user encounters one of the exit sprites, use a `_root.gotoAndStop()` command to move the program's focus to the appropriate new frame.

Enhancements to Zelda

You have limitless ways to enhance this style of game. The most important element is the story, but you can also consider these features:

- ✔ **Some type of combat system:** An adventure game needs monsters, and those monsters must be slain. Of the many types of combat systems, the most common ones use random numbers, the player's abilities, and the monster's capabilities to determine the results of an encounter. You can also use some type of arcade action (such as shooting fireballs) to handle encounters with monsters.

- ✔ **The ability to improve:** As the player gets farther along in the game, he or she should become more powerful. This can be done by adding experience (which then makes the player capable of handling more difficult opponents) or through improved equipment. (For example, after a player picks up the magic sling, he can hurl fireballs at enemies.)

- ✔ **An inventory system:** One fun thing about adventures is all the virtual equipment, tools, weapons, armor, and useless junk you can pick up. The player should have to make some kind of decision about what to carry and what to drop, or he'll just drag everything around all the time.

- ✔ **A sense of urgency:** Adventure games tend to be slower paced than arcade games, so you need something to keep up the excitement level. Many adventure games achieve this through some sort of time limit. Maybe a level must be completed in a certain number of turns, or the user gets hungry and must find food to continue.

✔ **A tile-based approach:** If you want a more sophisticated variant of Zelda, look ahead to the section called "Tile-Based World Games," later in this chapter.

Platform Scroller Games

The platform scrolling genre was made famous by games like *Mario Brothers, Donkey Kong,* and countless others. In this style of game, as shown in Figure 15-8, the user controls some sort of character that's viewed from the side. Usually, the character progresses through the game by traversing screens from left to right, and the player can typically jump to reach higher platforms. Often the character can also fire some sort of projectile, duck, and run. Too, some kind of enemy typically appears onscreen to impede the player's progress.

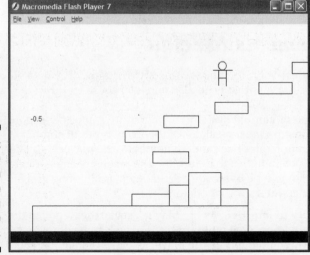

Figure 15-8: The humble yet fun platform scrolling adventure game.

Building a platform scroller game

Here is perhaps the easiest technique to build platform scroller games:

1. **Design your world.**

   Begin by sketching the type of game you're building, what typical screens look like, how the player acts, and the types of enemies the player encounters. For now, have each screen be a separate frame. That way, simply swapping to a new frame is easier than scrolling, but you can easily convert this technique to a scrolling system after you master the basics.

2. Create a movie clip to represent the terrain.

Use one movie clip to represent anything the player can stand on. You can make this clip as visually complex as you want, but make sure that it includes white space for the user to walk around on.

3. Build the player sprite.

The player sprite should start out simple but will probably involve multiple visual states (running, crouching, jumping) as you improve the game.

4. Set the registration point at the bottom of the player movie clip.

Most of the time, you design sprites so that the registration point is the center of the clip. In this type of game, you're really more concerned where the player's feet are, so design your sprite so that the registration point is at the bottom center, as shown in Figure 15-9. Placing the registration point at the player's feet makes landings easier to calculate.

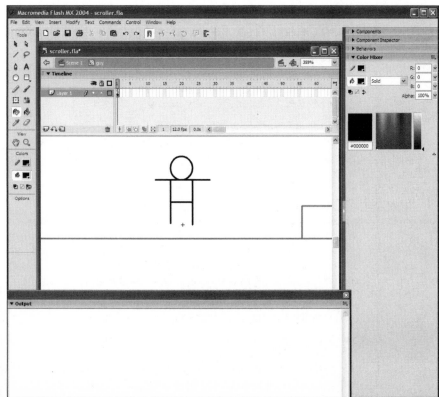

Figure 15-9:
Place the registration point at the player's feet.

5. **Add keyboard control to the player.**

   Begin with basic left and right motion based on the arrow keys (or some other keyboard command). Usually the player moves only frontward and backward while a key is pressed and stops motion when the key is released. Add a jumping command, which sets a value to the player's dy so the player begins moving upward.

6. **Incorporate gravity.**

   If the player is in the air, incorporate gravity to pull the player downward. If the player is on the ground (touching the platform sprite), set dy to 0.

7. **Build trigger sprites to let the user move off the screen.**

   When the player collides with one of these sprites (which can be invisible or just off the Stage), call the _root.gotoAndStop() method to transfer program control to a new state.

8. **Add enemy characters.**

   These can be movie clips running under program control.

Enhancements to a platform scroller game

Some possibilities to enhance this style of game are

- **Give the player a weapon.** Let the player fire some sort of weapon at the enemies. Weapons usually follow a straight left-to-right trajectory.

- **Add enemy types.** Be creative with the kinds of enemies you use to challenge players. Give different types of enemies different behaviors. Enemies might fly, crawl, explode, or fire bullets. Part of the fun of this style of game is learning strategies to defeat the various enemies. Be sure that each enemy has a weakness that can be exploited, or the game won't be fun.

- **Add player abilities.** Use power-ups to give the player new capabilities, such as invincibility, *teleportation* (moving to a new random spot onscreen), flying, a new weapon, or inverse gravity. Special abilities should last for a short time and should also be placed so that players can use them to solve otherwise impossible layers.

- **Go backward.** Let the user move and shoot from right to left as well as the typical left-to-right orientation.

- **Add more rooms.** Although there is an action element, scrolling games are essentially puzzles. Be creative in your room design. Be sure the puzzles are interesting and varied by mixing the background themes, music, enemy types, and style of rooms.

Breakout

The *Breakout*-style games emerged immediately after *Pong*. This style of game is much like *Pong*, but it's intended to be a single-player game. The player controls one paddle near the bottom of the screen and moves the paddle via the mouse or keyboard. A series of bricks is placed at the top of the screen. When a brick is hit by a missile (ball) guided by the paddle, it is removed from the screen. The level is finished when all the bricks are eliminated. Figure 15-10 illustrates a very basic version of this program.

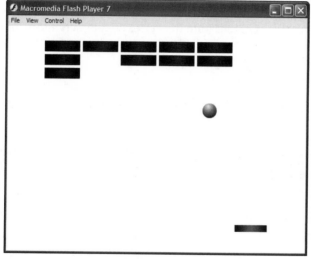

Figure 15-10: Bounce the ball to destroy the bricks.

Building Breakout

The seemingly simple Breakout game has a surprisingly challenging design. The ball and paddle can be completely borrowed from the Pong game in Chapter 6, but there are a lot of bricks to control in the game, and you need some sophisticated techniques to manage them well.

1. **Create the ball sprite.**

   Add code to move the ball onscreen using dx and dy. Have the ball bounce off all four walls. Check Chapter 5 for a refresher on these techniques.

2. **Create the paddle sprite.**

   The paddle follows the mouse, so build it much like the one in Chapter 5.

3. **Build one brick.**

When you are building several instances of one object, begin by creating one instance that works properly. After you get the first one acting correctly, you can add the code that clones that one individual. The bricks need to be removed from the screen, and you need several of them, so use the `attachMovie` method to create your first brick. Chapter 13 explains this technique.

4. **Make more bricks.**

Use a `for` loop around the brick creation code to assemble a series of bricks. As you look at the code for this program on the companion Web site, you'll actually see two `for` loops. I organized the bricks by row and column to make them easier to manage. Look carefully at the code to see that it isn't that different from the sprite creation code you've already written.

5. **Write the brick-ball collision code.**

In each brick's definition, instruct the brick to self-destruct when a ball collides with it. Also, the ball's `dy` should change when it encounters (and destroys) a brick.

Enhancements to Breakout

The Breakout code is functional as it appears on the companion Web site, but you'll have to tweak it to make a fully functional game. Consider the following improvements:

- **Improve the ball-paddle collision routine.** As written, the ball-and-paddle collision doesn't give the user much control. Modify the routine shown in Chapter 7 to give the same kind of control to the breakout paddle that you create in the Pong game.

- **Create different brick types.** To add visual appeal, make many colors of bricks. Also consider using special bricks that alter the game play. For example, you can create super bricks that require multiple hits to destroy, invisible bricks, and unbreakable bricks.

- **Add power-ups.** Periodically (randomly or when you hit a certain type of brick) have various special elements available. If the user touches this power-up, something happens to change the game play. You can change the paddle size or ball speed, invert the paddle directions (drives players crazy!), destroy all the bricks onscreen, or devise some other devious scheme.

- **Build more levels.** When the player clears all the bricks from one screen, move to another with different challenges. You can create each new level on a different frame, or you can use a data structure to build new levels dynamically.

Space Invaders

The classic form of *Space Invaders* involves an array of aliens marching at the top of the screen. After each pass, the aliens creep lower, coming closer to the planet (the bottom of the screen), where the user controls a ship via keyboard input. The player can fire bullets at the encroaching aliens, which removes them from the screen when they are hit. A very simple version of this game is illustrated in Figure 15-11.

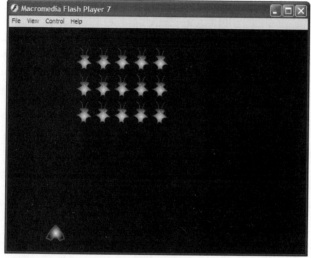

Figure 15-11: I still have nightmares about hordes of aliens slowly descending on my house.

Building Space Invaders

The *Space Invaders*-style game is quite similar to the Breakout game. Both games feature a collection of objects. The Breakout bricks are stationary, but the aliens move in a herd. If you've already created the Breakout game (see the preceding section), you can modify it to make Space Invaders, or you can start from scratch.

1. **Create the ship.**

   Build a sprite to represent the player's ship. Usually such games use keyboard input to control the ship's motion, so add a keyboard handler to incorporate left- and right-arrow keys. You don't need to track the ship's dy because it moves along only the x axis.

2. **Make a bullet.**

   The bullet is a small movie clip object. Create an instance of the bullet object but move it offstage until you need it. When the user hits the spacebar, fire the bullet upward from the ship.

3. **Build aliens.**

   Build alien creatures dynamically so that they can be removed from the screen when they're hit by a bullet. Create the aliens in the same type of 2-D structure described earlier in the Breakout game. Move all the aliens at one time by using global dx and dy variables.

4. **Move the aliens.**

   The aliens are unlike most sprites I use throughout this book. Usually, each entity has its own dx and dy. However, the aliens are not so independent. Rather, they all move in the same direction at the same time, so rather than moving by the brick's dx and dy properties, they move by global motion variables called globalDX and globalDY.

5. **Move down the aliens when they encounter an edge.**

   When one of the aliens encounters the edge of the screen, all the aliens should move down closer to the planet. The easiest way to do this is with a special moveDown() function, which uses a pair of for loops to specify each alien and then move that alien down 20 pixels.

Enhancements to Space Invaders

Although the basic functionality is there, the game is not yet complete. Some enhancements bring the game to a functional level, and others can add entirely new challenges.

✔ **Recognize when all aliens have been defeated.** To this point, the program keeps spinning along after all the aliens have been eliminated from the screen. Modify your program to recognize the player for winning the level and add a new level.

✔ **Code alien destruction of the Earth.** If the aliens reach a certain level, they win. Put some code in place to handle this eventuality. Inform the player of his score and then start the destruction of the Earth all over again.

✔ **Add special targets.** Periodically place special targets onscreen. If the player strikes these targets, reward him with points or special abilities.

✔ **Add special weapons.** Maybe the aliens have advanced technology, such as a confusion ray that causes the player's controls to be reversed. Maybe the player can have an occasional "smart bomb" that can be steered or a mega-bomb that clears the entire screen.

✔ **Give the aliens weapons.** In the original game, the aliens occasionally dropped bombs on the player. This made timing more important because the player could no longer simply wait for the aliens to come right above him.

✔ **Add shields for the player.** Add destructible shields that can protect the player from a certain number of hits.

✔ **Generate more original alien behavior.** Let the aliens act in new ways in later layers. Some aliens might break out from the pack and dive-bomb the player, or maybe the aliens sometimes break off into random motions.

Orbit Matcher

Orbit Matcher is an original game of mine based on the planetary orbit simulation described in Chapter 12. The player controls an orbiting spacecraft that must rendezvous with a satellite in a different orbit. The player can control the spacecraft with the keyboard and must try to match orbits with the satellite. You can't just fly right to the satellite: You have to try to match orbits with it. A rendezvous is successful if the two craft are near each other and are heading in nearly the same direction. The game is shown in Figure 15-12.

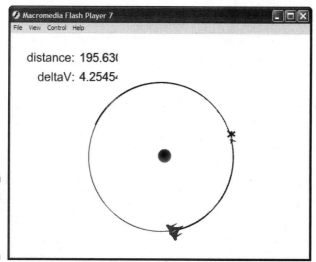

Figure 15-12: Match orbits with the satellite.

Building Orbit Matcher

As usual, this game takes bits and pieces from examples throughout the book. The Orbit Matcher game is based heavily on the `planet` program shown in Chapter 12. To make this new game

1. **Begin with the `planet` program.**

   Build a ship that can be controlled by the keyboard. Add a planet and then build a `gravitate` function that allows the ship to maintain a reasonable orbit. See Chapter 12 for lots of information on building this type of game.

2. **Tone down the ship's performance.**

   The ship in the `planet` game developed in Chapter 12 has a ridiculous amount of power. To make the game more interesting, tone down the ship's `thrustSpeed` from 1 to 0.10. This forces the player to use finesse rather than simply powering up to the satellite.

3. **Add the satellite.**

   The satellite is essentially a second ship. You can copy most of the ship code to make the satellite. The satellite doesn't require keyboard input or a `turn()` method, but it will still need `move()` and `gravitate()` methods. Make sure that the satellite is moving properly: You might have to play with the satellite's initial `dx`, `dy`, and position to start it in a reasonable orbit.

4. **Check for rendezvous.**

   I define a rendezvous by determining the distance between the ship and the satellite. (I also calculated the relative velocity, but I'm not yet using that value as part of the rendezvous calculation.)

Enhancements to Orbit Matcher

The game is pretty interesting as it stands, but there are always things that can be done to improve it:

✔ **Add scorekeeping.** To this point, only a `trace` statement marks a successful rendezvous. Make something more interesting happen when the user docks with the satellite. You might generate a new orbit to reach or perhaps require the user to return to an orbit within some distance of the planet.

✔ **Use more realistic thrusting.** Most actual orbital maneuvers are performed by firing in the current direction of orbit (a *prograde burn*) or in the opposite direction (a *retrograde burn*). Modify your program so that the ship's direction always follows the current orbital path. Use the up arrow for a prograde burn and the down arrow for retrograde.

✔ **Add a fuel limit.** Spacecraft carry very limited amounts of fuel. Reduce the fuel every time the player fires the main thrusters. The turn thrusters burn much less fuel, so you can ignore them if you wish.

✔ **Check for relative velocity.** If two objects touch, it could be a docking or a crash. Use the relative velocity of the objects to determine whether the objects are heading close to the same direction. A good rendezvous is determined by a small distance and a small *deltaV* (space talk for relative velocity). I already calculated a simple form of deltaV in the sample program.

Tile-Based World Games

Tile-based worlds aren't a particular type of game but rather a technique that you can apply to many styles of games. Figure 15-13 shows an adventure game built using the tile-based technique.

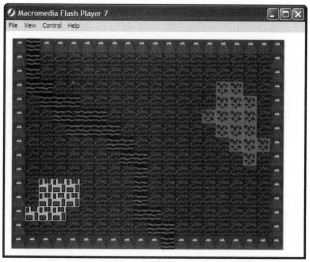

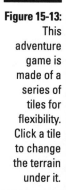

Figure 15-13: This adventure game is made of a series of tiles for flexibility. Click a tile to change the terrain under it.

Rather than using Flash tools to generate game details, all the information for a game is stored in a memory structure. The visual output is generated from this structure while the game is played. The playing surface is broken into a series of (usually rectangular) tiles. Each tile can be represented by a movie clip. A movie clip that can represent many different states is duplicated once for each square of the map. The main advantage of a tile-based approach is flexibility. After you design the basic structure, you can easily build new levels by modifying the data. Changing the visual feel of the program (by modifying the movie clips) is easy and makes your program smaller because small amounts of information are being reused efficiently.

Building a tile-based world game

The example in Figure 15-13 is a *Zelda*-style adventure game. This particular version allows the user to change the terrain in any square by clicking the cell. To build this style of game by using a tile-based approach, follow these steps:

1. **Draw some sample maps, using graph paper.**

   Think about the kinds of terrain you want to represent and then draw maps using colored pencils or initials representing each terrain type in each square of the graph paper.

2. **Determine which terrain types you need.**

   Drawing the sample maps tells you what kinds of terrain types you want. My sample contains town, grass, mountain, trees, and water. Each terrain type has a different appearance, but it might also have an effect on game play. For example, you might not let the player cross water spaces without a boat, or you might give the player a defensive advantage if he's fighting in a tree tile.

3. **Build a movie clip to represent one tile.**

   Make one movie clip and add a state for each terrain type you want. At first, you should make the various terrains relatively simple, but after you get the basic operations working, you can add animation and fancier graphics. The tile should be relatively small because you'll use many copies of it in your game. My tile is 25 x 25 pixels. Be sure to name each state so you can determine and change the terrain type of the tile easily.

4. **Create an instance of the movie clip using code.**

   Test your movie clip by writing code that creates the clip, moves it to a particular part of the screen, and sets its state to represent a particular terrain type.

5. **Build a 2-D array to store the map.**

   Look at the sample code to see how I made an array of arrays. This structure seems complex, but it's an ideal way to make maps because it corresponds easily to rows and columns on the map. Notice that for brevity, I store numbers in the array representing the terrain types.

6. **Make an ordinary array to retrieve terrain type names.**

   Because numeric values are used in the terrain array, I use another array called `tileName` to help me remember which type of terrain is associated with which number.

7. **Use a pair of nested loops to generate the map.**

   Each tile of the map is created with an `attachMovie()` command. The `for` loops are used to figure out where each element goes and what type of data it should represent.

8. Add the player sprite on top of the map.

The player sprite and monster sprites should be generated above the tiles so that they're visible to the user. The easiest way to ensure this is to build these sprites dynamically and assign them a very high z-order. You'll probably want to move the player around via the keyboard or mouse. Have the player move one tile at a time or do a `hitTest()` to determine which tile he's on as well as what that might do to his behavior.

Enhancements to a tile-based world game

After you understand the tile-based technique, you can use it to create and improve many kinds of games:

- ✔ **Build a board game.** Checkers, chess, and reversi *(Othello)* are usually programmed using a form of tile-based world.

- ✔ **Create a strategy game.** Most war games and other strategy games have tile-based worlds at their heart.

- ✔ **Make a side scroller.** If you build a side scroller using a tile-based metaphor, it's much easier to create new levels than using the technique described in the platform-scroller section of this chapter.

- ✔ **Build a level editor.** Many games now come with a *level editor,* which allows users to generate new levels of the game on their own. Your game can then have all kinds of new levels, and you won't have to write them! With a tile-based approach, a level editor is simply a visual tool that changes the underlying 2-D array. My version of the game has an extremely simple level editor that lets you switch terrain types by clicking on cells. Take a look at the code to see one way to accomplish this feat.

Whack-an-Author

The *Whack-a-Mole* game has been popular for many years in arcades and carnivals. In the classic version of the game, each player takes a large hammer and stands over a series of holes. Moles randomly pop out of the holes, and the user must pound the defenseless animals back into their underground refuge. Hundreds of computerized variations abound. No doubt they are popular because they allow players to vent their aggression. Figure 15-14 shows my version of the game — Whack-an-Author — that lets you abuse the likeness of a certain computer book author, who shall remain nameless.

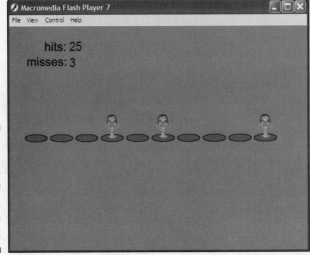

Figure 15-14:
When the
offender
pops out of
his hole,
smack him
down.

If you find you're really good at beating up on authors, you should consider a career in the publishing industry.

Building Whack-an-Author

After you can build one target, building several of them is easy. The targets are largely autonomous. To build the game

1. **Create a target sprite.**

    The target sprite should have two states:

    - up: The up state shows the target sticking his head up.
    - down: The down state shows an empty hole.

    Notice that I use an actual raster graphic. I usually avoid raster-based images, but in this case, it makes the game a lot easier to write. Because the image is small and is never rotated, it doesn't hurt the game's performance or download time in a significant way. To add a raster graphic, simply import it to the library just as you do for audio files.

2. **Generate the sprite dynamically.**

    The target is an ideal candidate for an external class definition (as described in Chapter 13) or more traditional generation (as I do in the example code on the companion Web site).

    www.dummies.com/go/flashgameprogrammingfd1e

In either case, define the sprite using the `attachMovie()` method. (If you want to place the sprites by hand, be sure to name the instances `target_0`, `target_1`, and so on to make the remaining code work correctly.)

3. **Make the sprite pop up randomly.**

   Add code to each target's `enterFrame` method. If the target is in the `down` state, make a random possibility that the sprite will pop up. I use a property called `popUpRate`. By default, I set `popUpRate` to `.05`, meaning that each target has a five percent chance of popping up on every frame that it is down. Change this value to make the targets pop up more or less frequently.

4. **Have the target retreat after some time out of the hole.**

   When the target pops up, have it wait a certain number of frames and then go back to the `down` state. I use a property called `resetFrames` that indicates how many frames the target hangs around before returning to the hole. If the target retreats without being whacked, increment the number of misses.

5. **Respond to mouse clicks.**

   The target should ignore mouse clicks if it's in the hole. If the target is in the `up` state and the user releases the mouse over it, move the target back to the `down` state and increment the number of hits.

6. **Repeat for as many targets as you wish.**

   After you have one target working correctly, use a `for` loop to build several instances of the target, as described in Chapter 13.

Enhancements to Whack-an-Author

The inherent violence of this game makes it a lot of fun for your users, but you can do many things to improve it:

- ✔ **Provide your own target.** The easiest and most satisfying change to this game is to modify the target sprite so it contains a picture of some suitable target of your aggressions.

- ✔ **Add a hammer, or a mallet, an axe, a deadline, or whatever else you want to smack the targets with.** Use the mouse-replacing techniques described in Chapter 8 to replace the mouse with a movie clip of your own design.

- ✔ **Change the difficulty level.** You have many ways to make the game easier or harder. Begin by messing with the `popUpRate` and resetFrames properties. These properties allow you to change the rate at which the targets appear and the length of time each target stays onscreen. You can also manipulate the game by changing the size and position of the targets. Larger targets are easier to hit than smaller ones, and targets in a cluster are easier to hit than those in a straight line.

✔ **Add ending conditions.** As it stands, the game goes on forever. Provide a time limit, with a penalty for each miss; time how long it takes to hit 100 targets; or continue until the player misses five times. These conditions encourage the player to try again to beat his high score.

✔ **Move the targets.** Moving the targets makes the game more challenging. Move them slowly or keep them onscreen longer — moving targets are much harder to hit than stationary ones.

Index

• G •